Shaker Recipes and Formulas for Cooks and Homemakers

By William Lawrence Lassiter

Illustrations by Constantine Kermes

Bonanza Books · New York

To all my beloved Shaker Friends

This book was originally published as *Shaker Recipes for Cooks and Homemakers*.

Copyright ©MCMLIX by William Lawrence Lassiter.
All rights reserved.
This edition is published by Bonanza Books,
a division of Crown Publishers, Inc.,
by arrangement with William Lawrence Lassiter, Jr.
a b c d e f g h
BONANZA 1978 PRINTING
Manufactured in the United States of America

Library of Congress Cataloging in Publication Data
Lassiter, William Lawrence.
  Shaker recipes and formulas for cooks and homemakers.
  Reprint of the ed. published by Greenwich Book Publishers, New York, under title: Shaker recipes for cooks and homemakers.
  Includes index.
  1. Cookery, Shaker. I. Title.
TX715.L348   1978   641.5′66   59-8620
ISBN 0-517-26388-2

CONTENTS

FOREWORD

Many visitors to the New York State Department of Education, of whose staff I am a member, and personal friends have for a number of years urged me to assemble a collection of Shaker recipes. When this task was started, it was not so arduous as had been expected, for when once the work was begun the response was generous. All recipes have been faithfully copied from their original sources without changes in spelling or punctuation, and it is with sincere hope that, in this form, they will serve the historian as well as the culinary hobbyist and the gourmet.

Thanks are given to the late Mrs. Charles Fayerweather and Mrs. Laura Lindholm of New Lebanon, New York, and to the Shaker Sisters of the Pittsfield, Massachusetts, and Sabbathday Lake, Maine, and Canterbury, New Hampshire, colonies, who contributed recipes for this book. Other recipes were gathered by perusal of Shaker manuscripts and printed materials in the New York State Library and the New York State Museum at Albany; the Wayside and Fruitlands Museums, Inc., at Harvard, Massachusetts; the New York Historical Association at Cooperstown, New York; and the Grosvenor Library at Buffalo, New York. I express gratitude to the librarians of these institutions for their cooperation.

To Mrs. Emily Dixon, who typed the manuscript and gave many valued suggestions, and to Mrs. Marguerite F. Melcher and Dr. Frederick H. Bair, who read the manuscript, I give profound thanks.

I am also grateful to Miss Helen Fraser, who made the index.

The drawings are by Constantine Kermes, one of America's most promising young artists, of Crafton, Pennsylvania. His most recent presentations of his studies were under the title *American Saints,* represented in three New York one-man-shows at the Jacques Seligmann Gallery. Mr. Kermes, on invitation, has exhibited his characterizations of American religious folk groups at the New York State Museum, the New York Historical Association, Rutgers University, and the Dayton Art Institute. His paintings are in the permanent collections of the Everhart Museum in Scranton, Pennsylvania, and the Shaker Heights Public Library, Cleveland, Ohio, as well as in numerous private collections.

—WILLIAM LAWRENCE LASSITER

Albany, New York

INTRODUCTION

The Shakers, despite their efforts to shun publicity, became not only a local but an international subject of conversation and writing from the days of their beginning in America to the present day. Their success as a prospering communal group brought visitors from home and abroad to investigate their way of living, their homes and shops. During the nineteenth century, many socio-religious groups began in North America, but none has existed so long as the Shakers, who were given this name in derision by the public, who attended their religious services and saw them perform their religious marches and dances. They have been known, most generally, and have distinguished themselves by this name, the Shakers, for over a hundred and seventy-five years.

Twenty years ago, when the antique collectors sought new interest in items to collect, they discovered Shaker furniture. Exhibits of Shaker art and crafts were opened in museums in many cities in northeastern United States; photograph exhibits, lectures, newspaper and periodical articles followed, giving the present generation an insight into the Shaker communities. As a result of this propagation of interest, all roads led and are still leading to the remaining Shaker homes at Sabbathday Lake, Maine, Canterbury, New Hampshire, and Pittsfield, Massachusetts.

The United Society of Believers in Christ's Second Appearing or the Shaking Quakers, or Shakers, who first settled in Watervliet, Albany County, New York, in 1776, migrated from Manchester and Bolton, England, in May 1774, to establish in America their new religion, which they hoped would give spiritual satisfaction to many as it had to them.

Their religions were derived from the early teachings of the persecuted French Camisards, who came to England from France in 1706, and the English Quakers of Manchester. These two groups met at the home of James and Jane Wardley, and formed a Society in 1747 for the propagation of their combined beliefs. It was the Wardleys who predicted that the second appearing of Christ on earth was soon to be, and would come, in the form of a woman. When Ann Lee joined this group with her special revelation, she was acclaimed the female expression of the Christ Spirit.

Ann Lee (1736-1784) dreamed and saw visions, as Jacob and Moses of the Old Testament had. She claimed that while incarcerated in the Manchester jail on charges of disturbing the peace and spreading the doctine of celibacy, Jesus appeared to her and directed her to take the group to the New World to spread their faith. Eight of her followers did venture across the sea with her on May 19, 1774, on board the ship *Mariah*. The old ship sprang leaks enroute, but by a miracle the pilgrims survived and landed in New York City, August 6th, 1774, after enduring many storms and a near shipwreck. Those who remained in England, being without a leader, since the Wardleys were taken to the almshouse, lost their inspiration and became absorbed in the ordinary courses of religion and living.

John Hocknell, the only person of means in the group of Believers in Christ's Second Appearing, visited Albany and procured a tract of land at Niskayuna from Stephen Van Rensselaer, Lord of the Manor of Rensselaerwyck, where the group might live and work without molestation. Hocknell returned to England to settle his business affairs and to bring his family. Mother Ann Lee remained in New York, where she was employed as a laundress, and the remaining members found employment in or near Albany.

On December 25th, 1775, John Hocknell, with his family arrived in Philadelphia, and from there went to New York, where they consulted Mother Ann. Shortly afterwards, he went to Niskayuna (Watervliet), Albany County, New York, to develop those swamp lands already rented from Squire Van Rensselaer. During the spring of 1776 Mother Ann joined them, and the group of the "Shaker Quakers" were all together in their "New World" home. Here they cleared the land and drained the swamp to provide agricultural land and a tract for their homes. The group was without funds but so boundless was their love for the life they chose, that they did not complain. They lived here in seclusion and apart from the world for several years.

The Believers, who had done nothing to propagate their faith since their arrival in America, were relieved of a sense of selfishness when many flocked to Niskayuna, or Watervliet, from various quarters, to inquire about the religion of Mother Ann. Joseph Meacham and Calvin Harlow from a New Lebanon, New York, group of revivalists, came to make inquiries. These men were followed by others from the New Lebanon revival, and they became convinced the Shakers were the disciples of the New Creation they sought. Joseph Meacham, a Baptist minister, and his wife joined. Samuel Johnson, a Presbyterian, and other leaders of this revival joined later. It was Joseph Meacham, the first American convert who, with the assistance of Lucy Wright, a convert from Pittsfield, Massachusetts, formulated the "Millennial Laws" which guided all Shaker activities and individuals, as well as group conduct.

This seeming success of "gathering in" of members and proselyting, soon met with public disapproval, since many of the leaders representing the Presbyterian, Baptist and Methodist faiths had joined the Shakers and left the other sects without able leaders. The Shaker idea regarding the celibate existence of its members was misinterpreted, and it was thought that they aimed at the annihilation of the human race. Also, they were accused of being English spies, since they were then the most recent immigrants to North America prior to the Revolutionary War, and were thrown into jails at Albany and Poughkeepsie. It was Governor George Clinton who freed Mother Ann and the Elders when no just reason for incarceration was established.

William Lee, brother of Mother Ann, died July 21st, 1784. A few weeks later Mother Ann died also as a result of injuries received during mob attacks on visits to New England in 1784. At the cost of their lives, a triumphant mission of proselyting ended. From this time on members came into the order "like doves," as Mother had predicted before the first revivalist visited Niskayuna.

Lucy Wright suggested that the Believers be brought together in Communes, where they could be free from world influence. This would allow them to practice their faith unmolested, since they were away from the world's people. This ideal community was established at New Lebanon, New York, at the foot of the Lebanon Mountain, in 1788, on lands consecrated by David Darrow and John Bishop. This is the beginning of what was the oldest of the Communal Groups in the United States. It served as a model for eighteen other Shaker settlements, established in seven states of the United States. It was here that the ministry, or the presiding group over all Societies, was located, and it was here that the largest number of members resided during the heyday of the movement.

The cardinal principles of Shakerism are celibacy, community of goods, confession of sin, and withdrawal from the world. As a result of these beliefs, all persons, regardless of education, contribution of material goods to the Society at the time of joining, or position held with or in the organization, shared alike, all laboring for each and each for all. True democracy reigned, regardless of different opinions or race.

The practical issues which grew out of those beliefs were a comfortable home, manual labor for each according to strength and ability, opportunity for intellectual development within the necessary limits prescribed by common good, sanitation, purity of thought expressed in speech and personal habits, freedom from debt, worry and competition. These conditions could not have been achieved, except in a commune that embraced such ideals.

GOVERNMENT

The Shaker Government was vested in Christ and His human representatives, a dual order of leaders. The spiritual leaders, both the men and women, of the Ministry, were over the Societies, the Elders and Eldresses over the "family" or groups. The temporal leaders, men and woman, in charge of the business and industrial interests were the trustees, deacons and deaconesses and care-takers.

The Shakers adore God as the Almighty Creator, the fountain of all good, life light, truth and love. He, the eternal Father-Mother, is expressed in Christ, the head of a Shaker Group or "family." Jesus of Nazareth represented the male and Mother Ann Lee, the founder of Shakerism, the female expression of this Christ Spirit. All who accepted this belief were Sons and Daughters of God. The living of the life of these Christ spirits, and not the form of expression, was essential.

Shakerism was established at a time when it was most needed in this country. The source for members was from the world's plain, middle-class people, who sought the satisfying ways of the Society's communal life. A Shaker home was a haven of comfort to those who had been victims of the world's injustices. This does not mean to say that within a Shaker home there were no periods of anxiety for individuals or the group, for the Shakers stood prosperity and adversity alike with the calm that their Christian nurture had taught them.

The men and women who lived as brothers and sisters in the family of Jesus Christ had no personal interest to be satisfied, since there was equality of the sexes in all departments of their life, equality in labor, and common ownership in the "family" property.

The decline of membership came after the Civil War, which brought about great changes in the economic and social system of America. Few persons were interested in the rigidly disciplining life of the Shakers, and young people upon reaching majority withdrew from the Society. Orphans, one of the chief sources of potential members, were more and more provided for by state institutions and others privately endowed. By this time business opportunities in offices and factories opened new means of employment for men as well as women. With the invention of the typewriter and other office machines, women who earlier might have joined the Shakers for economic security and protection, went to work as typists, stenographers, and clerks, since the prejudices that once surrounded them in business and shop were gradually being diminished.

The industrialization of the South and West after the Civil War, likewise, took many from the Shakers who might have joined. With all these contributing factors the Shaker Society lost future great leaders like Frederick Evans, Henry Blinn, Benjamin Youngs, Antoinette Doolittle, Lucy Wright, Henry Eads and Anna Case, who would have kept alive the Society even against these great odds. Certainly it was not celibacy alone that caused the decline of the organization, as many suspect, but the social, industrial, and economic changes and indifference to spiritual life.

Continuance as a member of the Shaker Society was not obligatory, even though members over twenty-one years of age signed the Covenant of their own free will to conform to the practices of the Shaker Society and dedicate themselves and their services to it. However, upon making known to the Ministry their desire to withdraw from the Society, they would receive a release together with sums of money and goods to begin life anew. Likewise, those whom the Ministry dismissed for nonconformity to the Covenant they had signed, received similar treatment.

CLOTHING

At the beginning of the Society, the Shakers did not devise a style of their own in costumes for either men or women, but during their advancement distinctive costumes were designed. In these costumes many of the features of the antique were retained from the style in vogue at the time of the inception of the organization. The women's dresses, the caps and neckerchiefs, with modification, were fashioned after the English peasants' clothing of nearly two hundred years ago. The fitted bodice and wide ankle-length pleated skirts of the one piece dress were likewise of past style, changed solely on the grounds of convenience and modesty.

The cap, made of thin muslin, and later of machine-made net, was worn by the Sisters and older girls indoors. A poke bonnet of hand-woven straw, or a cloth bonnet, was worn over this when going out of doors.

The Brethren exchanged their knee breeches of the Colonial period for long trousers, and on Sundays wore to the meetings long frock coats with vests. In their work, often a smock of hand-woven linen in white, blue, or brown was worn in place of a coat or vest.

Both the Sisters' and Brethren's clothing was made of hand-woven cotton, wool and linen material from their own looms. Their shoes were made by the Shaker cobbler, of home-tanned leather and cloth. Wide brimmed hats of felt and straw for the brethren were made by Shaker hatters over their own hand-fashioned wooden blocks.

As the membership of the Society of Believers diminished, the distinctive Shaker costume likewise was discontinued by many of the members, since it became cheaper to buy clothing in the neighboring city store, than to make this special garb. Even though departing from the community tradition, the members still select clothing that is becoming to the quiet, plain life of the sect. Style is not, and never has been, an engrossing theme among the Shakers.

BUILDING

It was beween 1790-1864 that the membership of the Shakers increased. Religious revivals were opening all over the country and more and more people were seeking the religious experience that would give spiritual satisfaction. Knowledge of the Shaker faith spread and the Shaker ministry was sent far and wide to make known their philosophy of the "New Creation." Shaker societies were opened north, south, west and east, and thousands of persons joined who were willing to abide by their laws, confess their sins, live a celibate life, and share and contribute to their use of all goods. As Mother Ann predicted, they came like "doves."

During this great period of "gathering of the order" the Shakers built the great meeting house at Mount Lebanon, work shops and dwelling houses in the various communities, which are now greatly admired.

The stone barn at Mount Lebanon, known the world over for its size and many conveniences, was built in 1857. It was designed by Brother George Wickersham, and he also directed its construction to the last detail. It is built of native field stone and measures 296 feet long, fifty feet wide and five stories high. Each floor was made accessible by means of a driveway that opened at various levels on the hill side. This eliminated bridges and steps which require repair and are often unsafe. That the Shakers took advantage of natural topography in their building program can be noticed in every community where they lived.

The circular barn at Hancock, Massachusetts, was built in 1826, and had many unusual features, as did the barns at Canterbury, New Hampshire, and Shirley, Massachusetts. These communities were engaged in a lucrative dairy business, and well-built barns with features that diminished labor and furnished time-saving devices were of utmost importance. Such innovations were self-feeding haymows, arrangements for facilitating the cleaning, and built-in silos to prevent freezing of ensilage.

The meeting house at Mount Lebanon, the home of the Central Ministry, was built in 1825, and was designed to accommodate the large number of members then in that Shaker village, and visitors. The main meeting room measured eighty by seventy-nine feet and was without supporting pillar or other obstruction that might interfere with the religious marchers and dancers. The segmented ceiling, which is twenty-five feet above the floor, is curved to conform with the barrel roof. It is supported from above by seventy-two laminated beams, which form lintels spanning the distance between the prince posts to which are attached the lateral walls of the building.

All of the community buildings, whether of brick, stone or wood, are recognizable as Shaker architecture. They are devoid of unnecessary decorations, useless pinnacles, or decorative doorways. They are rectangular structures, with doors and windows arranged in symmetrical fashion. Depending upon the use of the building, they are conveniently located on the lot: thus the herb houses are near the gardens; the laundry and shops are placed where water power could be harnessed to operate the machinery.

Throughout the various structures are special features for convenience. Window sashes that could be lifted out by the cleaners, who were sisters and aged men, were thought of and built long ago by the Shakers. These provided for safety and did not take the valuable time of younger brethren, whose strength could be used elsewhere. The "off center" doors, which opened in two sections when needed, were to admit large articles that could not be carried through the door of ordinary width.

FURNITURE

Shaker furniture, which is now in demand by collectors of Americana, is limited in its quantity. Household furniture, with the exception of chairs and beds, was not made to sell to the world's people, hence its scarcity. This furniture, made for their home use only, was reduced to its simplest form. It did not depend upon decorations, carvings or fancy architecture to give it beauty, for the Millennial Laws forbade all of such useless display of vanity. Every piece of furniture was to serve its purpose without waste of time or material, but the pent-up feeling for beauty found its expression in rightness of line and proportion, in selection of wood, and in superb workmanship. The woods commonly used in furniture such as tables, both movable and built-in chests of drawers, storage chests, and cupboards, were of pine, maple, cherry, and butternut. Late in the 19th century some communities used chestnut and black walnut, and their use was accompanied by a decadence in design. This furniture attracts little or no attention at present, since it does not follow the design of older pieces.

The finish of these pieces of furniture was a thin coat of varnish, or an oil finish that contained ocher or venetian red pigments. Artificial graining and the veneering of woods was prohibited by the Millennial Laws.

It is to be remembered that the furniture was to serve a plain and simply living people, and not the wealthy, who preferred the elaborate designs of Chippendale, Hepplewhite, Sheraton, and the other master designers. Many examples of the Shaker furniture are to be found in a few museums and few private collections.

MUSIC

Shaker music and literature have been criticized as not being of the highest quality. This criticism, of course, is made by persons who know nothing of the Shaker background. The Believers built their literature and music on the same principle as they did their houses and their furniture. The music and literature are forceful, direct, and without embellishments, and are simply another expression of the way in which they chose to live. Shaker music was confined to hymns, and the literature chiefly to Shaker history, religious discourse, and the application of religion to the current world problems.

In the early days of the organization musical instruments were not allowed, but as the years passed, new members who had training in music and were players of instruments, encouraged the use of instrumental accompaniment. Isaac N. Youngs, nephew of Benjamin Youngs, the well-known Shaker clockmaker, of the New Lebanon Society, and Abraham Whitney of Shirley, were teachers of music among the Believers. Youngs wrote on the theory of music, while Whitney was an instrumental music teacher among the several Societies. In 1815 an anthem was written with notes and sent to the Ohio Society by a Mount Lebanon member, and about this time the Harvard Society began to make use of the letters of the alphabet in special musical notation. This device was adopted and used for many years in the Society. The first seven letters of the alphabet were employed, the Roman letters designated quarter notes, the italic letters the eighth notes. Half notes had the addition of a single line by the side of the letter. This method of notation was developed and perfected by Brother Isaac N. Youngs of Mount Lebanon and Brother Russell Haskell of Enfield, Connecticut. In 1847 Haskell issued "Musical Expositor" for teaching this method, and the results were prodigious. Songs were exchanged among the various societies, and these were copied in books by the members who learned them by heart, for no books were taken into the meeting house, except by the leaders. Many of these copy books are extant. About 1870 this letter notation was abandoned and the regular musical note system was used, since confusion had crept into the special system of writing.

By 1870 pianos, organs and other musical instruments were used freely in the Shaker societies, and without objection. Today, at Canterbury, New Hampshire, there is a pipe organ in the meeting room. It is played by Sisters who are well trained as organists and vocalists. A member of the original and well-known Shaker quartette, Sister Helena Sarle, is still living at Canterbury, New Hampshire.

Many printed volumes of music have been published since "Millennial Praises" was issued by the Hancock Society (now West Pittsfield, Massachusetts) in 1812. Other important music books are "Millennial Hymns" which appeared in 1847, and "Canterbury Book" or "Hymns and Anthems for the Hour of Worship," published in 1892. At Mount Lebanon, New York the Society's musicians published "Original Inspirational Shaker Music" in two volumes, dated 1881 and 1893. Nowhere in any of these books is there an indication as to the author of the music or words of the hymns but to these two volumes Eldress Rosetta Stephens made a great contribution.

Today a group of singers, headed by Mrs. Fred Parker Carr of Enfield, New Hampshire, interprets these Shaker songs with great feeling and accuracy. Despite Mrs. Carr's public announcement at every peformance that she and her singers are not Shakers, and they never had any connection with the Shaker Society, they are referred to as "Shakers." The results of these recitals are so successful that there is no wonder that Mrs. Carr and her fellow singers are known as the Shaker singers.

No mention can be made of Shaker music without reference to Miss Estella T. Weeks, Musicologist, of Washington, D. C., who for many years has been a persistent researcher in this

field. She is truly a dedicated person who has worked unstint-
ingly and often at great personal sacrifice, to increase knowledge
of the unexplored field of Shaker music, or inquire into this
realm, and as a result has amassed a wealth of materials on
Shaker music and musicians.

INDUSTRY

Shaker manufacturing was at its height during the period of
greatest membership. The public demand for their goods
regulated the output, which was large, since the dependable
quality of Shaker products made them acceptable anywhere.
The name "Shaker" associated with any ware was a guarantee
of honesty and fair dealing

Agriculture was the basic occupation of the early Shakers,
but with economic changes, both from within the society and in
the outside world, the manufacturing of various commodities
became necessary. Overproduction beyond the needs of the
community was inevitable, and products had to be bought
from the outside and theirs sold to the outside; consequently,
great businesses and business acumen were developed.

The Shakers grew garden seeds that they put in packages to
sell to home gardeners and farmers. The demand for seed became great because of the quality of the product and the high
germination count. The Shaker brethren traveled beyond the
immediate environs of the community peddling seed to farmers
and gardeners. The Shaker records show that this garden seed
business was instituted about 1789, which made them the first
to commercialize this product. By 1830 the Shaker seeds were
familiar in all parts of the country. Shaker seed wagons were
familiar. Seed catalogs were issued, posters were seen in the
general stores, and seed boxes were on hardware and general
store counters. The advent of the steamship in 1807, the opening

of the Erie Canal in 1825, and transportation by railway made it possible to ship seeds to all parts of the nation and in large quantities. This industry alone resulted in large incomes for the various Shaker societies, until the outside world business men built up their own seed business through greater advertising and investments. Thus was ended this business for the Shakers. It should be remembered that competition was forbidden in the Shaker doctrine.

The medical herb business followed closely and was established at Mount Lebanon, New York, about 1800. This business grew to such an extent that the Center Family, Mount Lebanon, built a special herb and herb extract building which was set up with the latest equipment from the world and of Shaker invention. Under the management of competent botanist Elias Harlow, and Brother Barnabus Hinkley, a graduate of the Pittsfield, Massachusetts, Medical College, this business flourished.

Dessicated medical herbs, extracts, powder, essential oils, salves, syrup compounds, and pills were sold all over the world to druggists and doctors. To meet the demand for these products the Shakers were forced to buy roots, and barks, and herbs from neighboring farmers, whose products were closely inspected by Shaker botanists.

Rafinesque, in his trip to America, visited the botanical or physic gardens of the Shakers, both in New York and Kentucky. (C. S. Rafinesque (1783-1840) — "A Life of Travels," printed 1836). He wrote, "The best medical gardens in the United States are those established by communities of Shakers, or Modern Essenians, who cultivate and collect a great variety of medicinal plants. They sell them cheap, fresh and genuine."

Shaker chairs were the earliest of the products made by the Society to sell, and are still sought by collectors. More chairs will be found in antique shops and homes than any other pieces. The reason is that chairs were made by the thousands by the several Societies, and shipped all over the United States, Canada, and even to Europe, Africa, and South America. Other furniture was limited since it was made for home use only. Eldress Sarah Collins, the last to carry on the chair business at Mount Lebanon, New York, with Sister Lillian Barlow, told the writer, "Yea, I shipped Shaker chairs all over the world during my day."

These chairs, both straight and rockers, were of a simple New England slat back type. The upper rear post terminated with a pine cone shaped finial, but without imitation carving. The rockers were with and without arms. The early types of rockers had graceful curved arms that were held to the front post by being doweled into it. The front post ran through the bored hole in the arm and the hole was covered by a morticed biscuit finial. The seats of the chairs were commonly woven in by a woven "listing tape" about three-fourths of an inch wide, in a basket-like or checkerboard pattern. Split maple and white oak bottoms were also used. The chairs were noted for their graceful contour, lightness in weight, and durability. The Shaker craftsman knew the physics of stress and strain, and applied this knowledge to chair building.

Many of the side chairs, or "tilting chairs," were fitted with a special Shaker innovation, the ball and socket in the lower rear post. The ball, flattened on the floor end, is attached in the socket by a leather thong. This device prevents slipping and the damaging of floor or carpet. Chairs like these are now being reproduced by non-Shaker craftsmen.

Many other businesses were engaged in by the various Shaker communities, such as the making of tin ware for the kitchen and dairy, tanning of leather and making of shoes and leather goods, weaving of cloth, making of hats, fans, cloaks, and the canning of vegetables and fruits. The Shakers were forced to discontinue these occupational pursuits when they could not compete with outside industry, or when the reduction in membership did not permit them to continue. The Shakers could not employ labor in the shops, since this was contrary to the plan to withdraw themselves from the "world's people."

28

Sister Sadie Neale (1849-1948), nonagenarian member of
the Believers, remembered when the Church Family, Mount
Lebanon, New York, was producing eighty different types
of baskets. These ranged in size from small button baskets,
made by the Sisters, to large storage baskets measuring six
feet, made by the Brethren. The materials, used in basket-mak-
ing were maple splints, white oak splints, and willow. Many
baskets with designs on the splints found by collectors at Shaker
communities were probably exchanged by Indians for Shaker
products.

INVENTIONS

Today many of the household and industrial objects we
now use are of Shaker origin, but have lost their association,
since the Believers did not patent their inventions.

The circular saw was invented by Sister Tabitha Babbit,
of the Harvard Society, Massachusetts, who noticed that one
half of the motion of straight sawing was lost, so designed
a saw in tin and attached it to her spinning wheel and sawed
a shingle. One of the Brethren made a steel saw under her
direction, and this was as accredited the first circular saw the
world knew ("Gleaning from Old Shaker Journals," by Clara
E. Sears, 1916; "Simonds Guide for Millmen," Simonds
Manufacturing Company, Vol. XIV, No. 2, March-April, 1922).
The metallic pen, the clothespin, babbit metal, apple-parers
and the first one-horse wagon used in the United States are
also among the many Shaker inventions, but not so known to
the general public.

The flat corn broom, such as we use today, and a decided
improvement over the round bundle type, was invented by
Brother Theodore Bates, of the Watervliet, New York Society.

This business was established at Watervliet in 1789. Brooms of all sizes and hairbrushes were made in the various communes for every purpose. Shaker brooms and brushes were known in thousands of households in the United States.

These are but a few of the Shaker inventions that contributed to the industrial and economic history of the United States.

THE END

The great Shaker building stands today as monuments to consecrated labor, thrift, and ingenuity. The decay that now surrounds the dwelling houses, barns and shops, shows that the end came with no resistance. In the barns are the reminders of days of great activity and labor. The hay rigs and mowing machines driven in during the last days of use are now covered with dust; the cradle scythes, that once were swung by sturdy young Brethren, hang from pegs, rusty and wrapped in cobwebs. The cattle stalls are worn and untenanted, but bear a sign giving the pedigree of their last occupant: Marian, April 1, 1924; Dam, Canterbury Bell, Sire King Juba.

As the membership grew smaller in a community, it became impractical to carry on, and those few members left migrated to live in other Shaker homes. The surviving Shaker colonies are at Canterbury, New Hampshire, Sabbathday Lake, Maine, and West Pittsfield, Massachusetts. Other groups in Maine, New Hampshire, Connecticut, New York, Ohio, Florida, Kentucky, and Indiana have long been closed. To the present younger generations, who now live near these former settlements, Shaker Heights, Shaker Road, Ann Lee Home, mean little or nothing, since such names do nothing to bring back the memories of those peaceful people who once were neighbors.

The total Shaker population in the extant colonies is now under thirty persons, and the prospects are that soon these people will all be transferred to one community. The end is inevitable, and the Shakers' history will close within the life time of the reader of this story.

Footnote:— Noteworthy collections of materials dealing with Shaker life are to be found in the Western Reserve Historical Society, Cleveland, Ohio; the Fruitland and Wayside Museum, founded by Miss Clara Endicott Sears, at Harvard, Massachusetts; the New York State Museum at Albany, and the Good Hope Farms, Shaker Museum, Old Chatham, New York, founded by John S. Williams. Literature and manuscripts are to be found in the New York State Library at Albany; Williams College, Williamstown, Massachusetts; the Grosvenor Library, Buffalo, New York; the New York Public Library at 42nd Street and Fifth Avenue, New York City; and the Library of Congress at Washington. The most comprehensive record of Shaker Arts will be found in the Federal Index to Design, National Art Gallery, Washington, D. C. These are chiefly watercolor renderings made by the artists working under the Federal Works Progress Administration during the economic recession of 1929 to 1937.

KITCHEN HINTS

A small piece of charcoal put into the pot with boiling cabbage removes the smell.

In boiling meat for soup use cold water to extract the juices. If the meat is wanted for itself alone plunge into boiling water at once.

A smart girl on shipboard found out from the cook how to peel and slice onions without crying over them. Very simple:

Just hold them under water.

Soaking salt fish in sour milk will freshen them speedily.

Salt curdles new milk; hence, in preparing milk porridge, gravies, etc. the salt should not be added until the dish is prepared.

Manifesto — 1879

In *grating nutmeg* begin at the flower end; if you commence at the other, there will be a hole all the way through.

Manifesto — 1882

Never allow salt meats of any kind to boil hard.

Manifesto — 1882

Tough meat may be made quite tender by soaking it in vinegar and water for six or seven hours.

Manifesto — 1882

A lump of bread about twice the size of an egg tied in a linen bag and inserted in the pot which boils vegetables, will absorb the gases which oftentimes send such an insupportable odor to region above.

Sabbathday Lake Shakers

Cooking does not render diseased or putrefying meat wholesome.

Manifesto — 1883

A correspondent asks how to keep fresh meat from tainting. Pour a little good vinegar into a spoon, dip a finger into it, and pass it over the entire surface of the raw meat.

Manifesto — 1879

Vinegar should be kept in glass or wooden jars. The acetic acid acts on stone or earthen vessels.

Manifesto—1881

Inhale the fresh air freely before partaking of the morning meal, it gives zest to it.

Manifesto — 1878

STORAGE

Keep tea in a closed chest or canister.
Keep coffee by itself, as its odor affects other articles.
Bread or cake should be kept in a tin box or stone jar.

Manifesto — 1881

VALUE OF FOOD

One pound of corn is equal, as food, to four pounds of potatoes, and more than equal to eight pounds of cabbage, or twelve and a half pounds of turnips. Meat is not fattening, but is muscle yielding and strengthening. Grains are fattening.

Manifesto — 1878

SANITARY RULES

Never eat or drink contrary to your own conscientious principles even though others may deride you.
Never drink unless you are thirsty, and then nature's wholesome and healthful beverage will be agreeable and delightful.
Never wear more clothing than is sufficient to keep the body warm.
Never let a day pass by without shedding on some one a ray of the sunshine of good will and kindly cheerfulness.

Manifesto — 1885

Never eat what you do not need because it pleases your taste. It is better to bear the cross and be saved from dyspepsia.
Never eat between meals.

Manifesto — 1878

WEIGHTS AND MEASURES

Wheat flour, one pound is one quart.
Indian meal, one lb. two oz. are one quart.
Butter, when soft, one lb. is one quart.
Loaf sugar, broken, one lb. is one quart.
White sugar powdered, one lb. one oz. are one quart.
Ten eggs are one lb.
Flour, eight qts. are one peck.
Flour, four pecks are one bushel.

Manifesto — 1878

LIQUIDS, ETC.

Sixteen large tablespoons are half a pt.
Eight large tablespoonfuls are one gill.
Four large tablespoonfuls are half a gill.
Two gills are one pint.
Two pints are one quart.
Four quarts are one gallon.
A common sized tumbler holds one half pt.
A common sized wine-glass, half a gill.
A teacup holds one gill.
A large wine glass is two ounces.
A tablespoonful is half an ounce.
Forty drops equal one teaspoonful.

Manifesto — 1878

PART I

BEVERAGES

WATER

Pure cold water is the best drink that God ever gave to man, and foolish are they who do not avail themselves of the blessing.

Manifesto — 1879

MEAT, TEA AND COFFEE

Meat, tea and coffee are not suitable for young children, neither are cake and candy, except in small quantities.

Manifesto — 1895

COFFEE

Take one tea-cup of Java, or whatever kind you have, break in one egg, stir together, add cold water, then turn on boiling hot water, set on the back of the stove, let it stand fifteen or twenty minutes, and I will warrant you to have a good dish if plenty of sugar and cream are added. I have a coffee-pot that holds about three pints.

Manifesto—1881

SHELLS

Put one quart of cold water and half a cupful of shells into the pot and boil gently four or five hours, add boiling water occasionally. About 20 minutes before serving, add one pint of new milk and boiling water enough to make three pints in all; let this boil a few minutes, strain and serve. The milk may be omitted and more water used.

Sister Mary Whitcher's
Shaker Housekeeper

NOTE: The shells mentioned are the outer covering of the
cocoa bean and make a delicious drink, something
like chocolate or cocoa, but it is not so heavy or
rich. We used a great deal of them for our children's
breakfasts and how they loved it on cold winter
mornings. We never boiled them more than an
hour and usually made it half and half milk and
water.

Sister Jennie M. Wells

TEA

At first, the Society used but a small amount of foreign
tea, but in place of this used Sage, Redroot, Aven's-root and
Liberty tea. In a few years the tea from China was accepted
and used with milk and sugar, particularly for breakfast. In
1808 tea was used, largely, without sweetening and this continued for several years. In 1840 all foreign tea was removed
from the table and used only by direction of the physicians.
Domestic tea was now used by the family. Some preferred
to drink milk while others accepted milk and water. Foreign
tea and coffee were again introduced in 1855 and Believers
have been more or less affected by the prevailing sentiment
around them. Several persons accepted the reform views of
Sylvester Graham, and abstained from the use of tea and
coffee, and from the eating of meat, and all animal fats. The
vegetable diet had found some earnest advocates, who believed that all food should be prepared in a simple and healthful manner.

Manifesto — 1879

COMPOSITION TEA

This almost universal remedy of the Shakers, and which
has been sought for by so many thousands as a panacea for
colds, coughs, lung irregularities and inflammations, is now
made public. Take two pounds of bayberry root bark, one

pound of the inner bark of hemlock, one pound of ginger, two ounces of cayenne pepper, all reduced to a powder and sifted through a fine sieve. Mix well together.

DOSE: One teaspoonful in a half-teacupful of hot water; add milk and sugar to please the taste and drink, as warm as consistent.

Manifesto — 1878

BEER

Take three gallons of water blood warm, three half-pints of molasses, a tablespoon of essence of spruce, and the like quantity of ginger-mix well together, with a gill of yeast, let it stand over night, and bottle in the morning. It will be in good condition to drink in 24 hours, it is a palatable, wholesome beverage.

A Collection of Useful Hints for
Farmers and Many Valuable Recipes
by James Holmes

A RECEIPT TO MAKE STRONG BEER

Two lbs. of hops put in six or seven pales of water and boil till it is strong then strain off and put the hops into the same quantity of water going over the same process. Then if the strength of the hops are not all out put in enough fresh water to make a barrel and strain it off and mix all together then take as large a kettle as you have, put in five galons of molasses and fill it up with liquor and boil it one hour then mix all together and set it off in coolers to cool. Now put it into the barrel and add half a pint of emptains that is good then set it by to work and fill it up every day, let it stand six months before it is used. The best time to brew it is in November or the first of December.

Shaker Manuscript,
Fruitlands and Wayside Museum,
Harvard, Mass.

COCOANUT DRINK

To two grated cocoanuts, with their milk, add two quarts of pure water; place over the fire and boil for five or six minutes, stirring constantly with a wooden spatula; then strain. Add to the liquid twelve ounces of pulverized sugar, mix well and ice. This is delightfully cooling.

Manifesto — 1879

CHOCOLATE

With four spoonfuls of grated chocolate mix one of sugar, and wet with one of boiling water. Rub this smooth with the bowl of the spoon, and then stir into one quart of boiling milk. Let this boil up once and serve.

Sister Mary Whitcher's
Shaker Housekeeper

BOILED CIDER

Take four gallons of cider and boil it to one gallon.

Sister Mary Whitcher's
Shaker Housekeeper

DANDELION WINE

Four quarts blossoms, pressed in measure, twelve quarts boiling water. Let stand until cool and strain. Seven lbs. sugar, grated rind of three lemons, boil one hour. Let cool and add yeast cake, let stand four days, then add juice of three lemons and strain into jug. Do *not* cork tight for a week and then let it stand for four months and bottle.

Eva C. Josselyn

GRAPE WINE

Select nice ripe grapes, remove them from their stems, reject all specked ones, mash the grapes to a pulp, and press out all the juice. Add to every quart of grape juice two quarts

of cold water and three and one half pounds of sugar. Put
the mixture into a clean keg or barrel, lay the barrel in a cool
cellar and let it ferment. The barrel should be kept full all
the time while the fermentation is going on, leaving the bung-
hole open Add every morning some sugar syrup to keep the
barrel full (the sugar syrup may be made by dissolving one
pound of sugar in one quart of water). When fermentation
has run its course and no noise can be detected in the barrel,
drive in the bung, and let the barrel lie for three or four
months; then draw off the wine; either fill into bottles or
put it in a clean barrel. Small quantities may be made in
large demijohns or five or ten gallon kegs In draining off
the wine can be drawn off through the slough without disturbing the bottom. If the wine were to be drawn through
a faucet it would be muddy as there is always a settlement
at the bottom. The settlement should be filtered through a
canton flannel bag.

Sabbathday Lake Shakers

TURKISH BEVERAGE

Put ripe grapes, picked from their stems, into an earthen
pan or dish, and cover them with boiling water. Set the pan
in a warm situation for four or five hours then strain off the
liquid, sweeten to taste, and place in a freezer and half freeze.
Grated pineapple, treated in the same way forms also a delicious
beverage.

Manifesto — 1879

COCOA PASTE

Cocoa paste is made the same as chocolate, omitting the
sugar. Never boil chocolate or prepared cocoa more than one
minute. Boiling makes it oily. The quicker it is used after
making the better. Chocolate and cocoa that is made with all

or part water, is never rich and smooth. After using all milk you will never go back to the water again.

Sister Mary Whitcher's
Shaker Housekeeper

SYRUP OF COFFEE

This preparation is of great use to those who have long journeys to make. Take half a lb. of the best ground coffee, put into a sauce-pan containing three pints of water, when thoroughly steeped, pour off into another clean vessel and boil until reduced to one pint. As it boils, add white sugar enough to give it the consistency of syrup. Take it from the fire, when cold, put into a bottle and seal. When traveling, if you wish for a cup of good coffee, you have only to put two or three teaspoonfuls of the syrup into an ordinary cup, then pour boiling water upon it, and it is ready for use. We have proved it to be good.

Manifesto — 1878

SOUPS

THE CUISINE

Asparagus a la creme is one of the most delicious of soups. It is not difficult to prepare. First cut the points of the bunch of asparagus, and lay them aside. Cut the remainder in small pieces, add to it a pint of white stock with a few onions and cook until tender enough to press through a flour sieve. After straining the soup, add a pint of boiling milk, two table-spoons of butter, mixed with two tablespoons of flour, finally the asparagus peas. Let the soup cook 10 minutes longer stirring carefully all the time if the "peas" are large, it is better to parboil them in a little stock before putting them in to the soup for the last boiling. Add a cup of boiling cream last of all, and serve the soup with dropped eggs, if you wish, it is more delicate with toasted bread.

Sister Abigail Crossman

BLACK BEAN SOUP

Add to a large knuckle of veal four quarts of water and one quart of black beans that have been soaked in water over night, and let them boil with the veal four or five hours; add also, a small bit of onion, a dozen whole cloves, some salt and pepper, cut three hard-boiled eggs and two lemons into slices and put into the bottom of the tureen and strain the soup, boiling hot, upon them. If the water boils away, keep adding to it, as this recipe ought to make a gallon of soup. It should be of the consistency of pea soup. If you have no veal, the bones of salt pork make a good substitute.

Sister Mary Whitcher's
Shaker Housekeeper

BEEF TEA

We find in the Boston Journal of Chemistry—most excellent authority by the way—the following directions: Beef tea is too well known to need any special recommendation, but it is too often spoiled in the making. One ounce of beef to six tablespoonfuls of water is a fair proportion for a good article. Cut the meat into dice, put it into a stew-pan and add the water cold. Certain components of the beef are soluble in cold water; therefore let it stand ten minutes. Chicken for broth should be boiled for six hours in a covered stone jar set into a pan of boiling water. Gelatine (which for a long time considered as absolutely innutritious, but is now recognized by the best authorities, as valuable food) renders beef tea or chicken broth more nourishing, and, as a change, more acceptable to the patient. Soak a quarter of an ounce of

gelatine in a quarter of a pint of cold water, add to it a cupful of the tea or broth, and stir it over the fire till the gelatine
is dissolved, when cold it will be a firm jelly.

Manifesto—1881

BEEF TEA

Take beef of a good quality, very fresh, and guiltless of a
particle of fat, cut it into pieces one-fourth of an inch square,
put them in an earthenware vessel; add cold water until the
beef is a little more than covered. Let it soak three hours at
least; for a very dainty person five hours is better; then let
it cook on a slow fire for 10 minutes. Never strain it. Serve
up with pepper and salt to taste and with a bit of dry toast,
well browned.

*Sister Mary Whitcher's
Shaker Housekeeper*

BEEF SOUP

Break up the bones of a roast of beef, and lay them in the
pot; dredge with salt, pepper and flour. Cut into pot one small
onion, and add two and one-half quarts of cold water. Set the
soup on the fire, and when it comes to a boil, skim it. Let it
boil gently three hours, then add eight sliced potatoes and
boil 20 minutes more. Have ready dumplings; put them in
and cover tight and boil 10 minutes longer, then dish. First
take out dumplings, and place in a small platter; then turn
the soup into a tureen being careful to take out the bones,
and serve.

*Sister Mary Whitcher's
Shaker Housekeeper*

CLAM SOUP

To two quarts of the broth, add ten quarts water, salt, pepper and half an onion. Boil this till onion is tender, skim and
strain through a sieve. To a pint of cream add seven table-

spoons of flour, to thicken the broth. Just before dishing up, add the finely chopped clams and some rolled crackers.

Sister Marian Scott

CLAM SOUP

To two parts clam juice add six parts water. Cook thoroughly with a little onion, salt and pepper. Skim. When cooked, strain through a cloth. Thicken with cream to which has been added a little flour, and, just before serving add the finely chopped clams. Serve with oysterettes.

Amelia Calver,
Lebanon Valley Cookery — 1926

CLAM CHOWDER

Put in a pot a layer of sliced pork, chopped potatoes, chopped clams, salt, pepper and lumps of butter, and broken crackers soaked in milk, cover with the clam juice and water, stew slowly for three hours, thicken with a little flour, it may be seasoned with spices if preferred.

The story of the Shakers and some of their
favorite cooking recipes. Calendar 1882-3

CORN SOUP

A quart of milk, a pint of grated green corn, the same quantity of water, two tablespoonfuls of butter, a heaping tablespoonful of flour, a slice of onion, pepper and salt to taste. Cook the corn in water for half an hour. Let the milk and onion come to a boil. Mix the butter and flour together, and add a few tablespoonfuls of the milk. When perfectly smooth stir into the remainder of the milk and cook 8 minutes. Take out the onion, add the corn, season to taste, and serve.

Sister Mary Whitcher's
Shaker Housekeeper

FISH CHOWDER

Cut half a pound of salt pork into slices and put into the
stew-pan. Fry slowly for 12 minutes, then add two onions, cut
fine, and fry 10 minutes longer. Have about four pounds of
fresh fish freed of skin and bone and cut into pieces, have
also one quart of potatoes pared and cut in thin slices. Put a
layer of the fish and then a layer of the potatoes on top of the
pork and onions. Dredge well with salt, pepper and flour. Continue this until all the fish and potato are used; then cover
with boiling water, and simmer gently for 15 minutes. Mix one
pint of milk with two tablespoonfuls of flour and add this to
the chowder, together with six crackers, split. Cook 10 minutes
longer and serve. The milk may be omitted if not liked. In
that case, however, be a little generous with the boiling water
when you begin the chowder.

Sister Mary Whitcher's
Shaker Housekeeper

GREEN PEA SOUP

Cover a quart of green peas with hot water, and boil, with
an onion, until they will mash easily. (The time will depend
on the age of the peas, but will be from 20 to 30 minutes).
Mash, and add a pint of soup stock or water. Cook together
two tabespoonfuls of butter and one of flour until smooth,
but not brown; add this to the peas, and add also a cupful of
cream and one of milk. A cupful of whipped cream added
the last minute is an improvement.

Sister Mary Whitcher's
Shaker Housekeeper

OKRA SOUP — EQUAL TO TURTLE SOUP

One leg of beef, quarter to a package of okra, two carrots,
eight tomatoes, two onions, cut fine, nine quarts of water. Boil

six and one half hours. Cut the meat off the bone in small pieces. Take the most glutinous parts of the leg and a little of the flesh and mix with the soup when it is made. Cut the okra in small pieces round wise. Boil steadily, but not hard.

Sister Mary Whitcher's
Shaker Housekeeper

OYSTER SOUP

Take one quart of water, one teacup of butter, one pint of milk, two teaspoonfuls of salt, four crackers, rolled fine, and a teaspoonful of pepper. Bring to full boiling heat as soon as possible, then add one quart of oysters. Let the whole come to a boiling heat quickly and remove from the fire.

The story of the Shakers and some of their favorite
cooking recipes. Calendar 1882-3

OYSTER SOUP

Drain one quart of oysters, and to the liquor add one quart of boiling water; let it boil, skim carefully, season with a little Cayenne pepper and butter, size of an egg; add the oysters and let it boil up once, and season with salt and serve in a hot soup tureen.

Manifesto — 1880

MOCK OYSTER SOUP

Peel twelve good-sized tomatoes, and boil in a little water until quite soft. Let two quarts of milk come to a boil and thicken with two large crackers that have been rolled fine. Add one teaspoonful of soda to the tomatoes. When these are well broken up, season with salt, pepper and three tablespoonfuls of butter. Add to the milk, and serve immediately. The tomato may be strained if you prefer.

Sister Mary Whitcher's
Shaker Housekeeper

POTATO SOUP

The water in which the potatoes are boiled makes a delicious soup, by adding a little egg batter, a pinch of parsley, seasoning, a cup of milk, cream, or a bit of butter.

Sister Martha Anderson
Manifesto — 1892

TOMATO SOUP

One pint of canned tomatoes or four large raw ones, cut up fine. Add one quart of boiling water, and let them boil ten minutes or until done. Remove from the stove and stir in one teaspoonful of soda. While foaming add one pint of sweet milk, salt and pepper and a small piece of butter. To be eaten hot with crackers, like oyster soup, to which it is almost equal.

Manifesto — 1881

TOMATO SOUP

Three pounds of beef, one quart tomatoes, one gallon water. Let the meat and water boil for two hours or until the liquid is reduced to a little more than two quarts. Then stir in the tomatoes and stew all slowly for three-fourths of an hour longer. Season to taste, strain and serve.

The story of the Shakers and some of their favorite cooking recipes, Calendar 1882-3

TOMATO SOUP

Put a quart can of tomatoes and a pint of water on to boil. Mix a large tablespoonful of butter with two of flour and gradually stir into this mixture half a cupful of boiling tomato. When perfectly smooth, add to the greater quantity of tomato, and add, also, a teaspoonful of salt and one of sugar. Simmer fifteen minutes, and season with pepper. After straining through a fine sieve or steamer, serve with toasted bread.

Sister Mary Whitcher's
Shaker Housekeeper

TURKEY SOUP

Take the turkey bones and cook for one hour in water enough to cover them, then stir a little of the dressing and a beaten egg. A little chopped celery improves it. Take from the fire, and when the water has ceased boiling add a little butter, with pepper and salt.

The story of the Shakers and some of their favorite cooking recipes. Calendar 1882-3

SALADS

CABBAGE SALAD

One small head of cabbage, half a bunch of celery, one-fourth cup of vinegar, one tablespoonful of mustard, one egg well beaten, one tablespoonful of sugar, pepper and salt. Take a little of the vinegar to wet the mustard, put the rest over the fire; when boiling stir in ingredients and cook until it becomes thick; pour it over the cabbage while hot and mix it well. When cold, it is ready for the table. The same sauce, when cold will do for lettuce.

The story of the Shakers and some of their favorite cooking recipes. Calendar 1882-3

CABBAGE SALAD

Shave a hard white cabbage into small white strips, take the yolks of three well-beaten eggs, a cup and a half of good cider vinegar, two teaspoonfuls of white sugar, three table-

spoonfuls of thick cream, one teaspoonful of mustard mixed
in a little boiling water, salt and pepper to suit the taste. Mix
all but the eggs together and let it boil, then stir in eggs rapidly;
stir the cabbage into the mixture and stir well. Make enough
for two days as it keeps perfectly and is an excellent relish to
all kinds of meat. The regular French salad dressing is composed of three parts of salad oil to one of vinegar, with a
palatable seasoning of pepper and salt.

*The story of the Shakers and some of their
favorite cooking recipes. Calendar 1882-3*

COLD SLAW

Slice one quart of cabbage fine, take one teacup of vinegar,
one tablespoonful of butter, one of sugar, one teaspoon of salt,
a little pepper; put in cup and cook; it is done when it com-
mences to thicken; pour over cabbage.

Manifesto — 1879

RAW CABBAGE

A nice way to prepare raw cabbage is as follows: Select a
fine, good head; chop finely in a bowl what you think will be
needed, and to every quart add one half teacupful of thick
sweet cream; two tablespoonfuls of strong vinegar or lemon
juice, one cupful of white sugar and mix thoroughly.

Manifesto — 1880

SLAW

Cut a small head of cabbage in two, chop half very fine
and put in a bowl, put two tablespoonfuls of vinegar in a
saucepan and set on the fire. Beat two eggs light, add them
to half a cup cream and a tablespoon of melted butter. Stir
into boiling vinegar. Season with salt and pepper, mix with
the chopped cabbage and set on ice.

Sister Marian Scott

50

CHICKEN SALAD

For one good-sized chicken taken one bunch of celery chopped fine, a little pepper and salt. For dressing for the above quantity take the yolks of two eggs boiled hard, make them fine, and add mustard, vinegar, oil and a little cayenne pepper and salt to suit taste, and the liquor of the chicken boiled in is very nice to use, mixing it. Put in just enough to moisten it nicely. When it becomes cold, it is just like a jelly, but it is a great improvement to the salad.

The story of the Shakers and some of their favorite cooking recipes. Calendar 1882-3

HAM SALAD

Take the lean part of three pounds of cold boiled ham and chop fine (cut three or four bunches of celery in small pieces.) Three tablespoons of olive oil, half a small cup of vinegar, yolks of five hard boiled eggs, one tablespoon mustard, half a teaspoonful of pepper and one teaspoonful each of sugar and salt. Pour over the ham just before serving.

Sister Marian Scott

POTATO SALAD

Slice thin six or eight medium-sized boiled potatoes, mince fine two silver-skin onions, so as to get the flavor and not detect the onions in pieces, mix parsley and the potatoes with the onions, and season with salt and cayenne pepper. Moisten one-third teaspoonful of dry mustard with a teaspoonful of hot water; put the yolks of two eggs in same dish, beat together with an egg-beater until well mixed, then drip in sweet oil beating all the time until it thickens like a custard, add one and one half tablespoonfuls of vinegar. Put this dressing over the potatoes and mix all together. The dish can be garnished with celery tops and made very pretty.

Sister Mary Whitcher's Shaker Housekeeper

POTATO SALAD

Chop fine six boiled potatoes and three small onions. Mix with a tablespoonful of chopped parsley and three or four stalks of celery. Pour over French dressing.

Sister Marian Scott

SALMON SALAD

Mince one pound of salmon either fresh or canned. Cut up one-third as much celery. Boil four eggs, separate the whites from the yolks and lay aside. Mash the yolks to a smooth paste with two tablespoonfuls of olive oil, one teacup of good vinegar with one tablespoon of sugar and one teaspoonful of salt, two teaspoonsfuls of mustard and a little pepper. Pour lightly over the salmon and celery. Garnish the dish with the celery tops and the rings of the hard boiled eggs. Set on ice.

Sister Marian Scott

VEGETABLES

CLEANING VEGETABLES

Peas and beans may be prepared for canning by simply cooking them as you would for the table, leaving out the seasoning and filling the cans quite up to the top while boiling hot. Have the peas rather young and tender. Add the seasoning when you open the cans to use them. Keep them in a cool, dark place, free from dampness. Corn, to can, should be young and tender, but full grown. Strip off the outside leaves and silk, but leave on the inner leaves, this will keep the sweetness in. Let it boil 15 minutes. Take it up, cut the kernels through the middle, and then take a cob that will fit in the jar without its being broken, and press it into the middle of the corn, and screw the tops on. Have the cans and the corn as hot as possible.

Manifesto — 1882

How To Cook Stringbeans

There is a way to cook this vegetable—a method always practiced at our house by which it is very much improved both in appearance and flavor. The pods are split (not opened at the edges, but in an opposite direction) from end to end, and then cut into short pieces as in the usual way; they are then boiled in any suitable vessel separated from meat or other vegetables, a small quantity of pearlash or saleratus having been thrown into the water. When taken from the water after having been sufficiently cooked, they are of a beutiful bright green color, and will be found much more tender and delicate than when cooked without saleratus. They are of course to be seasoned.

A Collection of Useful Hints For
Farmers and Many Valuable Recipes,
by James Holmes

Beets

One of the most satisfactory ways to cook beets is to to bake them. When boiled, even if their jackets are left on, a great deal of the best part of the beet is dissolved, and so lost. It will, of course, take a little longer to bake than to boil them; but this is no objection. Allow from fifteen to twenty minutes more for baking; slice them, and heat as you would if they were boiled. After they are cooked, season with pepper, salt and butter and a squeeze of lemon.

Manifesto — 1881

Beets

No knife should ever touch a beet previous to boiling, rub the leaves off by hand, for if there is a wound made in the beet, the best of its juices will be lost in boiling. Drop the beets into boiling water with a handful of salt. Most cooks take beets from the boiling kettle and place them in cold water for the ease with which the skin peels off. This should never be done, as they part with one half their flavor. When taken from the pot let them drain, then peel and slice them, butter and salt them, or pour good vinegar over, which many prefer.

A Collection of Useful Hints for Farmers
and Many Valuable Recipes
by James Holmes

TURNIPETTS

The true way to cook a beet is to bake, not boil it. Thus treated and sliced either in vinegar or in butter, it is much sweeter than when boiled, and said to be more nutritious. I save the vinegar in which my beets were pickled for dinner, the next day boiled a few small young turnips and sliced them up in the same vinegar. I added a little fresh vinegar, pepper and salt, and no one at the table knew that they were not eating white beets, until I called their attention to the fact.

Manifesto — 1879

CAULIFLOWER

Remove the green leaves and wash the cauliflower clean. Place in a deep saucepan, head downward, and cover with boiling water. Simmer gently one hour, serve with a cream and butter sauce.

Sister Mary Whitcher's
Shaker Housekeeper

COOKED CELERY

The green stalks of celery are cut up in small pieces and cooked until tender, which takes several hours. Season when well done; when ready to take up add a little thickened milk or cream, and put on nice fresh slices of toasted bread.

Sister Martha Anderson
Manifesto — 1892

ONIONS

From our own experience and the observation of others, we can fully indorse the testimony of the St. Louis Miller of the healthful properties of the above esculent. Lung and liver complaints are certainly benefitted, often cured, by a free consumption of onions, either cooked or raw. Colds yield to them like magic. Don't be afraid of them. Taken at night, all offense will be wanting by morning, and the good effects will amply compensate for the trifling annoyance. Taken regularly, they greatly promote the health of the lungs and the digestive organs. An extract made by boiling down the juice of onions to a syrup, and taken as a medicine, answers the purpose very well, but fried, roasted or boiled onions are better. Onions are very cheap medicine, within everybody's reach; and they are not by any means as "bad to take" as the costly nostrums a neglect of their use may necessitate.

Manifesto — 1881

FRIED PARSNIPS

After scraping the parsnips boil them gently for about three-fourths of an hour. When they are cold cut them into long slices about one-third of an inch thick, and season with pepper and salt. Dip in melted butter and then in flour. Put two table-spoonfuls of butter in frying-pan, and as soon as hot lay in slices enough to cover the bottom. Fry brown on both sides. Serve on a hot dish.

Sister Mary Whitcher's
Shaker Housekeeper

HOW TO TELL GOOD POTATO

Here is a good place in which to impart what is a secret to the vast majority of people, and it is one well worth knowing. It is simply how to tell a good potato; that is, as well as it can be done without cooking it, for sometimes even experts are deceived. Take a sound potato, and paying no attention to its outer appearance, divide it into two pieces with your knife and examine the exposed surfaces. If there is so much water or "juice" that seemingly a slight pressure would cause it to fall off in drops, you may be sure it will be "soggy" after it is boiled. These are the requisite qualities for a good potato, which must appear when one is cut in two: For color a yellowish white, if it is a deep yellow the potato will not cook well; there must be a considerable amount of moisture, though not too much, rub the two pieces together and a white froth will appear around the edges and upon the two surfaces, this signifies the presence of starch, and the more starch, and consequently froth, the better the potato, while the less there is the poorer it will cook. The strength of the starchy element can be tested by releasing the hold upon one piece of the potato, and if it still clings to the other this in itself is a very good sign. These are the experiments generally made by experts, and they are ordinarily willing to buy on the strength of their turning out well, though as stated above, these tests are by no means infallible.

Manifesto — 1881

Soaking Potatoes

The common practice of paring potatoes and leaving them for hours, and sometimes for days, reduces their value exceedingly as food. Solon Robinson in "How to Live" tells us that meat, fish, potatoes, and else, when left for twelve hours in water, impart to the water half their value. If, then, they are left to soak longer than twelve hours, there is more value in the water which is commonly thrown away, than in the article to be cooked. So far as the cooking of potatoes is in question, those who soak them for hours, are worthy of being called very poor cooks; as a comparison between tubers soaked and unsoaked will abundantly testify.

Manifesto — 1878

Boiled Potatoes

Pare the potatoes, cover them with boiling water, and boil 30 minutes. When they have been cooking 15 minutes add one tablespoonful of salt for every dozen potatoes. When cooked, drain off every drop of water and place the kettle on the back part of the stove for a moment. If you are not ready for the potatoes as soon as cooked, cover with a clean towel, but do not put the cover of the kettle on. The steam must pass off, or the potatoes will be soggy and strong flavored. It takes a good cook to boil a potato.

Sister Mary Whitcher's
Shaker Housekeeper

Baked Potatoes

Wash and nip good sized potatoes and bake in a moderate oven 45 minutes. They are spoiled by being over-cooked.

Sister Mary Whitcher's
Shaker Housekeeper

How to Cook Potatoes

There are two ways of boiling potatoes—both are good. The first fashion is to put them into well salted cold water; having let them boil until they are nearly done, pour off nearly all the water, set them back on the fire, cover and let them steam until thoroughly done. Take off the cover and let them stay a moment or two to evaporate the moisture.

The other way is to drop the potatoes into enough boiling water to cover them, and as soon as they are done pour off the water entirely and put back on the range to evaporate the moisture, put the cover on the kettle so that about a quarter of the mouth is left open to the air. They must boil from thirty to thirty-five minutes. Always select potatoes as nearly of a size as possible. New potatoes with delicate skins, should not be pared for boiling. Take a sharp knife and scrape off the skins. In the country new potatoes, just brought in from the garden, do not even need scraping; a few smart turns with a rough-textured cloth takes off the fine skin in a twinkling. But the dwellers in towns don't get these ideal potatoes. For perfect mashed potatoes, pare and boil them as above, and after every trace of the water has evaporated, mash them with your pestal still in the kettle over the fire; they are naught if not kept hot. Get out every suggestion of a lump, and as you mash them put in a generous quantity of fresh butter, and, if you have it, some cream—if not cream—enough milk to make the potato rich and moist. Salt it to taste, and serve fresh and hot piled up and smoothed over in a hot dish with a little black pepper sifted on top. Mashed potato which stood on the stove for a while before serving is poor stuff. If you want the top brown, hold over it a salamander or a very hot stove lid—don't push the dish into the oven; that only makes the contents watery.

Manifesto — 1881

SHAKER CREAMED POTATOES

Slice cold potatoes thin, place on stove in an iron frying pan in which a generous lump of butter has been heated (not browned). Pour in milk to half fill the pan, heat to boiling point and then pour in sliced potatoes, salt and let simmer. Turn once in a while till milk is absorbed.

Sister Jennie M. Wells

POTATO CAKES

Roast some potatoes in the oven. When done, skin and pound in a mortar with a small piece of butter, warmed in a little milk. Chop a shallot and a little parsley very finely, mix well with the potatoes, add pepper and salt; shape into cakes; egg and bread them, crumb them and fry a light brown.

The story of the Shakers and some of their favorite cooking recipes. Calendar 1882-3

POTATO CROQUETS

Boil and mash a dozen potatoes; add a piece of butter size of an egg, tablespoonful of white sugar, a little salt, and two well-beaten eggs. Mix well, Make them up into Cones; dip them into raw eggs, sift on plenty of bread crumbs, and fry brown like crullers.

Manifesto — 1878

MASHED POTATOES

Pare and boil for 30 minutes. Mash light and fine with a wooden masher. To every twelve potatoes add one teaspoonful of butter, half a cupful of boiling milk, and salt to taste.

Sister Mary Whitcher's
Shaker Housekeeper

POTATO PIE

Potato pie may be made by lining pie tins with ordinary pie crust, and filling with mashed potatoes seasoned with a little fried onion and summer savory. Put on an upper crust and bake from twenty to thirty minutes. Serve hot.

Manifesto — 1897

SWEET POTATOES

Wash and wipe. Bake in a moderate oven, if they are of medium size, one hour, but if they are large, one hour and a quarter.

Sister Mary Whitcher's
Shaker Housekeeper

SARATOGA FRIED POTATOES

Peel good-sized potatoes, slice them as evenly as possible, and drop them into ice-water; have a kettle of very hot lard, and after putting a few of the slices at a time into a towel and shaking in order to get out the moisture, drop into the boiling lard. Stir them occasionally, and when of a light brown take them out with a skimmer and they will be crisp and not greasy. Sprinkle salt over them while hot.

Sister Mary Whitcher's
Shaker Housekeeper

SQUASH

Pare the squash and boil in a little water for 30 minutes; or, better, steam it for forty. Mash well, and season with salt, pepper and butter.

Sister Mary Whitcher's
Shaker Housekeeper

DAILY USE OF TOMATO

Cut up with salt, vinegar and pepper, as you do cucumbers, and eat.

A Collection of Useful Hints for
Farmers and Many Valuable Recipes
by James Holmes

TOMATOES AS FOOD

Tomatoes, remarks an authority, are not without some defects as an article of food. They are not, like milk, a perfect diet of themselves, and besides, like most other articles of food, they contain some obnoxious qualities. But they need not be thrown aside on that account. Nature has provided us with such sufficient excretory organs that the obnoxious matter in our food, if in moderate amount, is readily cast out, and the body is protected against any material injury. Were it not so we should be obliged to throw out of our dietary many kinds of food now eaten, not only with impunity, but with advantage. Thus, red cabbage, cherries and peaches contain prussic acid, which is a deadly poison when taken in sufficient quantities. The very small amount of the poisoning acid these vegetables contain is cast out of the system without any material injury to the

person using them. A positive good may actually be derived
from the use of food containing some such foreign matter, by
way of giving increased activity and strength to the excretory
organs from their exercise in casting such foreign matter from
our bodies, provided the quantity is not so great as to over-
burden them. Since we are all the time liable to take in our
food substances the tendency of which is harmful, a good
development of efficiency in our excretory organs is necessary
to protect us against the pernicious effects which might otherwise occur. Almost every kind of grain and fruit in use contain
more or less things which in a larger amount would prove hurt-
ful. Unless we closely study our food, we are taking much ill
when we little suspect it. A Frenchman, not many years ago,
discovered a substance in wheat bran which under the high
heat used in baking, dissolved out and spread over the crumbs
of bread, of which bran forms a part, and discolored it, and
hence the brown stain peculiar to graham bread. But from this
discovery such bread has not been rejected but continues to be
accounted among the most wholesome kinds of food. Rye
is seldom the most healthful. Tea contains tannic acid, apples
contain malic acid, lemons and oranges citric acid, no one of
which is used either in nutrition or respiration but they only
become objectionable when used excessively.

Manifesto — 1882

SHAKER TOMATOES

To one quart of boiling tomato add one quart of cold milk
(if it all strings together do not be alarmed it will boil out);
when it foams up well, add some rolled cracker or bread crumbs,
let it boil the third time, season to taste with salt and pepper,
add a little cream or butter and serve boiling hot from a covered
dish.

Sister Martha Anderson
Manifesto — 1892

How to Stew Tomatoes

Take your tomato from the vine, ripe; slice up, put in the pot over the fire without water; stew them slow, and when done put in a small lump of butter, as you do apple sauce. If you choose, a little crumb of bread or pulverised crackers may be added.

*A Collection of Useful Hints for
Farmers and Many Valuable Recipes
by James Holmes*

Baked and Broiled Tomatoes

Baked tomatoes are very nice when prepared in the following manner: Place solid large tomatoes in a deep dish; open each tomato at the top and put in a few bread or cracker crumbs, pepper, salt and a little butter. Bake for about one hour in a moderately hot oven until the crumbs and tomatoes are a nice brown. To broil tomatoes, take solid "beef steak" tomatoes, cut in rather thin slices, broil them until brown, season with pepper, salt and butter, and serve plain or on toast.

Manifesto — 1881

Scalloped Tomatoes

Pare and slice fine ripe tomatoes; put into a bake-dish with alternate layers of buttered bread-crumbs; season each stratum of tomato with pepper and salt. Bake covered until very hot, then brown. The upper layer should be of crumbs.

Manifesto — 1879

Sliced Tomatoes

Take good ripe tomatoes, cut them in slices and sprinkle over them freely pulverized white sugar, then add claret wine sufficient to cover them. This method of preparing tomatoes for the table, we are assured by one who has made the experiment, is superior to anything yet discovered for the preparation of this excellent article.

Sister Abigail Crossman

MASHED TURNIPS

Pare, cut into slices. If the white turnips be used and they are fresh, they will cook in 40 minutes, but if they be the yellow kind, they must boil for two hours in plenty of water. Mash, and season with butter, salt and pepper.

Sister Mary Whitcher's
Shaker Housekeeper

DRIED SWEET CORN

The business was started in 1828, at Mt. Lebanon, New York. It was cooked by boiling on the cob, in a large iron kettle, taken from there, cut off with knives and dried in the sun on boards. In 1840 the first dryhouse was erected, having runways extending out from it, for large platforms on wheels to pass in and out, thus more easily caring for the corn, exposing it to the sun and preserving it from the rains, or dews by night. On these platforms the corn was spread very thinly, and raked at intervals to let the warm air percolate every kernel. It was a slow tedious process, the dissication finding great impediments in the fall of the year by cold, cloudy day—perhaps several rainy days in succession. Then the whole "batch" would sour; extra help would be added to stir it more frequently; and when the sun did favor it with his rays, and a slight breeze would blow, the entire settlement would be "regaled" with a hope at least, that the corn would be saved, because of the extensive, unpleasant very sour smell departing the corn, in the atmosphere.

Manifesto — 1879

VEGETARIAN DISHES

BOILED RICE

Wash in two waters one cupful of rice. Put it to boil in two quarts of boiling water and one tablespoonful of salt. Boil rapidly, with the cover off the sauce-pan, for 25 minutes. Turn into a colander to drain, and place where it will keep warm while the steak is broiling. The water in which it was boiled may be used to starch prints.

Sister Mary Whitcher's
Shaker Housekeeper

LUMBERMAN'S TOAST

Put over the fire one pint milk in double boiler. When hot, stir in one teaspoon flour mixed with two tablespoons cold water. As the milk gets hotter, add slowly two ounces grated cheese, then one ounce butter, teaspoon salt, dash Cayenne pepper, one egg well beaten and mixed with two tablespoons cold milk. Simmer 5 minutes and serve hot on buttered toast.

Lebanon Valley Cookery — 1926

A NICE DISH FOR BREAKFAST

Beat an egg and add a little salt. Pour in about two-thirds of a pint of water. Slice some bread, dip it, and fry in butter.

Sister Mary Whitcher's
Shaker Housekeeper

MOCK CREAM TOAST

This is a delicious side dish for breakfast. Melt in one quart of morning's milk about two ounces of butter, a large teaspoonful of flour, freed from lumps, and the yolks of three eggs, beaten light. Beat these ingredients together several minutes. Strain the cream through a fine hair sieve, and when wanted, heat it slowly, beating constantly with a brisk movement. It must not boil or it will curdle and lose the appearance of cream. When hot dip the toast. If not sufficiently seasoned with butter, add salt. Send to the table hot.

Sister Mary Whitcher's
Shaker Housekeeper

WHITE MONKEY ON TOAST

Six nicely browned buttered slices of toast. One pint of new milk in a double boiler. As soon as warm, mix one teaspoon flour with two of cold water. As the milk gets hotter, add slowly so as to dissolve it, two oz. of grated cheese, one oz. of butter, one teaspoon salt, a dash of cayenne pepper, and one egg well beaten and mixed with two tablespoons of cold milk. Let the mixture simmer 5 minutes and serve.

Sister Marian Scott

MACARONI WITH BROWN SAUCE

Break one-fourth of a pound of macaroni in pieces two inches long. Put one quart of soup stock on to boil. Add the macaroni, boil rapidly half an hour. Take up and drain. Brown a tablespoon of butter, add one tablespoon of flour, mix smoothly. Add half a pint of the stock and stir till it boils. Put in two tablespoons grated cheese with the macaroni. Let boil up once, season to taste and serve

Sister Marian Scott

Welsh Rarebit

Half a pound of cheese, two eggs, a speck of cayenne, a tablespoonful of butter, one teaspoonful mustard, half a teaspoonful of salt, half a cupful of cream. Break in the cheese in small pieces and put it and the other ingredients in a bright sauce pan, which put over boiling water. Stir until the cheese melts; then spread the mixture on slices of crisp toast, and serve immediately.

Sister Mary Whitcher's
Shaker Housekeeper

Macaroni

Break up a quarter of a pound of macaroni. Wash quickly in cold water and put into saucepan with two quarts of boiling water and teaspoonful of salt. Boil rapidly for 20 minutes. The saucepan must not be covered. Serve with butter and salt or with tomato sauce.

Another way would be to put it in a dish as soon as boiled, and pour over it one cupful of milk and a tablespoonful of butter, and then cover with grated cheese and brown in the oven.

Sister Mary Whitcher's
Shaker Housekeeper

SWEET CORN PUDDING

Take a dozen ears of sweet corn that is nearly ripe is the best, grate it into a pan then put six eggs, one half nutmeg, three quarts of milk, one teaspoonful of salt, one teacup of sugar and half cup of butter, bake in a milk pan at least two hours and a half, as it begins to bake stir it occasionally if the corn is too soft to grate, it can be shaved and scraped off the cob, and is very nearly as nice. The nutmeg can be omitted by those who do not like it as a flavoring.

Sister Abigail Crossman

EGGS

Wouldst Know Fresh Eggs

Les Mondes gives the following old recipe for testing the age of eggs which, it thinks, seems to have been forgotten. As *Nature* thinks so too, we may reproduce the recipe for our younger readers and also as having other possible applications. Dissolve 120 gramm. of common salt in a liter of water. An egg put in this solution on the day it is laid will sink to the bottom; one a day old will not reach quite to the bottom of the vessel; an egg three days old will swim in the liquid; while one more than three days old will swim on the surface.

Manifesto — 1881

Eggs

Eggs, when softboiled, are easily digested, but when hardboiled they require very strong powers of the stomach to digest them. If a person in health is going on a journey where he will be long in getting food, one or two hardboiled eggs, taken before setting out, will keep off the sensation of hunger for a considerable time. An egg for healthy child, is a good article of diet, but ought to be softboiled, and a due quantity of bread eaten with it. In cooking an egg with the shell on, place in boiling water and set off the fire. Let it stand six or seven minutes, when it will be much superior to one that is steadily kept boiling from two to four minutes. Eggs rubbed over with fat grease of any kind will keep fresh much longer than if this is not done. Perhaps there is no better way to prepare eggs for breakfast than to break them in to a large dish, season, pour in a little cream or milk; stir while cooking, and be sure and take off before it gets the least bit tough.

Manifesto — 1878

A good egg will sink in water.

A boiled egg which is done will dry quickly on the shell when taken from the kettle. The boiled eggs which adhere to the shell are fresh laid.

Manifesto — 1882

"Boss" Way to Cook Eggs

Butter a tin plate and break in four eggs, set in a steamer; place over a kettle of boiling water and steam until the whites are thoroughly cooked. They are very ornamental broken into patty tins, as they keep their form better. The whites when cooked in this manner are tender and light.

Manifesto — 1879

Brine for Eggs

One quart of unslaked lime, one teaspoonful of soda, one tablespoonful of salt, one gallon of water. Let it settle, place in another jar the eggs with the small end down, pour the thin liquor over them.

Sister Abigail Crossman

Devilled Eggs

Boil six eggs ten minutes, then lay in cold water till cold; then cut in halves, slicing a little off the bottom of each, so they will stand upright. Remove the yolks, and rub a smooth paste with a little melted butter, a bit each of cayenne and mustard, and a teaspoonful of vinegar. Fill the hollow whites with this, and send to the table upon a bed of chopped white cabbage. Lettuce may be used instead of cabbage, if in season, and a spoonful should be used half an egg.

Manifesto — 1879

Dropped Eggs

Have ready the skillet half-filled with salted water scalding hot, break each egg into a cup, and slip carefully into the hot water, so as not to break the yolk. While the eggs are boiling, throw the water over the yolk with a spoon. When the white looks firm, take them out with a perforated skimmer. Trim them neatly, place each on a piece of buttered toast, and send them to the table hot. About one-third of the egg is solid nutriment.

Manifesto — 1879

Egg Toast

Beat thoroughly four eggs. Put two tablespoons of butter in a saucepan and melt slowly, add a pinch of salt and pour in the eggs. Heat without boiling stirring constantly. When hot, spread on slices of nicely browned toast.

Sister Marian Scott

Omelette

For each egg four tablespoonfuls of rich milk, one scant teaspoon of flour in which is a little baking powder, also a little salt and pepper. Beat the yolks add to the milk, then stir in smoothly with the flour. Beat the whites to a stiff froth and add just before frying. Cook only on one side and turn half over. Cook rare. Three eggs with its added flour and milk is enough for four people.

Sister Amelia J. Calver

Omelette

One cup sweet milk, in which strain two teaspoonfuls of cornstarch, salt to taste. Four eggs, white and yolks beaten separately; butter half size of an egg. Put it in a frying pan, make hot but not scorched. Stir quickly together milk and yolks, and lastly whites, stir lightly and pour all into the hot butter. When browned lightly at bottom, turn one-half over the other and serve.

Manifesto — 1879

OMELETS

Take one teacupful of milk, one egg, one tablespoonful of flour. Bake in small tin pans. They require baking about 20 minutes. Eat warm with butter.

Sister Abigail Crossman

DELICATE OMELET

Mix a cupful of warm milk with a tablespoonful of melted butter, a tablespoonful of flour, wet with a little cold milk, a teaspoonful of salt, a little black pepper, and the yolks of six eggs, Add the whites last, beaten to a stiff froth. Bake 20 minutes in a deep dish.

Sister Mary Whitcher's
Shaker Housekeeper

TOMATO OMELET

When stewed, beat up a half dozen new laid eggs, the yolk and white separate; when each are well beaten, mix them with the tomato, put them in a pan, and heat them up; you have a fine omelet

A Collection of Useful Hints for
Farmers and Many Valuable Recipes
by James Holmes

QUAKER OMELET

Three eggs, a tablespoonful of butter, one and one half tablespoonfuls of corn starch, a teaspoonful of salt, one half cupful of milk. Heat the omeletpan (a frying pan may be used), together with a cover that will fit closely. In the meantime beat the yolks of the eggs, the cornstarch and the salt. Beat the whites to a stiff froth; add to the beaten yolks. Stir all together very thoroughly, and add the milk. Put the butter in the hot pan; when melted, pour in the mixture. Cover, and place on the stove, where it will brown but not burn. Cook about seven minutes; then fold it, turn on a hot dish and serve immediately.

Sister Mary Whitcher's
Shaker Housekeeper

SCRAMBLED EGGS

Beat well ten eggs, have your spider quite hot; put in a piece of butter the size of an egg, and when melted turn the eggs in and stir every minute until all are cooked; be careful not to cook too much.

Manifesto — 1879

SCRAMBLED EGGS

Six eggs, one coffee-cup of milk, one teaspoonful of butter, one teaspoonful of flour, and salt. Beat the eggs very light, rub the butter and flour together, add this to the milk after it has been placed on the stove, and becomes a little warm. Salt to taste. Add the eggs, and cook until the whites are cooked, and serve while hot, or with toast.

Manifesto — 1879

SPANISH EGGS

Add to two quarts of boiling water a tablespoonful of salt, and in it cook a cupful of rice for half an hour. After draining through a colander add a tablespoon of butter. Spread lightly on a hot platter, and on it place six dropped eggs.

Sister Mary Whitcher's
Shaker Housekeeper

STUFFED EGGS

Cut carefully in halves six hard-boiled eggs, take out their yolks and mash them with parsley and onion finely chopped, a teaspoonful of butter, the yolk of a raw egg, and salt and pepper; refill the white halves with the mixture and place them in a baking-dish, add white sauce, sprinkle over a little pound crackers, and set the dish in an oven a few minutes.

Sister Mary Whitcher's
Shaker Housekeeper

EGG PUFFS

Six eggs, one pint of milk, three spoonsful of flour, four ounces of butter melted, a spoonful of yeast; mix, and fill cups half full, bake 15 minutes, wine sauce.

Sister Abigail Crossman

TO BEAT WHITES OF EGGS

To beat the white of eggs quickly put in a pinch of salt. The cooler the eggs the quicker they will froth. Salt cools and also freshens them.

Manifesto — 1882

SHAKER FISH AND EGG

In a common saucepan heat one pint of new milk, or thin cream if you have it. Season with salt and let it simmer for a few minutes. Remove a portion of this gravy into another vessel and dissolve therein a small piece of butter. Into the saucepan slice a layer of boiled potatoes, making the slices say three-eights of an inch thick; to this add a little salt codfish, boiled and picked very fine, then a layer of boiled eggs, each egg cut in four or five slices. Alternate with another layer of potato, fish and egg, until the desired quantity is obtained. Now pour on the reserved gravy and cover for a few minutes, or until ready to place upon the table. When dished up, place upon the top of some of the sliced eggs. The eggs should be boiled six minutes and then immediately immersed in cold water. This prevents them from becoming too hard, and also toughens the shell, thus rendering it more easily removed. For four persons, about eight eggs and eight medium sized potatoes are needed. This quantity will require of salt fish about three tablespoonfuls, when nicely prepared this is really a delectable dish.

Sister Mary Whitcher's
Shaker Housekeeper

MEATS, POULTRY AND GAME

How to Bake Meat

Place it on a grate, in the dripping pan. Sprinkle on salt sufficient to season half through. Cover lightly with flour from the dredging box. The latter seals the pores, thus preserving the juice. Add water about one half inch deep, to absorbe the juices of the meat, and prevent its drying or burning upon the pan. When browned on one side turn over very carefully, aiming not to puncture it with knife or fork, thus letting the juice escape. Season and flour on this side, and leave to brown. During the process of baking occasionally dip up the juice with a large spoon, and pour over the meat. Beef should be cooked rare, other meats thoroughly. The oven should be tempered to bake quickly, but not hot enough to scorch.

Manifesto — 1878

Recipe for Curing Meat

In his last issue, Maj. Freas, the long-time editor of the Germantown *Telegraph*, says: "As the season has arrived when curing meat is in order, we republish as of old our famous recipe for curing beef, pork, mutton, hams, etc., as follows: 'To one gallon of water take 1½ lbs. of salt, ½ lb. of sugar, ½ oz. of saltpetre, ½ oz. of potash. (Omit the potash unless you can get the pure article Druggists usually keep it). In this ratio the pickle can be increased to any quantity desired. Let these be boiled together until all the dirt from the sugar rises to the top and is skimmed off. Then throw it into a tub to cool, and when cold pour it over your beef or pork. The meat must be well covered with pickle, and should not be put down for at least two days after killing, during which time it sould be slightly sprinkled with powdered saltpetre, which removes all the surface blood, etc., leaving the meat fresh and clean. Some omit boiling the pickle, and find it to answer well, though the operation of boiling purifies the pickle in salt and sugar. If this recipe is strictly followed it will require only a single trial to prove its superiority over the common way, will not soon be abandoned for any other. The meat is unsurpassed for sweetness, delicacy, and freshness of color.' "

Manifesto — 1881

To Make Tough Meat Tender

Soak it in vinegar and water; if a very large piece, for about 12 hours. For 10 pounds of beef use ¾ of water to ¾ of a pint of vinegar, and soak it for six or seven hours.

The story of the Shakers and some of their favorite cooking recipes. Calendar 1882-3.

Cold Meat

By the following method is cold roast beef or mutton as good the 2nd day as the 1st day. It is to be cut in thin slices, each slice dipped in flour and dusted with pepper and salt and sweet herbs if you like, then placed in layers in a deep dish, and covered with gravy and water. Catsup poured over or canned tomatoes are added, the dish filled with water then cover tightly and baked two hours or three. This makes even the poorest and toughest part of a roast tender and delicious.

Sister Abigail Crossman

MEAT PIE

Rub through a quart of flour 2 teaspoonfuls of cream of tartar, a piece of butter or lard the size of a large egg, well beaten first, and at least a tespoonful of salt. Dissolve 1 teaspoonful of soda in 1 cupful of milk or water, and mix with the flour, adding enough more to make the crust stiff enough to roll. Roll it half an inch thick, and use no bottom crust. Cover with cold water, bits of bone, gristle, and pieces of meat which are not nice for the pie, and simmer gently for a long time; strain off the gravy so made; thicken it with a small piece of butter and tablespoonful of flour, previously rubbed together. If you have plenty of gravy, save a part of it to serve in a tureen. Cut the cold meat into small square pieces, lay it in a baking dish (without an under-crust), add tiny bits of butter, pepper and salt, sprinkle a little bit of flour over the top and add a cupful of gravy or hot water; then cover with crust; bake about ¾ of an hour. A little onion, finely minced, is an improvement; or a few spoonfuls of canned tomatoes may be used.

Sister Mary Whitcher's
Shaker Housekeeper

MEAT HASH

Dredge with salt and pepper any kind of cold meat and chop it fine. This is always the best manner of seasoning hash, as all parts will be seasoned alike If you have cold potatoes, chop fine and mix with the meat, if they are hot, mash. Allow one pint of meat to two of potatoes. Put this mixture in the frying-pan with a little water or soup stock to moisten it, and stir in a spoonful of butter; or if you have nice beef dripping, use that instead of butter. Heat slowly, stirring often, and when warmed through, cover and let it stand on a moderately hot part of the stove or range twenty minutes. When ready to serve, fold as you would an omlet.

Sister Mary Whitcher's
Shaker Housekeeper

A LA MODE BEEF

Cut deep gashes in a piece of round of beef, weighing six pounds, and rub into them a handful of salt, a spoonful of cinnamon, half a spoonful of cloves, half a spoonful of allspice, a spoonful of mace, one of pepper and half a cupful of flour. Fill the gashes with dressing made as for turkey, with the addition of a little chopped onion. Sew the gashes together, and bind the beef with strips of cotton cloth. Lay the meat in a small kettle that can be covered tight; put in a whole onion, a slice of carrot, and one of turnip, and add boiling water enough to cover the piece. Simmer three hours and then make a thickening with four spoonfuls of flour, and stir in, and at the same time stir in two spoonfuls of either mushroom or walnut catsup and simmer one hour longer. Some persons think the addition of a glass of claret or Madeira an improvement, but it is nice without.

Sister Mary Whitcher's
Shaker Housekeeper

BEEFSTEAK ROLLS

Cut a beefsteak quite thick, then split it open lengthwise, and cut in strips four or five inches wide, rub over the inside with an onion and in each strip roll up a thin slice of bread, buttered on both sides; stick two cloves in the bread, and sprinkle with salt, pepper, celery seed (cut or thin slices of nice celery stalk if in season), and put into gravy. Tie each roll with a thread; dredge it with flour, and fry in hot butter. Then put these, when a delicate brown into a stewpan with only water enough to stew them. Make a nice thickened gravy from the liquor in which the steaks were stewed, and serve with rolls, very hot. The rolls should stew slowly two hours. Veal or mutton is good prepared in this way.

The story of the Shakers and some of their favorite cooking recipes. Calendar 1882-3

BOILED FLANK OF BEEF

Wash the flank, and make a dressing as for turkey which spread over it, first having salted and peppered it well; then roll up and tie. Wind the twine round it several times, to keep it in place, then sew into a cloth kept for that purpose. Put a small plate in the pot, and put in the meat; then pour on it boiling water enough to cover; and boil gently six hours. When done, remove the cloth, but not the twine until stone cold; then cut in thin slices, and you will have alternate layers of meat and dressing. This is a nice dish for breakfast or tea.

*Sister Mary Whitcher's
Shaker Housekeeper*

BROILED BEEF STEAK

Have the steak cut three-quarters to an inch thick Dredge it with salt and flour and cook over clearcoals for ten minutes —this gives it rare—then place on a warm dish and season with salt, pepper and butter. Have the vegetables ready to serve as soon as the steak is cooked, as it spoils by standing.

*Sister Mary Whitcher's
Shaker Housekeeper*

COLD BEEF WITH PUREE OF POTATOES

Pare, boil and mash twelve large potatoes. Add to them salt, pepper and two tablespoonfuls of butter, then beat in gradually one pint of boiling milk. Spread this preparation on a warm dish and then place on it handsome slices of cold roast beef. Put one tablespoonful of gravy on each slice. Place the dish in the oven for five minutes. Garnish the edge of the dish with any kind of green, likely parsley, carrot, or celery. Other kinds of cold meat can be served in this manner.

Sister Mary Whitcher's
Shaker Housekeeper

FRENCH BEEFSTEAK

Cut the steak two-thirds of an inch thick from a fillet of beef; dip into melted fresh butter, lay them on a heated gridiron and broil over hot coals When nearly done sprinkle pepper and salt. Have ready some parsley chopped fine and mixed with softened butter. Beat them together to a cream and pour into the middle of the dish. Dip each steak into the butter, turning them over, and lay them round on the platter. If liked, squeeze a few drops of lemon over and serve very hot.

The story of the Shakers and some of their
favorite cooking recipes. Calendar 1882-3

FRICASSED BEEF

Put a pint of clear water in a frying pan, and when it comes to boil, thicken with one heaping spoonful of flour, and season with salt, pepper and a little butter. Cut cold roast beef into slices and put into this gravy; let them boil five minutes. If there be any cold beef gravy, add it to the other, in which case you will not need quite as much butter. Boiled potatoes, tomatoes, boiled rice or macaroni, and squash may be served with the fricassee.

Sister Mary Whitcher's
Shaker Housekeeper

Pressed Corn Beef

The thin part of the ribs, the brisket and the flank are the best parts to press. Wash the meat and if it is very salty, cover with cold water; but if not thoroughly salted, cover with boiling water. Let it come to a boil, and skim; then cover and simmer six hours, unless the piece weighs more than ten or twelve pounds; in which case allow fifteen minutes for every additional pound. No matter how small the piece, it will require six hours to cook. When done, take from the fire and let it stand one hour in the water in which it was boiled; then take out the bones, place the meat on a platter or cake pan, put a tin sheet on top of it, and on the sheet a weight, and set in a cool place. In the morning trim the edges; use the trimmings for hash. If the beef be boiled rapidly it will be dry and stringy, but if it is allowed only to bubble it will be tender and juicy. This is true of all kinds of meat.

Sister Mary Whitcher's
Shaker Housekeeper

Roast Beef's Heart

Soak four hours in cold water. Remove the muscles and wash out all the blood. Make a dressing of one cup of bread crumbs, one tablespoonful chopped parsley, a little salt and pepper, one tablespoonful of melted butter. Mix, and stuff the heart. Tie together with twine and wrap in cloth. Boil two hours. Remove the cloth, put in a baking pan, baste with melted butter and bake until brown. Make a brown gravy and pour over it.

Sister Marian Scott

Steamed Beef Steak Pudding

One quart of flour, one large teaspoonful of lard, two teaspoonfuls of cream-of-tartar, one teaspoonful of soda, two cupfuls of milk or water, a little salt, one and half pounds of beef steak. Roll out the crust and line a deep earthen dish; then lay in part of the steak, with a few pieces of butter, a little salt, and few whole cloves; then lay on the rest of the steak, with seasoning as before. Turn the crust up over the whole. Steam two hours.

Sister Mary Whitcher's
Shaker Housekeeper

BAKED CHICKEN

Split and prepare as for broiling. Dredge with salt and flour on both sides, and place in a baking dish with the split side down. Rub two tablespoons of soft butter over the top and again dredge thickly with flour. Put in water enough in the pan to just cover the bottom. Bake in a quick oven for half an hour. Take up the chicken and add one cupful of hot water to the gravy in the pan. Thicken with one table-spoonful of flour. Season with salt and pepper.

Sister Mary Whitcher's
Shaker Housekeeper

CHICKEN HASH

Take the remains of any cold chicken, cut the meat from the bones, put in a pint of boiling water in a sauce pan. Add a teaspoonful of salt and tablespoonful of butter, with a sprig of parsley. Let come to a boil put in the chicken, season with pepper, thicken with a little flour. Serve hot.

Sister Marian Scott

FRIED CHICKEN

Cut the chicken into six or eight pieces, and season well with salt and pepper. Dip into beaten egg, and then in fine bread crumbs, in which there is a teacupful of chopped parsley for every cupful of crumbs. Dip once more in the egg and crumbs, and fry ten minutes in boiling fat.

Sister Mary Whitcher's
Shaker Housekeeper

Broiled Partridges

Time, fifteen to twenty minutes. Partridges, gravy, butter, pepper, salt, Cayenne. Thoroughly pick and draw the partridges, divide each through the back and breast, and wipe the insides. Season them highly with pepper, salt and a very little Cayenne, and place them over a clear, bright fire to broil. When done, rub a piece of butter over them, and serve them up hot with brown gravy.

The story of the Shakers and some of their favorite cooking recipes. Calendar 1882-3

Hash of any kind of Meat

Cut any cold lean meat in small squares. To every pint of meat, add one tablespoonful of butter, one tablespoon of flour and one half pint of boiling water. Let butter melt and brown, add flour, and boiling water. Let boil. Add meat, season with salt and pepper, and, if desired, one small minced onion.

Sister Marian Scott

To Keep Ham Through Warm Weather

Use one or more hams. Cut off the fat and boil it out for lard. Prepare the lean meat in the ordinary way of curing ham; then slice it nicely and cook until done (but not brown.) Take out into a sieve, to drain out all the moisture that may remain. Have ready jars about a third full of warmed lard, and into these closely pack the thoroughly drained meat. Be sure to have lard at least an inch above the last layer of meat. Closely cover and set in a cool, dry place. When any is taken up for use, the lard that is removed should be warmed and strained over the remaining meat, always keeping at least one inch of lard above the meat. Ham served in this way is safely and nicely kept through the whole summer. Sausage

82

meat can be cooked and packed in the same way. It will keep equally as good.

Sister Mary Whitcher's
Shaker Housekeeper

BOILED HAM

Let the ham soak twenty-four hours, put in a kettle, cover with cold water and set on the back of the stove. Simmer gently five or six hours. Set off the fire. Let it remain in the water it cooked in until cold. Take up and skin.

Sister Marian Scott

BROILED HAM

Cut the ham in thin slices, cut off the rind, and broil over clear coals ten minutes. When the ham is very salty or hard, slice and let stand in boiling water ten minutes before frying or broiling.

Sister Mary Whitcher's
Shaker Housekeeper

DEVILLED HAM

One pint of boiled ham chopped fine with a good proportion of fat, one tablespoonful of flour, one half cup of boiling water. Press in mould, and cut in slices.

The story of the Shakers and some of their favorite cooking recipes. Calendar 1882-3.

FRIED HAM

Cut the ham in very thin slices, and cut off the rind. Have half a spoonful of boiling drippings in the frying-pan. Lay the ham in this, and fry quickly eight minutes. It will then be brown and crisp.

Sister Mary Whitcher's
Shaker Housekeeper

HAM AND EGGS

Fry the ham as before directed, and when it is all cooked, turn the fat into a basin, and scrape the salt from the frying-pan. Turn back the fat, and add to it half a cupful of lard. When this comes to a boil, break in the eggs, leaving room to turn them, if you prefer them so. They look much nicer, however, when they are not turned. If they are not fried on both sides, dip up the boiling fat while they are cooking and pour over them. They will cook rare in three minutes, well done in four. Lay them on the slices of ham, and serve.

Sister Mary Whitcher's
Shaker Housekeeper

SCOTCH HAM

To a round of beef of thirty pounds, from which the bones have been taken, add one ounce of saltpetre, one pint of sugar, one pint of table-salt. Pulverise the saltpetre and mix with half a teacupful of the sugar and half the salt. Rub thoroughly into the beef, so it will penetrate well, and let it lie twenty-four hours. Mix the rest of the sugar and salt and rub into the beef. Turn this each day for ten days and rub into the brine which has collected. Let it drain for twenty-four hours. Mix three large tablespoonfuls of black pepper, the same quantity of cloves, one and a half of alspice, one and a half of grated nutmeg. Rub these well into the "ham" and tie up. The meat is good to use in a week.

Sister Mary Whitcher's
Shaker Housekeeper

BOILED LEG OF LAMB

Time, one hour and a quarter after the water simmers. Select a fine fresh leg of lamb, weighing about five pounds; soak it in warm water for rather more than two hours, then wrap it in a cloth and boil it slowly for one hour and a quarter.

When done, dish it up and garnish with a border of carrots, turnips, or cauliflower around it. Wind a cut paper around the shank bone, and serve it with plain parsley and butter sauce poured over it.

The story of the Shakers and some of their favorite cooking recipes. Calendar 1882-3

ESCALOPED MUTTON

Chop some cold mutton rather coarse and season with salt and pepper. For one pint of meat use half a cupful of gravy and a heaping cupful of grated bread crumbs. Put a layer of the meat into an escalop dish, then some gravy, then a thin layer of crumbs. Continue in this way until the dish is full. The last layer must be a thick one of crumbs. Cook fifteen minutes in a hot oven.

*Sister Mary Whitcher's
Shaker Housekeeper*

HARICOT OF MUTTON

Take two pounds of cold roast mutton, cut into slices, and lay in a deep sauce-pan, and then put in half an onion, half a turnip, two potatoes, and one carrot, all cut into small pieces. Dredge with flour, salt and pepper. Cover with cold water, and boil slowly one hour; then add two spoonfuls of flour mixed with cold water, and boil one hour longer. Have a dish ready with an edging of mashed potatoes (brown them or not, as you please), and into the center of the dish turn out the meat. Serve mashed potatoes and turnips and boiled rice with the haricot.

*Sister Mary Whitcher's
Shaker Housekeeper*

ROAST MUTTON

Wipe the mutton with a damp cloth, then dredge with salt, a little pepper, and generously with flour. Place on a

meat rack in the baking-pan before dredging, with flour. Place
in a hot oven and as soon as the flour in the pan is brown
(which will be in about five minutes) pour in hot water
enough to cover the bottom of the pan. Baste every fifteen
minutes. Cook a leg weighing six pounds, one and one quarter
hours and give ten minutes for every additional pound. This
cooks it rare. If it is to be well done, roast one and a half
hours, with fifteen minutes for every pound over six. When
the meat is done, pour all the fat from the gravy and add a
cupful of boiling water to what remains in the pan. Thicken
this with a smooth paste made of a tablespoonful of flour
and a little cold water. Stir well, and boil two minutes. Season
with a salt and pepper. Strain and serve. All the dishes must
be very warm for a mutton dinner.

Sister Mary Whitcher's
Shaker Housekeeper

SADDLE OF LAMB

Time, a quarter of an hour to the pound, one hour and
a half to two hours. Cover the joint with buttered paper to
prevent the fat catching, and roast it at a brisk fire, constantly
basting it, at first with a very little butter, then with its own
dripping. Mint sauce.

The story of the Shakers and some of their
favorite cooking recipes. Calendar 1882-3.

PIG'S HEAD CHEESE

Boil pig's head until the bones will drop out. When cold,
chop fine and season highly with pepper, salt, and sage; then
put it into a kettle, and to every quart of meat add one half
pint of the liquor in which it was boiled. Simmer slowly
for one half hour and turn it into deep earthen dish, on
top of which place a plate with a weight upon it. Set in a
cool place, and when cold cut in slices.

Sister Mary Whitcher's
Shaker Housekeeper

How to Cook Salt Pork

If only a little extra care be given to preparing it for the table, salt pork may be made very palatable. The proper way to fry it is to cut it into slices one-quarter of an inch thick, and after removing the rind, pour on boiling water, in which let the slices remain for ten minutes; then turn off the water and fry them till they are nicely browned on both sides. In those places in the country where fresh meat cannot at all times be easily obtained, it is well to study various modes of serving pork. If it is liked broiled, prepare it the same as for frying, and keep it ten minutes over a fire of clear coals. Another mode that gives a most satisfactory dish is to fry it, then dip it in a batter, and fry again in the pork fat, to which should be added two spoonfuls of lard or drippings. The batter mentioned is made by mixing gradually together a cupful of milk and one tablespoonful of flour, and adding a well-beaten egg and a little salt.

Sister Mary Whitcher's
Shaker Housekeeper

Fried Sausages

After cutting the sausages apart, wash them, and laying them in a pan pour in boiling water over them. Let them boil two minutes; then turn off the water and prick the sausages with a fork, or they will burst open when they begin to fry. Put a small quantity of drippings in the pan with them, and fry twenty minutes. Turn them often, that they may be brown on all sides. Cut stale bread into fanciful shapes fry in the sausage fat and garnish the dish with them. Brown bread is very palatable fried in this way. Serve plain boiled potatoes, squash, mashed turnips, and apple-sauce with sausages.

Sister Mary Whitcher's
Shaker Housekeeper

Beef Stew

Three pounds of beef—the navel piece is the best—cut into inchsquare pieces. Peel and slice four or five onions. Put a layer of meat in the bottom of the stew-pan, then a layer of onions, and dredge well with salt, pepper and flour. Continue this until all the meat and onions have been used. Pour into the pan two quarts of potatoes, peeled and sliced, and three tablespoonfuls of flour mixed with one cupful of cold water. Add more salt and pepper if needs, simmer thirty minutes longer. Dumplings served with the stew are an improvement.

Sister Mary Whitcher's
Shaker Housekeeper

An English Stew

Cut roast beef into small and rather thin slices, season these highly with salt and pepper, and dip each lightly in bread crumbs moistened in gravy or melted butter. Dress them neatly on a dish, and lay over them a thin layer of cut pickles. Moisten the whole with a glassful of pickle vinegar, and the gravy of the beef. Heat in a Dutch oven, and garnish with fried sippets.

Sister Mary Whitcher's
Shaker Housekeeper

A Fine Irish Stew

There will be needed for the dish only two pounds of the neck of mutton, six large potatoes, four onions, three pints of water, two tablespoonfuls of flour and some salt and pepper; and then will prove an excellent one. Cut the meat into shapely pieces. Put about half the fat into the stew-pan with the onions and stir for eight or ten minutes over a hot fire; then put in the mutton, which sprinkle with the flour, salt and pepper. Stir for ten minutes, then add the water, boiling. Set the pan where it will simmer for an hour, and at the end of that time add the potatoes, peeled and cut in quarters. Simmer another hour before serving. Dumplings add to the attractiveness of the dish.

Sister Mary Whitcher's
Shaker Housekeeper

PENOBSCOT STEW

Use about one-quarter of a pound of cold broiled or roast meat, four potatoes, two onions, a quart of water, one-fourth of a cupful of barley, a tablespoonful of flour, salt and pepper to taste. Cut the meat into small cubes; cut the onions very fine, wash the barley. Put these all in a stewpan and dredge them with the flour, half a tablespoonful of salt, and one-eighth of a teaspoonful of pepper. Add the water and simmer two hours. Pare and slice the potatoes and add them to the stew and simmer an hour longer. Add more salt and pepper if there is not already enough.

Sister Mary Whitcher's
Shaker Housekeeper

VEAL LOAF

Three pounds of veal or fresh beef, half a pound of salt pork chopped fine, two beaten eggs, one teacupful of cracker crumbs, three tablespoonfuls of salt, two teaspoonsfuls of pepper. Mix and press hard into a tin. Bake one and a half hours.

Sister Mary Whitcher's
Shaker Housekeeper

ROAST SHOULDER OF VEAL

Time, twenty minutes for each pound. A shoulder of veal, some oysters or mushroom sauce. Remove the knuckle from a shoulder of veal for boiling and roast what remains as the fillet, either stuffed or not with veal stuffing. If not stuffed, serve it with oysters or mushroom sauce, and garnish with sliced lemon.

The story of the Shakers and some of their favorite cooking recipes. Calendar 1882-3.

FISH and SEA FOODS

Fish as Food

There is much nourishment in fish, little if any less then there is in meat, weight for weight. In fact it may be more nourishing, because as a rule it is much more easily digested. Fish is considered almost a specific against scrofulous diseases.

Manifesto — 1878

Shaker Fish and Egg

In a double boiler heat one pint of cream, season with salt, remove a portion of the gravy into a saucepan in which you have dissolved a small piece of butter; into the double boiler slice a layer of boiled potatoes cut very thin, to this add a little saltfish boiled and picked very fine, then add a layer of boiled eggs cut into four or five pieces, alternate with another layer of potatoes, fish and egg, until the desired amount is obtained, now pour on the reserved gravy and cover, let it remain for an hour or so until ready to serve, garnish with some hard boiled eggs. The eggs should be cooked six minutes then immerse them into cold water, this prevents them from getting too hard; fresh fish can be used, but it does not give the fine flavor as the salt fish. For four people use eight eggs, eight medium sized potatoes and three tablespoons of codfish. This can also be made in a casserole if preferred.

Eldress Prudence Stickney

Baked Fish

Take a fish weighing from four to six pounds. Scrape and wash clean and season well with salt. Make a dressing with five small crackers rolled fine; one tablespoonful of butter, one teaspoonful of salt, a little pepper, one half a tablespoonful of

chopped parsley and water enough to make very moist. Stuff
the fish with this preparation, which fasten with a skewer.
Cut slits in the fish and put small strips of salt pork into them.
Place the fish on a tin sheet in a baking-pan, and dredge well
with flour. Baking one hour, basting often. Serve with a tomato
sauce around it.

Sister Mary Whitcher's
Shaker Housekeeper

Turbot a la Creme

Boil either bass or cod with plenty of salt, flake it, removing
all skin and bones; boil a quart of milk or cream and, while
it is boiling, put in a bunch of parsley, an onion, and a little
celery; stir in also three tablespoonfuls of flour mixed perfectly smooth with a little cold milk. When boiled, take out
the vegetables, add a one-fourth lb. of butter to the cream.
Butter a deep dish, and put in a layer of fish, and then a layer
of sauce; continue this until the dish is full making a final
layer of the sauce. Cover the top with fine bread-crumbs, and
a trifle of grated cheese, if liked. Bake half an hour.

Sister Mary Whitcher's
Shaker Housekeeper

Fish Balls

Use the fish left from dinner. Put it in your chopping-tray,
being careful that there are no bones in it, and chop fine. Pare
and boil potatoes enough to have twice the quantity of potatoes
that you have of fish; when cooked, turn them into the tray with
the fish, mash fine, and make into balls about the size of an egg.
Have the fat boiling hot, and fry a light brown. Have slices of
pork a nice brown to serve with the fish balls.

Sister Mary Whitcher's
Shaker Housekeeper

FISH CAKES

One pint of salt codfish, picked very fine, two pints of whole, raw, peeled potatoes; put together in cold water and boil till the potatoes are thoroughly cooked, remove from the fire and drain off all the water, mash with potato-masher, add piece of butter the size of an egg; two well beaten eggs and a little pepper; mix well with a wooden spoon; have a frying-pan with boiling lard or drippings, into which drop the mixture by spoonfuls, and fry brown, do not freshen the fish before boiling potatoes, and do not mould cakes, but drop from a spoon.

Sister Mary Whitcher's
Shaker Housekeeper

SALT COD

First wash the fish, in the evening, and soak it over night in cold water. In the morning put it in fresh water and put it on to cook. Just as soon as the water is at the boiling point set back where it will keep hot but not boil. A hard dry fish will cook in from four to six hours, and some will be done in half an hour.

Sister Mary Whitcher's
Shaker Housekeeper

STEWED LOBSTER

Open a lobster weighing two and one half pounds and cut the meat into little dice. Heat two tablespoonfuls of butter and add the dry flour, stirring until perfectly smooth; then gradually add the water, stirring all the while. Season to taste. Add the lobster and beat thoroughly.

Sister Mary Whitcher's
Shaker Housekeeper

SALT MACKEREL

Soak salt mackerel over night, after washing them carefully in plenty of cold water; lay them in a dripping-pan, cover with hot water and bake till tender, drain from the water and serve hot with butter gravy.

Manifesto — 1880

CREAMED OYSTERS

A pint of oysters, one of cream, a small piece of onion and a very small piece of mace, one tablespoonful of flour and salt and pepper to taste. Let the cream, with the mace and onion, come to a boil. Mix the flour with a little cold milk or cream and stir it into the boiling cream. Let the oysters come to a boil in their own liquor. Skim carefully, drain off the liquor and turn the oysters into the cream. Skim out the mace and onions and serve.

Sister Mary Whitcher's
Shaker Housekeeper

SCALLOPED OYSTERS

Crush and roll several handfuls of Boston or other friable crackers. Put a layer in the bottom of a buttered pudding dish. Mix this with oyster liquid and milk slightly warmed. Next have a layer of oysters; sprinkle with salt and pepper and lay small bits of butter upon them. Then another layer of moistened crumbs, and so on until the dish is full. Let the top layer be of crumbs thicker than the rest and beat an egg into the milk you pour over them. Stick bits of butter thickly over it, cover the dish, set in the oven, bake half an hour. If the dish is large, remove the cover, and brown by setting it upon the upper grating of the oven or by holding a hot shovel over it.

The story of the Shakers and some of their
favorite cooking recipes. Calendar 1882-3

FRIED OYSTERS

Select the largest, dip them in beaten egg, and then bread or cracker crumbs; fry in equal parts of butter and lard until they are brown. They are very good dipped in corn meal instead of crumbs.

Manifesto — 1880

PICKLED OYSTERS

One quart vinegar, one ounce of allspice, one half ounce of cinnamon, one ounce of cloves, one ounce of mace; scald all together; when cold put in the oysters; next day scald together.

Manifesto — 1880

OYSTER STEW

Put two quarts of oysters in the saucepan with the liquor, and when they begin to boil, skim them out and add a pint of cream or rich milk and seasoning; skim well, add the oysters, butter to taste and pour the hot liquor over them and serve.

Manifesto — 1880

OYSTER PIE

Line a dish with puff paste or a rich biscuit paste, and dredge well with flour, drain one quart of oysters, season with pepper, salt and butter, and pour into the dish; add some of the liquor, dredge with flour and cover with a top crust, leaving a small opening in the center.

Manifesto — 1880

OYSTER FRITTERS

Time, five or six minutes. Some good-sized oysters, four whole eggs, a tablespoonful of milk, salt and pepper, crumbs. Bread some good-sized oysters, make a thick omelet batter with four eggs and a tablespoonful of milk, dip each oyster into the batter and then into the grated bread, fry them a nice color and use them to garnish fried fish.

The story of the Shakers and some of their favorite cooking recipes. Calendar 1882-3

BREAD, CAKE, COOKIES

BAKING POWDER

Thoroughly dry separately by gentle heat, one half lb. pulverized tartaric acid, three-fourths of a pound of pure bicarbonate of soda, three-fourths of a pound of pure pulverized potato farina. Mix them in a dry room. Pass the mixture through a sieve and at once put into dry cans and cover securely so as to exclude the air and moisture. One or two teaspoonfuls are mixed with the dry flour or other ingredients, which are then made into dough as quickly as possible with cold water, and at once baked or boiled, as the case may be.

Sister Mary Whitcher's
Shaker Housekeeper

EXCELLENT YEAST

Boil a single handful of unpressed hops a few minutes in one quart of water. Strain, and return to the kettle. Add half a teacupful of white sugar, two tablespoonfuls of salt and four good-sized potatoes, pared and grated fine. Boil up once and set away to cool. When milk-warm add half a cupful of baker's yeast of *this* kind and put in a warm place to rise. Half a teacupful is sufficient for four small loaves of bread, and the bread with no additional salt.

Sister Mary Whitcher's
Shaker Housekeeper

HOW TO MAKE YEAST

Take two oz. hops, one dozen middling size potatoes, pare and slice the potatoes, boil the hops and potatoes two hours in a pail of water then strain the liquor boiling hot, on five quarts of rye flour and one of Indian, rinse the hops with a little cold water, when cool enough to put your hand into, add one quart rye flour, one pint Indian, one gill molasses, one spoonfull ginger, and a handful fine salt with one quart yeast. Let the whole stand in an open vessel in a warm place for two hours, then dip the yeast into a tight firkin or keg, and it will be fit for use. We use about half a pint to a half bushel flour in warm weather, in cooler weather we use more.

A Collection of Useful Hints for
Farmers and Many Valuable Recipes
by James Holmes

LIQUID YEAST

Take a handful of hops boil in one quart of water for 10 or 15 minutes, then strain the liquor into a quart of flour, let it stand till cool, then add the yeast also a tablespoonful of sugar, one of salt and a little ginger; set to rise and when light—bottle up closely and set in a cool place. It will keep three or four weeks.

Sister Abigail Crossman

HOP YEAST

To make vegetable stock yeast, steep one quart malt and four cups full of flour or wheat bran with three quarts boiling water two hours, boil a half pound of hops in ten quarts of water two hours, strain into the malt and let it stand until milk is warm. Add one quart of stock yeast, let it ferment 10 or 15 hours in a warm room and then bottle for use. Any sweet hop yeast will answer to start the above.

Sabbathday Lake Shakers

A RECIPT FOR MAKING YEAST

Take one lb. of hops and thirty middling sized potatoes, cut them thin, put them into two pails and a half of water and let them boil two hours. Then take 12 quarts of rye flour, put it into a large wooden vessel, then strain in your liquor boiling hot, and be careful to have all your meal scalded thoroughly.

Then take your potatoes and hops and jam them together and
rinse them well in water. Have your composition as thick as
you can make, run through your funnel into your keg. Stir them
well when they are cooling until they are about milk warm, then
take one pint of rye flour, one pint of Indian meal, one teacupful of ginger, two teacups of molasses, three good handfuls
of salt and two quarts of good yeast, then stir them faithfully
and then let stand open until they get quite light then dip
off the top into your keg, be as careful as possible, the less you
stir them after they begin to rise the better they well be and
you can continue to dip off the top until you get them all into
your keg. Be careful to have your keg *iron hooped* and large
enough to hold your emptings. You may have your keg full
within five or six inches. You can have a large brass key to your
keg and when your emptings is in the keg, stop tight just turn
the key and let off the confined air, otherwise they would be
likely to burst, then set off your keg into the celler or some cool
place.

NOTE: You can put more water into your hops if you need it,
but be sure to have your first liquor boiling hot and
the water you rinse your hops and potatoes in. You
may put in cool if your meal is all scalded.

Sabbathday Lake Shakers

Patent Flour

Almost everybody knows of patent flour, but not everybody
understands what it is. Stripped of technicalities, this is about
the story of its manufacture. The best flour used to be made
of winter wheat. Spring wheat yielded either much less in quantity, or else so much of the bran got into the flour in its
manufacture that its color was intolerably dark. The wheat
would be ground and then bolted. In the refuse—the bran
and middlings—would be included a large proportion of the
spring wheat, and this would sell more particularly for feed for
horses. Now, the best of flour, and the most expensive, is made

of this very refuse of old fashioned process. It all came out of the discovery of a way to draw out the bran. Under the new process the wheat is ground about as before. The first result is an ordinary flour sold for exportation. Then the remainder is taken and put upon great horizontal sieves, and wheel agitation is going on there, an ingenious system of draft is rushing up through and carries off the bran. What is left is the glutinous portion of the wheat, the most nutritious and most productive and out of this purified now by the drawing off of the bran, we get our new process flour. The result of the discovery of the process has been to make the poor spring wheat of Minnesota and upper Wisconsin the most valuable of grain.

Manifesto — 1881

Rule for Making Bread

Take one handful of yeast, one large handful of salt, one quart or three pints of water (about milk warm) in cold weather, then mix in flour until your sponge will cleave off from the tin or pan or whatever your sponge is in. You must set this water sponge over night, if your room is warm, it will get light on the table and if not you must set a warm place.

Sabbathday Lake Shakers

Good Bread

I notice articles upon Graham bread in the Am. Agriculturist and other papers. Perhaps our experience at the North Family, Mt. Lebanon, may be of some interest and service to the public. For many years we have used bread made from wheat of our own raising. We wash the wheat thoroughly, kiln-dry, grind it ourselves, coarsely, use it unbolted, and bake it in a soapstone oven. No leaven in it. It is good wheaten bread. I doubt whether really good men and women, Christians, can be raised on poor bread, made of adulterated materials and chemically corrupted by leaven. If a clean thing cannot be brought out of an unclean then how can a good thing be made out of a bad materials? Have not a loaf to spare (unless to feed the hungry) a bushel of wheat, nor a barrel of flour to sell at any price.

Manifesto — 1882

To Make Sponge Bread without Yeast

Scald milk or whey—stir in the flour when it is about blood warm, until it is some thinner than pancake dough or like thick porridge, then put it in a warm place and let it rise 5 hours, or until it is light—then mix it some thinner than common bread—and put it into the pans, let it rise a little while and bake it. And if you have had good luck it will be very light, tender and sweet.

Shaker Manuscript
Fruitlands and Wayside Museum—Harvard, Mass.

Light Bread

Three good sized potatoes, pare and slice them and boil in one quart of pure water; when throughly done pour into a colander with the water in which they were boiled in; mash the potatoes through, when cool put in the flour and yeast, beat it all together until free from lumps, set it to rise; when light, add a little warm water with a bit of butter; work well and set it to rise, when light knead it down, let it rise and bake the second time.

Sister Abigail Crossman

Unleavened Loaf Bread

The Shakers claim to make the best unleavened loaf bread from pure Graham flour. Here is another recipe which makes a very nice composition bread. Mix the best of rye and Indian meal in equal proportions into a soft dough, with cold water in hot weather, but warm water in cold weather. Mix and knead it with the hands until light, and lay it softly, so as not to press out the air confined in it, in deep tin pans. Now smooth over the top wth the moistened hand so as to give it a neat appearance. Let it stand over night, then bake it in an oven, hot at first, but gradually cooling. If it could be made late enough in the evening to be allowed to remain in the oven over night, it would make a very nice breakfast bread.

Manifesto — 1879

CORN BREAD — SET OVERNIGHT

One pint corn meal in a deep dish. One teaspoon each of butter, sugar and salt. Pour over it one cup boiling milk. When cool enough to bear a finger, half a cup or one cake of yeast, half a cup flour, two beaten eggs. Thin to proper consistency. Keep warm 2 or 3 hours. Bake in a steady moderate oven.

Sister Marian Scott

SHAKER BROWN BREAD

Mix together two quarts of Indian meal, one quart of rye meal and one pint of "canaille" (coarse flour). To one pint of this mixed meal add water and scald thoroughly, and when cool, add a teaspoonful of stock yeast. Let it stand to rise. To the remainder of the meal add three quarts of sweet milk, scalding hot. Mix thoroughly with a pudding stick, and when cooled lukewarm, add the "yeasted" portion. Put in the oven immediately and bake with a steady heat for 7 or 8 hours.

Sister Mary Whitcher's
Shaker Housekeeper

STEAMED BROWN BREAD

One cup rye meal, one cup corn meal, half a cup flour, half a teaspoonful soda, half a teaspoonful salt, one-fourth cup molasses, one and one half cup sweet milk. Mix all the meals and flour, sift in the soda and salt, add the molasses and milk

and beat all together very thoroughly. Turn into a buttered pail
or mould with a tight cover and place the pail in a kettle of
boiling water. Cook two and one half hours.

Sabbathday Lake Shakers

STEAMED BROWN BREAD

Two cupsful of new milk, two of Indian meal, one and one
half of flour, one of molasses, one teaspoonful of soda. Steam
3 hours.

Sister Mary Whitcher's
Shaker Housekeeper

BROWN BREAD

Two quarts Indian meal. One quart rye meal, one pint
canaille (coarse flour), mix with scalding hot sweet milk, stir
with a pudding stick till quite a stiff batter. Bake in iron pans
7 or 8 hours. A soapstone oven is best; but if you bake in a
oven keep a steady heat.

Manifesto — 1878

BROWN BREAD

Two cupsful of sour milk, two-thirds of a cup of molasses,
two of Indian meal, one of rye meal, one egg, one teaspoonful of
soda, one of salt. Steam 4 hours.

Sister Mary Whitcher's
Shaker Housekeeper

BROWN BREAD

Two cupsful of sour milk, two of Indian meal, one of
graham, half a cupful of molasses, one teaspoonful of salt, half
a teaspoonful of ginger. Steam 2 hours and bake one.

Sister Mary Whitcher's
Shaker Housekeeper

GRAHAM BREAD

Make a stiff batter of half a pint of warm water thickened with graham flour and add to it one-third of a cupful of yeast. Let it rise over night and in the morning add a little piece of butter, half a cupful of sugar, and wheat flour enough to mould. Let the bread rise in pans and bake an hour.

Sister Mary Whitcher's
Shaker Housekeeper

GRAHAM BREAD

Three pints of Graham flour; one pint of wheat flour; one cup yeast; half cup molasses and a teaspoonful of salt. Mix with lukewarm water as stiff as you can, stir with a spoon. Let it rise over night, and bake in a moderately hot oven.

Manifesto — 1879

RYE BREAD

In one quart of warm water stir as much wheat flour as will make a smooth batter. Stir into it one yeast cake and set in a warm place to rise. In the morning, put three and one half pounds rye flour in a bowl, pour in the sponge, add a dessert spoon of salt, half a teaspoon of soda dissolved in a little warm water, make the whole into a smooth dough, cover well and set in a warm place 3 hours. Knead it again, make into three loaves, bake one hour. (I think she omitted to set it again after forming loaves,—M. D. F.)

Sister Marian Scott

INDIAN BREAD

One quart of Indian meal, one quart of white flour, one quart of buttermilk, half a cupful of molasses, one egg, one teaspoonful of soda. Steam 3 hours and bake half an hour. The above rule makes a delicious loaf of bread.

Sister Mary Whitcher's
Shaker Housekeeper

STEAMED INDIAN BREAD

Four cups of corn meal, two cups of flour, two cups of sweet milk, two cups of sour milk, one teaspoonful soda, a little salt, one cup of molasses. Steam 3 hours.

The story of the Shakers and some of their favorite cooking recipes. Calendar 1882-3.

STEAMED INDIAN BREAD

One egg, one cup buttermilk, one cup sweet milk, one cup flour, two cups cornmeal, half a cup molasses, one teaspoon soda, one teaspoon salt. Steam 2 hours. This will make a two-quart basinful.

Florida Shakers
Lebanon Valley Cookery — 1926

SALT RISING BREAD

Two cups corn meal, two tablespoons baking soda. Four cups hot milk. Set this mixture in warm place till morning.

Four tablespoons sugar, two teaspoons salt, one quart boiling water. Flour enough to make thick as pancake batter. Cover tightly, set in a warm place till it is full of bubbles. Add six tablespoons of butter and then add flour enough to make a firm dough. Knead lightly, place in greased bowl. Let rise in very warm place. Put in tins, let rise till double its size, bake in a moderate oven for one hour. Remove from pans wrap in towel, makes four loaves.

Sister Jennie M. Wells

BUNS

One-fourth cup yeast, one-fourth cup warm water, one cup milk, scalded and cooled, one tablespoonful sugar, half a teaspoonful salt, two cups flour. Mix these ingredients into a batter and beat it thoroughly. Place the bowl in pan of warm water to rise and when full of bubbles add one egg well beaten, one-fourth cup butter melted, half a cup currants, one-fourth teaspoonful cinnamon, flour to make a stiff dough. Knead it 20 minutes. Let it rise again as before and when light, shape it into small balls like biscuit. Place them close together in a shallow pan and when risen very high bake in a moderate oven. When done brush them over with a little beaten white of egg mixed with sugar.

Sabbathday Lake Shakers

BUNS

One cup sugar, one cup butter, one half cup ferment, one half cup milk, mix at night as for bread. In the morning add one cup sugar, one cup milk, one cup butter, cinnamon and currants, mould in flour so as to roll, or mould, let it stand where quite warm, until raised to twice its original size. Then beat one egg and wash them lightly over with a brush and bake in a hot oven.

Sabbathday Lake Shakers

BUNS

Half a cupful each of yeast, sugar and butter, one and half cupfuls of milk, half a nutmeg, and a little salt. Mix together at night and in the morning add half a cupful of sugar and some currants.

Sister Mary Whitcher's
Shaker Housekeeper

CROSS BUNS (GOOD, *I* BELIEVE)

Beat to a cream one large cup of granulated sugar and one scant cup of grease. Add gradually three well beaten eggs and one pint of scalded milk, blood warm. Put in flour to make a batter stiff as you can. Beat it. Add one yeast cake dissolved in half a cup of warm water, heat until it blisters well. In the morning, knead well with a half cup of flour, dough must be very soft.

Rub over the top with warm butter and let rise. When double in bulk, form into rolls, rub with butter and cut a cross on top with a sharp knife. Let rise one and a half or two hours and bake half an hour.

Sister Marian Scott

Hot Cross Buns

To one dozen, dissolve one yeast cake in one cupful rich milk, stir in enough flour to make a thin sponge, set in a warm place to rise till its bulk is doubled. Cream two heaping tablespoons of butter with four tablespoons sugar. Mix these ingredients thoroughly, then add, a little at a time, half a pound sifted flour. Mix this with the light sponge, cover closely with buttered paper and then with a tin cover. When risen, dredge with flour. Do not knead. Roll out, cut into buns, score with a sharp knife to form a cross, cover, let rise another hour, score again. Brush with caramel and bake in a hot oven 15 minutes.

Sister Marian Scott

White Mountain Rolls

Make the dough by the recipe for soup sticks. When risen and ready to shape, form it into rolls about five inches long, and plump in the middle and tapering at each end. Place them on the pan so they will not touch after rising. Let them rise in a warm place until very light, then bake in a hot oven, very hot at first, then check the heat that they may not become too brown before the inside is done. When they are taken from the oven glaze them with butter twisted in a cloth.

Sabbathday Lake Shakers

Pemigewasset Rolls

These are designed for breakfast. The ingredients are, a cupful of butter, one of yeast, half a cupful of white sugar, four cupfuls of boiled milk, the whites of four eggs beaten to a stiff froth, sixteen cupfuls of flour; the butter should be melted, and the milk blood warm. Mix the bread, and set in a warm place to rise over night. In the morning shape into long rolls. Let these rise for an hour and then bake half an hour.

Sister Mary Whitcher's
Shaker Housekeeper

PARKER HOUSE ROLLS

Boil together a pint of milk and a piece of butter the size of an egg, when cold, turn over it a quart or more of flour, add a little salt and half a cup of yeast, stir slightly and let it rise over night, in the morning work in flour as stiff as for bread, and leave it rise thro the day occasionally cutting it with a knife. About an hour before baking roll out and cut in round cakes, fold one side over and put in the baking pan. To be very nice they should be made 24 hours before baking, but may be made on the same morning. Bake in a hot oven.

Sister Abigail Crossman

GRAHAM ROLLS

Two cups of wheat meal, one and half cups of flour, salt, three-fourths of a cup of sugar, two and a half cups of sour milk, one teaspoonful of soda.

The story of the Shakers and some of their
favorite cooking recipes. Calendar 1882-3.

GERMAN ROLLS

One cupful of sugar, one of sour milk, half a cupful of butter, one egg, one teaspoonful of soda, flour enough to knead quite hard. Roll out, spread on sugar and butter, and spice to suit taste; roll up again, cut off thin and bake quickly.

Sister Mary Whitcher's
Shaker Housekeeper

DIRECTIONS FOR MAKING FRENCH TEA ROLLS

Dissolve half of a Clark's yeast cake in half a cup of warm water, thicken with flour, and set to rise 3 or 4 hours before using. When risen take two quarts of flour (sifted), one pint of boiled milk (cooled), two tablespoonfuls sugar, one of lard, a little salt and stir all together, then set to rise over night. Knead over in the morning; rise until 3 P.M. then make into rolls. Bake 20 minutes. In making the rolls a small piece of butter should be placed between the folds.

Sabbathday Lake Shakers

CREAM TARTAR BISCUITS

Stir into one quart of flour two teaspoonfuls of cream tartar, dissolve a teaspoonful of Super Carb of soda in a teacupful of milk. Mix the whole rather soft with milk and bake like biscuit.

Sabbathday Lake Shakers

RAISED BISCUIT

Two cupfuls of milk, half a cupful of yeast, half a cupful of shortening, half butter half lard is best, half a cupful of sweet cream, a little salt, flour enough to make a soft dough. When light add half a teaspoonful of saleratus dissolved in a little warm water. Knead very thoroughly, roll out and cut into biscuits. When light, bake. In making bread and biscuits after the dough is made use as little dry flour as possible in kneading, otherwise the loaves will creack and be one-sided.

Sister Mary Whitcher's
Shaker Housekeeper

SODA BISCUIT

Rub up fine into five tumblers of sifted flour a lump of butter the size of a large egg, add salt. Before the flour is sifted stir in one teaspoonful of soda, two of cream of tartar, tho-

roughly mixed and enough sweet milk or water to make it
knead nicely, then either make into cakes or roll out and cut
up to suit the fancy, and bake in rather a quick oven.

Sister Abigail Crossman

SODA BISCUIT

Put into a sieve with a quart of unsifted flour a teaspoonful
of salt, one of saleratus, two of cream of tartar, and a tablespoonful of white sugar. Mix all thoroughly and run through the
sieve; then rub a spoonful of lard or butter, and wet with a little
more cut with a biscuit cutter, and bake in a quick oven 15 minutes. If you have no milk, use a little more butter, and wet with
water. Handle as little and make as rapidly as possible.

Sister Mary Whitcher's
Shaker Housekeeper

SODA BISCUIT

Eight tumblers of sifted flour with two teaspoonfuls of soda
and four of cream of tartar and butter the size of two eggs wet
with sweet milk enough to knead nicely. Sour milk and less
shortening may be used instead of cream of tartar.

Sister Abigail Crossman

SODA BISCUIT

One quart flour, one and a half cups of buttermilk, one teaspoon soda, piece of butter the size of an egg, pinch of salt.

Sister Marian Scott

CORN BREAD AND PUDDING

Take one quart of buttermilk and one pint of corn meal, one
teaspoonful of soda, one teaspoonful of salt, one tablespoonful
of sugar and three eggs. Have the stove very hot and don't bake
in too deep a pan. We use a dripping pan and we think of all
the cornbread we ever tasted, this is the best.

Sister Abigail Crossman

CORN BREAD OR CAKE

One quart sour milk or buttermilk, four eggs, two table-spoonfuls of sugar or molasses, one pint of corn meal, two table-spoonfuls of sour cream may be added, though it is good with-out. Bake about one hour.

Sister Abigail Crossman

CORN CAKES

Beat together one egg, two tablespoons of sugar, two of melt-ed butter, one-half teaspoon salt, two teacups of cornmeal, one tablespoon flour, one teaspoon soda, and two teacups of sweet milk. Dissolve the soda in the milk, and add last. Bake in a shallow pan about 15 minutes, in a well heated oven.

Manifesto — 1879

SALLY LUNN

A generous pint of milk, a quart of flour, two eggs, two tablespoonfuls of sugar, three of butter, a teaspoonful of salt, half a cake of compressed yeast. Have the milk blood warm, and add to it the butter melted, the eggs well beaten, and the yeast, dissolved in three tablespoonfuls of cold water. Pour on the flour gradually and beat into a smooth batter; then add the sugar and salt. Butter baking pans and into them pour the batter to the depth of about two inches. Let it rise for 2 hours in a warm place and bake half an hour.

Sister Mary Whitcher's
Shaker Housekeeper

POPOVER

Butter two cups of milk with two cups of flour add the yolks of two eggs, a little salt, lastly the whites. Bake in small pans.

Sister Abigail Crossman

RUSK

One pint bowl of light sponge, half a cup of melted butter, one cup of sugar and two to four eggs sponge. When light knead and form into biscuit when very light, bake. If washed over with sweetened milk when nearly done, it will give them a nice color. The same recipe will make nice doughnuts.

Sister Abigail Crossman

GRAHAM CRACKERS

Two quarts of graham flour, one-third white flour, one cup butter, one cup sugar, mix with buttermilk and enough soda to take the sour off.

Sister Marian Scott

RECIPE FOR MAKING CRACKERS

To two quarts of water, twelve pounds of flour, one of magnesia, one tablespoonful of salt. Firstly place the flour in a large wooden bowl leaving it hollowing in the middle, then carefully sprinkle the magnesia round on it also the salt, then lay on the lard and butter then carefully pour in the water minding that it will not touch the bowl, then mix it with your hands until it seems to be wet through and your bowl will be clean if done right. Then put it under the breaker, then work it until perfectly smooth and resembles putty, then roll it with your hands into little bits about the size you want the crackers having a cloth wrung out of cold water and lay over your dough, keep them from the air so that they do not dry and make them out about the size of a dollar, roll them in flat pans so that they will not touch each other, prick them about half way through having the oven about suitable for apple pies. Bake them 15 or 20 minutes. If the oven has flash enough to raise a reddish blister they will be the better.

Sabbathday Lake Shakers

Superior Johnny Cake

Take one quart milk, three eggs, one teaspoonful saleratus, one teacupful of wheat flour and Indian meal sufficient enough to make a batter of the consistency of pan cakes. Bake quick in pan previously buttered and eat it warm with butter or milk. The addition of wheat flour is a great improvement.

Sabbathday Lake Shakers

Johnny Cake

Eight cups buttermilk, six eggs, six small teaspoons soda, two pints flour, three and a half pints corn meal, one cup molasses, salt. Steam four and one half hours.

Sister Marian Scott

Steamed Johnny Cake

Two bowls corn meal, one cup molasses or brown sugar, eight cups sour milk or buttermilk, one tablespoon of salt, eight level teaspoons of baking soda, two cups of rye or wheat flour. Soak corn meal in milk over night. In the morning dissolve baking soda in half a cup of hot water, stir in corn meal mixture, add flour, sugar or molasses and mix thoroughly. It should be thin enough to pour into a well greased milk pan. Steam for 3 hours and then bake in oven till dry on top. Serve with plenty of butter and apple sauce. I suppose I have made over 100 pans of this and there wouldn't be a crumb left.

Sister Jennie M. Wells

CAKES

Rules to be observed in making Nice Cake

Cake to be good, must be made of nice material. The eggs,

butter and flour, should not be stale and the sugar should be of light color and dry. Brown sugar answers very well for most kinds of cakes, if rolled free from lumps and stirred to a cream with the butter. The flour should be sifted, and if damp, dried perfectly, otherwise it will make the cake heavy. The eggs should be beaten to a froth and the cake will be more delicate if the yolks and whites are beaten separately. Saleratus and soda should be perfectly dissolved and strained before they are stirred into the cake. Raisins should have the seeds taken out. Zante currants should be rinsed in several waters to cleanse them, rubbed in a dry cloth to get the sticks out, and then spread on platters and dried perfectly before they are put into the cake. Almonds should be blanched, which is done by turning boiling water on them, and letting them remain in it till the skins will rub off easily. When blanched, dry them, then pound them fine, with rosewater to prevent their oiling. When the weather is cold the materials for the cake should be moderately warmed before mixing them together, all kind of cake that are made without yeast are better for being stirred, till just before they are baked. The butter and sugar should be stirred together till white, then the eggs, flour, and spices added. Saleratus and cream should not be put in till just before the cake is baked—add the fruit last. Butter the cake pans well. The cake will be less liable to burn if the pans are lined with white buttered paper. The cake should not be moved while baking, if it can be avoided, as moving it is apt to make it heavy. The quicker most kinds of cake are baked, the lighter and better they will be; the oven should not be of such a furious heat as to burn them. It is not possible to give any exact rules as to the time to be allowed for baking various kinds of cake, as so much depends on the heat of the oven. It should be narrowly watched while in the oven, if it browns too fast cover it with paper. When cake that is baked on flat tins moves easily on them it is sufficiently baked.

Sister Abigail Crossman

ALMOND CREAM CAKE

Two cupfuls of powdered sugar, one of sweet milk, three of flour, one-fourth of a cupful of butter, whites of four eggs, well beaten, two teaspoonfuls of baking powder and half a teaspoonful of vanilla. Bake in four tins and put together in layers with cream made as follows: Whip one cupful of powdered sugar, a few drops of vanilla and one pound of almonds blanched and chopped. Spread quite thick between the layers of cake. Frost the top and sides.

Sabbathday Lake Shakers

AMBROSIA CAKE

Two-thirds of a cupful of butter, two of sugar, half a cupful of milk, three cupfuls of flour, four eggs, one teaspoonful of soda, two of cream-of-tartar. Bake in layers. Mix together one well-beaten egg, half a pint of whipped cream, one full cup of grated cocoanut, half a cupful of sugar, the juice of one orange and half the grated rind. Place this preparation between the layers and on the top of the cake.

Sister Mary Whitcher's
Shaker Housekeeper

ANGEL CAKE

Beat two eggs in a teacup and fill with rich sour cream, one teacup sugar, one cup flour, not quite half a teaspoon soda. Bake in four tins.

Sister Marian Scott

ANGEL'S FOOD CAKE

One and a half cups powdered sugar, whites of eleven eggs, one large cup flour, one teaspoon cream tartar (no soda). Sift flour six times, three times before and three times after putting in cream of tartar. Beat whites of eggs to a stiff froth having first put in a pinch of salt. Stir in the sugar very lightly, then add the flour in the same manner. Add a teaspoon of vanilla. Pour in a stemmed cake tin and bake one hour in a moderate oven.

Sister Marian Scott

BLUEBERRY CAKE

One cup milk, one cup sugar, one spoonful butter, one cup of blue or other berries, one-half teaspoonful soda, three cups of flour. This is a very nice breakfast or tea cake. The fixed air in the berries makes the cake light. It is best baked in patty pans.

Sister Mary Whitcher's
Shaker Housekeeper

NICE CHEAP CAKE

One cup sugar, half a cup butter, one cup flour, half a cup milk, two eggs, three teaspoons baking powder. Beat thoroughly.

Sister Martha Wetherill

HALF HOUR CHOCOLATE CAKE

One coffee cup granulated sugar, one tablespoon softened butter, three eggs unbeaten, reserving the white of one. Beat all together slowly. One cup flour, two teaspoons baking powder, half a cup milk. Spread thin in three tins, bake 5 minutes.

Filling: Melt one-third cake of sweetened chocolate in a cup set in a pan of boiling water. One cup milk, one tablespoon flour, two tablespoons sugar rubbed smooth in a little cold milk. Boil till it thickens. Add one tablespoon of the melted chocolate and one teaspoon vanilla. Spread between the layers as soon as baked. For the frosting use the white of one egg, one tablespoon water, one teaspoon vanilla. Stir in powdered sugar until thick enough. Then add the rest of the chocolate.

Sister Marian Scott

CHOCOLATE CAKE

One cup sugar, three eggs (reserve two whites for frosting), half a cup milk, two cups flour, half a cup butter, two teaspoons baking powder.

Frosting: One and one half cups sugar, three tablespoons chocolate, two tablespoons water. Let it come to a boil, then add the whites of two eggs beaten to a stiff froth. Add a little more chocolate, flavor with vanilla. Set aside to cool.

Sister Martha Wetherill

CIRCLE CAKE

One egg, one cupful of sugar, two cupfuls of flour, one-third of a cupful of butter, half a cupful of sweet milk, one teaspoonful of cream of tartar, half a teaspoonful of soda. Flavor with lemon.

Sister Mary Whitcher's
Shaker Housekeeper

COCOANUT CAKE

Three-fourths cup butter, two cups sugar, four eggs, one milk or water, three cups flour, two teaspoons baking powder.

Icing: Put 10 teaspoons sugar to the white of one egg with either prepared or fresh cocoanut, spread between layers and on top.

Sister Marian Scott

COFFEE CAKE

Five cupfuls of flour, one of butter, one of coffee, one of molasses, one of raisins and a teaspoonful of soda.

Sister Mary Whitcher's
Shaker Housekeeper

COFFEE CAKE

One cup molasses, half a cup sugar, three cups flour, half cup butter, one cup cold strong coffee, two cups raisins, two eggs, one tablespoonful saleratus. Spices to suit the taste.

The story of the Shakers and some of their favorite cooking recipes. Calendar 1882-3.

CHEAP CREAM CAKE

One cup white soft sugar, one egg, one cup sweet milk, two cups flour, one tablespoon butter, two heaping teaspoons baking powder, flavor to taste. Divide in three parts and bake.

Cream filling: Beat one egg and half a cup sugar, then add one-fourth cup flour, wet with a very little milk and stir this mixture in half a pint of boiling milk until thick. Flavor to taste. When cool, spread between the cakes, sprinkle the top with powdered sugar.

Sister Marian Scott

CREAM CAKE

One cupful of sugar, half a cupful of cream, two eggs, one cupful of flour, one large teaspoonful of cream of tartar, one level teaspoonful of soda and the same quantity of salt.

Sister Mary Whitcher's Shaker Housekeeper

BOSTON CREAM CAKE

The cake—One-half pint milk, five ounces flour, four ounces butter and five eggs. Boil milk and butter together, stir in flour while boiling then add eggs.

The story of the Shakers and some of their favorite cooking recipes. Calendar 1882-3,

CUP CAKE

One cup of butter, two of sugar, three of flour, four eggs, beat well together. Bake in pans or cups 20 minutes.

Sister Abigail Crossman

DELICIOUS CAKE

Two cupfuls of white sugar, one of butter, one of milk, three eggs, half teaspoonful of soda, one of cream of tartar, three cupfuls of flour. Beat the butter and sugar together. Add the yolks of the eggs and then the beaten whites. Dissolve the soda in milk. Rub the cream of tartar in flour and add last.

Sister Mary Whitcher's
Shaker Housekeeper

ELECTION CAKE

Take four pounds of flour (a pint is a pound the world around), three-quarters of a pound of butter, four eggs, one pound of sugar, one pound currants and raisins, half a pint of good yeast, wet it with milk and mould it on a board. Let it rise over night; bake three-quarters of an hour.

Sister Abigail Crossman

FEATHER CAKE

Two cups sugar, two-thirds cup butter, two-thirds cup milk, three cups flour, three eggs, two teaspoons baking powder.

Sister Marian Scott

FEATHER CAKE

One cup milk, one cup flour, one egg, half cup sweetened milk, one tablespoon melted butter, one teaspoon baking powder, one teaspoon lemon juice.

Sister Marian Scott

FRUIT CAKE

Three pounds raisins, three pounds currants, one pound citron, one pound sugar, one pound flour, three-fourths pound butter, one dozen eggs, three tablespoons molasses, one nutmeg, one wine-glass of brandy, one glass of wine, one orange or lemon. Bake one and half hours.

Sister Marian Scott

FRUIT CAKE

Three-fourths lb. butter	One lb. of raisins
One lb. of brown sugar	One lb. of currants
One and one-fourth lb. of flour	Three-fourth lb. of citron
	One cup molasses
Six eggs	Spice to taste

Manifesto — 1882

FRUIT CAKE

One pound fine sugar, one pound butter, half a pound citron, chopped fine. One pound flour, one pound currants, twelve eggs, one and one half pounds raisins, seeded or chopped; one tablespoonful cinnamon, two tablespoons cloves, wine-glass of brandy. Stir sugar and butter to a cream, add the beaten yolks of the eggs. Stir all well, then add half the flour. Then add spices next, the whipped whites stirred in alternately with the rest of the flour. Last the fruit and brandy. Bake 3 hours in a slow oven.

Sister Marian Scott

PLAIN FRUIT CAKE

Half a cupful each of milk and butter, one and one half cupfuls of sugar, two and one half cupfuls of flour, two eggs, half a teaspoonful of soda, spice and fruit.

Sister Mary Whitcher's
Shaker Housekeeper

LAYER FRUIT CAKE

One cup sugar, three-fourths cup butter, two cups flour, whites of five eggs, three teaspoons baking powder, vanilla to flavor. Take from this one large tablespoonful. Bake the rest in two tins. To this add half a cup of chopped raisins, citron, flour and molasses, two teaspoons cinnamon, half a teaspoon of cloves and a wine-glass of brandy or wine. Bake this in one layer. Put in the middle with soft frosting.

Sister Marian Scott

EXCELLENT GOLD CAKE

A cupful of sugar, half as much butter, half a cupful of milk, one and three-fourths cupfuls of flour, the yolks of three eggs and one whole egg, one-fourth teaspoonful each of soda and cream of tartar, half a teaspoonful of lemon flavor. Mix together the sugar and butter, and add the eggs, milk, lemon extract and flour in this order. Bake for half and hour in a moderate oven.

Sister Mary Whitcher's
Shaker Housekeeper

RECIPE FOR MAKING MOLASSES GINGER BREAD

Molasses, four cups, four large teaspoonfuls of saleratus, one teaspoonful pulverized alum, dissolved in hot water. A piece of butter the size of an egg; two tablespoonfuls of ginger. Boil your molasses and pour it boiling hot onto the flour, make it as hard as it can be rolled. Roll very thin and cut in squares.

Sabbathday Lake Shakers

GINGERBREAD

Melt a teacupful of butter and mix it with a pint of molasses, a tablespoonful of ginger, a pint of flour and two beaten eggs; dissolve one spoonful of saleratus in half a pint of milk and stir into the cake and add flour to make the proper thickness. Bake it in a deep pan half an hour.

Sister Abigail Crossman

Lancaster Gingerbread

One cupful of sugar, one of molasses, one of sour milk, two-thirds of butter, three eggs, and one half teaspoonfuls of soda, three and one half cupfuls of flour, ginger, cloves and raisins.

Sister Mary Whitcher's
Shaker Housekeeper

Sugar Gingerbread

One and one half cups of butter	Two teaspoonfuls of saleratus
One and one half cups of milk	Two teaspoonfuls of ginger
Four cups of sugar	Flour to roll out

Sabbathday Lake Shakers

Gingerbread

Four quarts of molasses	One lb. of shortening
Two of milk	Four ounces of saleratus
Flour to roll	

Sabbathday Lake Shakers

New York Gingerbread

One cupful of sugar, half a cupful of butter, half a cupful of milk, Two eggs, a teaspoonful of cream of tartar, half a teaspoonful of soda, a tablespoonful of ginger, a pinch of mustard, and two scant cupfuls of flour. Bake about 20 minutes.

Sister Mary Whitcher's
Shaker Housekeeper

Soft Gingerbread

Six teacups of four	One teacup of butter
Three teacups of molasses	One tablespoonful of pearlash
One teacup of cream	One tablespoonful of ginger

Sabbathday Lake Shakers

SOFT GINGER BREAD

One cup cream, one of molasses, one teaspoonful of ginger, one of saleratus dissolved in boiling water, a little salt. Bake half an hour.

Sister Abigail Crossman

SOFT GINGER BREAD

2 cups New Orleans molasses
2 cups brown sugar
1 cup shortening, melted
2 level teaspoons ground ginger
1 teaspoon ground cinnamon
2 cups water

8 cups flour
1 teaspoon salt
2 level teaspoons soda
Bake in dripping pan well greased
Bake 1 hour in slow oven

Sabbathday Lake Shakers

SPONGE GINGERBREAD

Three cups of flour, one cup molasses, one of sugar, one of sour milk, one heaping tablespoonful of butter, two teaspoons saleratus, two teaspoons ginger, one of cinnamon.

Sister Abigail Crossman

GINGER POUND CAKE

Three loaves of excellent cake can be made of two cupfuls of butter, two of sugar, two of molasses, nine of flour, two teaspoonfuls of cinnamon, two of saleratus, two tablespoonfuls of ginger, three eggs and a nutmeg.

Sister Mary Whitcher's
Shaker Housekeeper

HONEY CAKE

One quart strained honey, half a pint sugar, half a pint melted butter, one teaspoon of soda dissolved in one teacup of warm water, half a nutmeg, one teaspoonful of ginger. Mix and work in sifted flour till you can roll it. Cut thin and bake on buttered tins quick oven.

Sister Marian Scott

INDIAN CAKE

One pint of Indian meal, a cupful of flour, half a cupful of sugar, one-third of a cupful of butter, a teaspoonful of soda, one of cream of tartar, an egg and some salt. Mix in enough sweet milk to make a soft batter.

Sister Mary Whitcher's
Shaker Housekeeper

JELLY CAKE

Beat two eggs in a teacup and fill with rich sour cream, one teacup sugar, one cup flour, not quite half a teaspon soda. Bake in four tins.

Sister Marian Scott

JELLY CAKE

One and one half cups sugar, half a cup butter, one egg, one cup milk, three cups flour, three teaspoons baking powder. Spread thin, bake quickly.

Sister Martha Wetherill

JELLY ROLL

Four eggs, one cup sugar, three teaspoons baking powder. Spread very thin. Bake quickly, spread with jelly and roll while warm.

Sister Martha Wetherill

JELLY ROLL

Three eggs beaten with one cup of sugar. When light, add one cup flour, one teaspoon cream of tartar, half a teaspoon soda dissolved in hot water.

Sister Marian Scott

Jelly Roll Cake

Three eggs, one cup sugar, one cup flour, two tablespoons melted butter, two tablespoons water, one teaspoon baking powder. Bake in sheet and roll while hot.

Sister Marian Scott

Loaf Cake

Five eggs, one cup milk, four cups of brown sugar, five of flour, two of fresh butter, half lb. of raisins. Spice to taste.

Sabbathday Lake Shakers

Laconia Cake

A cupful of butter, a cupful and a half of sugar, half a pint of flour twice this quantity of flour, a teaspoonful of saleratus, six eggs, half a pound of currants, lemon extract. Bake in two loaves, in a moderate oven for nearly an hour.

Sister Mary Whitcher's
Shaker Housekeeper

New Layer Cake

Boil a cup of milk and stir into it a tablespoon of butter and set aside to cool a little. Beat two eggs light with a cup of sugar. Add half a teaspoon salt, two teaspons baking powder, two small cups flour and the boiled milk. Bake in two layers.

Filling: One beaten egg, grated rind and juice of one lemon, one cup sugar and three-fourths cup grated apple. Boil till thick.

Sister Marian Scott

Lemon Cake

Two-thirds cup butter, two cups soft or one and one half cups granulated sugar, one cup milk, three eggs beaten thoroughly, three cups flour, one and one half teaspoons baking powder.

Filling: Grated rind and juice of one lemon, one cup sugar, two eggs, beat thoroughly and cook.

Sister Marian Scott

LEMON CAKE

The rind and juice of a lemon, a teaspoonful of cream of tartar, half as much saleratus, a teacupful of butter, one of sweet milk, three of sugar, four and one half of flour and five eggs— the yolks and whites beaten separately. Bake in two loaves for 45 minutes in a rather quick oven.

Sister Mary Whitcher's
Shaker Housekeeper

MARBLE CAKE

Light part: One and one half cups sugar, half a cup milk, half a cup of butter, two and one half cups flour. Whites of four eggs, two teaspoons baking powder.

Dark part: One cup brown sugar, half a cup butter, half a cup molasses, half a cup milk (sour,) two and one half cups flour, one teaspoon soda.

Sister Martha Wetherill

MARBLE CAKE

Light part: One half cup butter, one cup soft white sugar, one cup milk, two and one half flour, whites of four eggs, flavor to taste, two teaspoons baking powder.

Dark part: One cup brown sugar, one cup milk, half a cup butter, two and one half cups flour, one teaspoon cinnamon, half teaspoon each of cloves and allspice, half of a grated nutmeg, yolks of four eggs, two teaspoons baking powder, five tablespoons chocolate.

Sister Marian Scott

MARSHFIELD CAKE

Two eggs, two cupfuls of sugar, one of butter, one of molasses, one of milk, one of chopped raisins or currants, four cupfuls of flour, one teaspoonful of soda, spice to taste.

Sister Mary Whitcher's
Shaker Housekeeper

124

Nut Cake

One and one half cups sugar, half cup butter, two and one half cups flour, half cup milk, three eggs, one at a time, beating well between. One cup walnuts, two teaspoons baking powder.

Sister Martha Wetherill

Poor Man's Cake

One cupful sugar, half of butter, stirred to a cream then add one egg and stir briskly, one cupful of milk, two of flour with two teaspoonfuls of baking powder added to it. Flavor with lemon or fruit and spices. This is a nice cake and easily made.

Sister Mary Whitcher's
Shaker Housekeeper

Pound Cake

Beat well the yolks of six eggs with a pound of white sugar and stir a half pound of fresh butter with another half pound of sugar. Dissolve one teaspoonful of soda in a pint of slightly soured cream and the gratings of two lemons. Stir these all together then add 1 lb. of flour and the whites of the eggs which have been beaten to a stiff froth. Mix in a third at a time of each.

Sabbathday Lake Shakers

Imitation Pound Cake

Cream a cupful of butter with one and one-fourth cups of sugar. Beat four eggs 5 minutes, and add to the butter and sugar, add two cups pastry flour measured after sifting once. Then add two level teaspoons baking powder, sift four times, one half cup water and one teaspoon orange extract (sic). Beat hard, then pour into tube cake tin and bake in moderate oven.

Sister Marian Scott

PUFF CAKE

Two cups sugar, three eggs, three-fourths cup butter, one cup milk, three cups flour, two teaspoons baking powder. Bake in loaf.

Sister Marian Scott

QUEEN'S CAKE

Half a cupful of butter, two cupsful of sugar, one of milk, three of flour, three eggs, half a teaspoonful each of cream of tartar and soda, flavor to taste. Two loaves can be made with these quantities.

Sister Mary Whitcher's
Shaker Housekeeper

RAISED CAKE

Three cups new milk, one cake yeast, two cups sugar, one cup butter, ten cups flour. Let it rise over night, add two cups sugar, two-thirds cup butter, two eggs, two cups raisins, season with nutmeg. Let it rise until light, put in pans, raise again very light. Bake slowly 1 hour.

Sister Martha Wetherill

SCRIPTURE CAKE

1 cup butter—1 cup Judges 5:25
3½ cups whole wheat flour—3½ cups Exodus 29:2
2 Cups figs—2 cups Nahum 3:12
1 cup water—1 cup Genesis 24:17
1 teaspoonful Corriander seed—1 teaspoonful Exodus 16:31
2 cups cane sugar—2 cups Jeremiah 6:20
2 cups raisins—2 cups Samuel 30:12
1 cup almonds—1 cup Numbers 17:8
6 eggs—6 of Isaiah 10:14
1 pinch salt—pinch Leviticus 2:13
3 teaspoons wine—3 teaspoons of Amos 8:14

Spices to taste
Beat well

Sister Jennie M. Wells

Seed Cakes

One cup butter, two cups sugar, one cup milk, eggs, two
teaspoons caraway seeds, two teaspoons cream tartar, one teaspoon soda, flour enough to roll smooth.

Sister Marian Scott

Silver Cake

The whites of six eggs, two and one half cups of flour, one
and one half cups of sugar, half cup of butter, two-thirds of a
cup of milk or cream, half a teaspoonful of cream of tartar and
a little soda.

Sister Abigail Crossman

Silver Cake

Half a cupful of butter, a cupful of sugar, half a cupful of
corn starch dissolved in nearly half a cupful of milk, the whites
of three eggs, one and one-fourth cupfuls of flour, half a teaspoonful of cream of tartar, one-fourth of a teaspoonful of soda
and a little vanilla or almond extract. After beating the butter
to a cream beat in the sugar gradually and add the flavor. Mix
together and sift the flour, soda and cream of tartar. Beat the
whites of the eggs to a stiff froth. Add the cornstarch and milk
to the beaten sugar and butter, then add the whites and the
flour. Mix thoroughly and as quickly as possible. Have the batter
in sheets about 2 inches thick. Bake in a moderate oven for
half an hour.

Sister Mary Whitcher's
Shaker Housekeeper

Silver Cake

Half a cupful of butter, one of powdered sugar, the whites
of six eggs, half a cupful of milk, two cupfuls of flour, one tea-

spoonful of cream of tartar, half of soda. Beat the butter and sugar to a cream; then add the whites of six eggs beaten to a stiff froth; then the milk, one cupful of the flour, in which is mixed one teaspoonful of cream of tartar, your cupful of flour, and lastly your soda, dissolved in a little of the milk. One cupful of English walnuts, broken. Very nice.

Sister Mary Whitcher's
Shaker Housekeeper

SPONGE CAKE

Twelve eggs, one pound of sugar, twelve ounces of flour. Beat the sugar and eggs together to a light froth and carefully stir in the flour.

Sabbathday Lake Shakers

BERWICK SPONGE CAKE

Beat six eggs 2 minutes. Add three cups sugar, beat 5 minutes. Add two cups flour, beat 2 minutes. Add one cup cold water, beat 1 minute. Add half a teaspoon salt, flavor with lemon, two more cups flour, three teaspoons baking powder. Beat all together another minute and bake in deep pans slowly 50 minutes.

Sister Martha Wetherill

A GOOD SPONGE CAKE

Into a froth of seven eggs and two cupfuls of sugar stir two coffee-cupfuls of flour, mixed with a teaspoonful of saleratus and two of cream of tartar. Flavor with the juice and grated rind of one lemon. Bake in sheets in a moderately hot oven.

Sister Mary Whitcher's
Shaker Housekeeper

MRS. HERBERT'S SPONGE CAKE

Stir the yolks of four eggs with one cupful powdered sugar for 15 minutes, add a half cup boiling water, one cup flour, one and one half teaspoons baking powder (heaping), the whites of the four eggs, beaten stiff, a little salt, the grated rind of a lemon. Bake slowly.

Sister Marian Scott

HOT SPRINGS SPONGE CAKE

Break two eggs into a dish, add a coffee cup of sugar, beat well, then pour into that one half cup of boiling water stirring briskly. Add one and one half cups of sifted flour and two teaspoonfuls baking powder. Bake three-fourths of an hour.

Manifesto—1878

TEA CAKE

Beat two eggs in a teacup. Fill the cup with sweet milk. Add one cup sugar, ten even teaspoons melted butter, one and three-fourths cups flour, two teaspoons baking powder. To be baked either in layers or loaf.

Sister Marian Scott

TEA CAKE

Four cups of flour, three cups sugar, one cup butter, one cup milk, one cup ferment, three eggs, one half nutmeg. Let it stand about one hour in a warm place, and bake into small pans when first mixed.

Sabbathday Lake Shakers

UNION CAKE

A cupful of butter, two of sugar, one of sweet milk, three of flour, half a cupful of corn starch, four eggs, two teaspoonfuls

SHAKER
HERB GARDENER

Constantine Kermes

"SHAKER WOMAN: HANDS TO WORK; HEARTS TO GOD"

Constantine Kermes

of lemon flavor one of cream of tartar and one half a teaspoonful of soda.

Sister Mary Whitcher's
Shaker Housekeeper

VELVET CAKE

One pound of sugar and half a pound of butter, four eggs, one cup of water and one half teaspoonful of saleratus. Lemon or other extract and one pound of flour, with one teaspoonful of cream of tartar.

Sabbathday Lake Shakers

SISTER HARRIET JOHN'S FRUIT CAKE

4 cups flour, 1 cup shortening (butter), 2½ cups sugar, 4 eggs—separate them, 1 cup sour milk, 3 tbsp. molasses, 1cup raisins, ½ cup currants, ½ cup citron, 1 tsp. soda, 1 tsp. baking powder, nutmeg.

Canterbury Shakers

BLUEBERRY CAKE

2 1/4 cups flour, 1½ cups blueberries (dust with flour), 1-¼ cups milk sweet, ½ cup sugar, 2 eggs beaten light, 2 tsps. cream tartar, 1 tsp. soda, piece of butter the size of a walnut. Bake one half hour.

Canterbury Shakers

COOKIES

One cup butter, two cups sugar, juice and rind of one lemon, three teaspoons baking powder. Flour to roll out easily.

Sister Martha Wetherill

BERKSHIRE COOKIES

One cupful of molasses, a teaspoonful of soda, dissolved in half a cupful of cold water, a dessertspoonful of salt, a like

of ginger, a teaspoonful of melted butter, flour enough to roll
out to the thickness of half an inch. Bake in a quick oven about
10 minutes.

Sister Mary Whitcher's
Shaker Housekeeper

BEST OUT COOKIES

One cup sugar, half a cup of butter, half teaspoon of soda,
four tablespoons of sweet milk, nutmeg, salt and flour to roll.
Bake in a quick oven.

Sabbathday Lake Shakers

BRISTOL COOKIES

A cupful of milk, one of sugar, half a cupful of butter, half
a nutmeg, two eggs, a teaspoonful of saleratus, and flour enough
to roll. Beat the butter and sugar to a cream; then add the eggs,
well beaten. Dissolve the saleratus in the milk, which stir into
the mixture. Finally add the flour.

Sister Mary Whitcher's
Shaker Housekeeper

BRISTOL COOKIES

One cup sugar, two-thirds cup milk, half a cup butter, two
eggs, half a nutmeg, three teaspoons baking powder. Flour to
roll.

Sister Martha Wetherill

DROPPED COOKIES

Four and one half cups flour, two and one half cups sugar,
one cup milk, one cup butter, three eggs, two teaspoons baking
powder. Cream sugar and butter, beat eggs till very light. Stir
thoroughly together, add one teaspoon cinnamon. Drop on
buttered tins, bake quickly.

Sister Marian Scott

Fig Filled Cookies

Half a pound figs, in a saucepan, four tablespoons water. Place over a slow fire, cover and let simmer till water is absorbed. Chop very fine. Half cup hot water, juice of half a lemon, then cook to a smooth paste.

Raisins

One cup chopped raisins, half a cup sugar, half a cup water, one tablespoon flour. Cook until thick. It burns easily.

Cooky dough

One cup sugar, half a cup shortening, half a cup milk, one egg, three and one half cups flour, two and one half teaspoons baking powder, one teaspoon vanilla. Roll the dough out thin, spread paste on one half, fold over and cut in squares. Bake in moderate oven.

Sister Marian Scott

Filled Cookies

Two cups of sugar, one cup of lard, one cup of sweet milk, three teaspoons of baking powder, one of vanilla. Mix as soft as can be handled and bake in a quick oven.

Filling

Two cups of chopped raisins, one cup of sugar, one cup of water, two teaspoons of flour. Cook until thick, being careful not to let the filling burn.

Sabbathday Lake Shakers

Fruit Cookies

Two cups of sugar, one cup of butter, half cup of molasses, half cup of sour cream, one large cup of chopped raisins, two teaspoons of cinnamon, one of nutmeg, and soda and flour enough to roll.

Sabbathday Lake Shakers

GINGER COOKIES

One cup molasses, one heaping cup butter, one scant cup hot water, two teaspoons soda, ginger, cinnamon to taste. Flour to roll.

Sister Martha Wetherill

GINGER COOKIES

Two cups molasses, one cup sour milk, five teaspoons of soda, well beaten with the above. One cup sugar, ginger to taste, a little salt, one cup butter, one cup cottolene (Crisco, etc.), four eggs, whites and yolks beaten separately. Flour to roll easily. Cut thin and bake in hot oven.

Sister Martha Wetherill

MOLASSES COOKIES FROM ALFRED

2 eggs, 2 cups molasses, 1 tbsp. ginger, pinch, of salt, 4 cups flour, 2 tsp. soda (heaping) dissolved in 2 tbsp. vinegar, 1 cup shortening. Beat well together. Makes about 60 cookies. Drop.

Canterbury Shakers

GINGER SNAPS

Three cupfuls of butter, six of molasses, three of hot water, three of sugar, six spoonfuls of ginger, six teaspoonfuls of soda, flour to roll.

Sister Mary Whitcher's
Shaker Housekeeper

GINGER SNAPS

Boil a teacup of molasses, add two spoonfuls of butter, one of ginger, one teaspoonful of saleratus, stir in the flour, when hot roll thin, cut it in rounds, bake quick.

Sabbathday Lake Shakers

Graham Cookies

One and one half cups of sugar, one and one half cups of sour cream, one teaspoon of soda, one of salt. Mix with graham flour to make stiff. No flavoring is needed.

Sabbathday Lake Shakers

Graham Puffs

Sift one pint of graham flour and one of wheat, add one heaping teaspoonful of baking powder and two teaspoonfuls of salt. Now beat three eggs well together add one quart of sweet milk and pour over the sifted flour. Beat hard for a minute or two, then pour into hot greased gem pans and bake in a hot oven until done or nearly 30 minutes.

Sister Marian Scott

Molasses Cookies

A cupful of brown sugar, one of molasses, one of lard, half a cupful of boiling water, one spoonful of ginger, one of saleratus, one of salt and flour enough to roll. Beat the sugar, lard, molasses, saleratus and ginger together; then pour on the boiling water and mix in the flour. Roll about three-fourths of an inch thick and cut with a round cutter. Bake in a quick oven.

Sister Mary Whitcher's
Shaker Housekeeper

Soft Molasses Cooky

One cup molasses, one tablespoon ginger, one teaspoon soda, two tablespoons warm water or milk, one-third cup cottolene (Crisco) softened, flour to mix soft dough. Sift ginger into molasses, dissolve soda in warm water, stir into molasses, add shortening quickly, one and one half teaspoon salt and flour to make a soft dough. Roll half an inch thick and bake in a quick oven. Bully good. (sic)

Sister Marian Scott

Molasses Drop Cakes

One cup molasses, half a cup butter, half a cup water, three cups flour two teaspoons ginger, one teaspoon soda. Drop with a spoon on buttered pans and bake quickly.

Amelia Calver,
Lebanon Valley Cookery — 1926

Very Nice Cookies

One cupful of butter, two of sugar, four eggs, juice of half a lemon, grated peel of one lemon, one teaspoonful of cream of tartar, half of saleratus, five cupfuls of flour. Save the white of one egg, beat it to a stiff froth, and spread upon the top of the cookies and sprinkle also with a little sugar. Bake quickly and roll thin. Teaspoonfuls in this rule are all even and not heaped.

Sister Mary Whitcher's
Shaker Housekeeper

Popcorn Cookies

Two well beaten eggs, one cup granulated sugar, one teaspoon vanilla, one and one half teaspoons baking powder. Flour to make dough stiff enough to roll out thin. Called "Popcorn" cookies because they taste like popcorn.

Lebanon Valley Cookery — 1926

Soft Cookies

One teacupful of sour cream, one of sugar, two eggs, one teaspoonful of soda, one of cream of tartar, a little salt, nutmeg, flour to roll.

Sister Mary Whitcher's
Shaker Housekeeper

Sour Milk Cookies

Two cups sugar, one cup butter, two eggs, half cup sour milk, one teaspoon soda dissolved in milk, flour to spank smoothly (sic).

Sister Marian Scott

Sour Cream Cookies

4 cups sugar	2 teaspoons baking soda
2 cups butter	1 whole nutmeg, grated
2 cups sour cream	8 cups flour

Mix, roll to half inch thickness and cut. Bake from 7 to 10 minutes.

Sister Jennie M. Wells

Spanish Drop Cookies

Cream together one cup butter, two cups sugar, five eggs beaten light, one cup currants, two cups sifted flour, one tablespoon lemon juice, grated rind of one lemon. Drop from a tablespoon 5 inches apart. Bake a light brown.

Sister Marian Scott

Cream Puffs

One cup cold water, half a cup butter boiled together. When boiling hot, add one cup flour, let simmer until thick. When partly cool add three eggs, one at a time, without beating the eggs. Drop by spoonful on a buttered pan and bake thoroughly in a hot oven.

Filling

One cup boiling hot milk, one cup sugar, two eggs and two small tablespoons flour. Flavor with lemon or vanilla and cook thoroughly. Cut the puffs as little as possible to fill.

Sister Marian Scott

HERMITS

A cupful of raisins, stoned and chopped; a cupful of butter, two of sugar, a teaspoonful each of cinnamon and cloves, half a teaspoonful of soda, dissolved in a little milk, one nutmeg, three eggs flour enough to roll out. Roll the dough to the thickness of one-fourth of an inch, and cut it with a round tin. Bake the cakes about 20 minutes in a rather quick oven.

Sister Mary Whitcher's
Shaker Housekeeper

SOFT HERMITS

One cup of butter, two cups of sugar, one cup of milk, four cups of flour, one cup of chopped raisins, one teaspoon of soda, one heaping teaspoon cream of tartar, two teaspoons of baking powder may be used instead, one teaspoon of all kinds of spice. Drop on buttered tin, about one inch apart and bake in a moderate oven.

Sabbathday Lake Shakers

JUMBLES

Three-fourths cup butter, one and one half cups sugar, three eggs, three tablespoons milk, one teaspoon baking powder, flour to roll. Sprinkle with granulated sugar, roll it gently in. Cut with hole in center and bake.

Sister Marian Scott

JUMBLES

Two cups of sugar beaten with two eggs and one cup of fresh butter. One teaspoonful of soda dissolved in one cup of sour cream or buttermilk. Put in any kind of flavoring you wish. Use sufficient flour to make them roll well, cut them in round cakes, and if you like, cut a little hole out of the center with a cutter the size of a pepper box cover. Lay them in white sugar before putting them in the tins. Bake in a quick oven 5 minutes.

They may be ornamented by dropping a spoonful of jelly on the top.

Sabbathday Lake Shakers

LAFAYETTE JUMBLES

Nearly half a cupful of milk, one half a cupful of butter, one cupful of sugar, three cupfuls of flour, two eggs, one half a teaspoonful of soda, half a nutmeg. Roll out and dust with the whit. of an egg. Sprinkle with sugar.

Sister Mary Whitcher's
Shaker Housekeeper

GRIDDLE CAKES and WAFFLES

SUPERIOR BATTER CAKES

Take one pint of flour; one teaspoonful lard or butter rubbed into the flour; two teaspoonfuls hominy or well boiled mush; one egg beaten; milk enough to make a tolerable batter and yeast sufficient to make it rise. Make the batter pretty stiff—being governed by the weather as to the heat to be applied to the batter when rising. The cakes should be half an inch thick and baked quick.

Sister Abigail Crossman

BOSTON RICE CAKE

Boil a cup of rice and while hot put into a large tablespoonful of butter. Beat the whites and yolks of three eggs seperately and stir them into the rice. Thicken with four tablespoonfuls of flour and bake either in muffin rings or upon a delicate greased griddle, salt to taste.

Sister Abigail Crossman

GREEN CORN GRIDDLE CAKES

Take twelve ears of green corn and grate then wash the cobs in a teacup of milk with three eggs, two spoonfuls of flour, one teaspoonful of salt and a little pepper if you choose. Bake. They have the flavor of oysters *very nice*.

Sister Abigail Crossman

SWEET CORN PANCAKES

Seven cups grated or chopped corn, three cups milk, five eggs, eight tablespoons flour, two teaspoons baking powder, salt to taste. To add pepper and fry in small cakes, they are mock oysters.

Shakers Mt. Lebanon, New York, 1926

CORN GRIDDLE CAKES

To one quart of sour milk add one teaspoonful of soda, the same of salt, and one egg, one-half cup of wheat flour; add corn-meal sufficient to make a batter thick enough to bake on hot griddle.

Manifesto — 1879

CORN GRIDDLE CAKES

Take eighteen ears of corn, grate off the kernels, season well with salt and pepper. Fry on a well greased griddle. This is a very decided improvement upon all other kinds of griddle cakes.

Sister Abigail Crossman

GRIDDLE CAKES

Two quarts of flour, a handful of Indian meal, two eggs, a teaspoonful of salt, one of soda, one quart of milk.

Sister Mary Whitcher's
Shaker Housekeeper

GRIDDLE AND INDIAN CAKES

For the griddle cakes use two coffee cupfuls of sour milk or buttermilk, one teaspoonful of saleratus dissolved in a little hot water, and flour enough to pour. Grease the griddle with a piece of salt pork, and fry the cakes a light brown. Indian cakes are made in much the same way, save that half flour and half Indian meal is used, and also a teaspoonful of salt. They require a somewhat longer time to fry.

Sister Mary Whitcher's
Shaker Housekeeper

INDIAN PANCAKES

One and a half cupfuls of sour milk, one teaspoonful of soda, one egg, a little salt, two tablesponfuls of melted butter, two tablespoonfuls of flour. Stir in enough Indian meal to make a good batter. Fry on a hot griddle.

Sister Mary Whitcher's
Shaker Housekeeper

PANCAKES

Into a froth made by beating three eggs, stir half a pint of milk, one teaspoonful of salt, and three tablespoonfuls of flour. Heat the frying pan, and grease well with butter. Turn a third of the batter into it, and fry a light brown on one side, shaking the pan frequently to prevent burning. When brown on one side, turn and brown the other. When done, spread with jelly, fold, and serve immediately. Sugar may be substituted for jelly, if you choose.

Sister Mary Whitcher's
Shaker Housekeeper

PANCAKES FOR DESSERT

Take one pint of sour milk, two tablespoonfuls of rich cream. Add soda sufficient to dispel the acid (about a teaspoonful), and add a little salt, and flour sufficient to make it of the consistency of common pancakes; then drop in one egg. When all is well beaten up, fry in hot lard, dropping in a spoonful at a time. These are eaten with white sugar and home-made wine or cider. These cakes are always relished by the family and guests.

Sister Mary Whitcher's
Shaker Housekeeper

RUTHLAND CAKE

Three cupfuls of boiling milk, one of Indian meal, two of flour, a teaspoonful of salt, a tablespoonful of sugar, two of butter, one-fourth of a yeast cake or one-fourth of a cupful of liquid yeast. Pour the milk upon the butter and meal, and when cool add the salt, flour sugar and yeast, which has been dissolved (if in cake form) in four tablespoonfuls of cold water. Let the mixture over night and fry like griddle cakes.

Sister Mary Whitcher's
Shaker Housekeeper

BRAN GEMS

Four cups bran, six cups white flour, half cup butter, one cup sugar, three eggs, two teaspoons soda. Sour milk to make a rather thick batter. Mix overnight, leaving soda and well-beaten eggs to be added in the morning.

Sister Martha Wetherill

GRAHAM GEMS

One egg, beaten well, one spoonful of sugar, one cupful of sour milk. One even teaspoonful of soda, a little salt. Make a stiff batter. Bake in iron pans, well heated.

Sister Martha Wetherill
Shaker Housekeeper

SUPERB GRAHAM GEMS

Superb graham gems are made from the following recipe:
Take half a pint of Graham flour; half a pint of wheat flour;
two fresh eggs, one pint of rich milk; a tablespoonful of salt.
Heat and butter the pans first and then bake in a quick oven.

Manifesto—1879

GEMS

Unbolted wheat or rye flour is mixed up with water and
made into a batter a little stiffer than for griddle cakes. It is
then dropped into sizzling hot gem pans and baked in a hot
oven for about half an hour, or until nicely browned. If not well
baked they are doughy and indigestible.

Manifesto—1879

FRANCONIA MUFFINS

A cupful of sugar, five of flour, a pint of milk, a teaspoonful
of saleratus, two of cream of tartar, two eggs, and butter the size
of an egg. Beat the butter and sugar together, and then add the
eggs well beaten, and with this mix the milk. Now beat in the
flour in which the saleratus and cream of tartar have been
mixed. Bake in a buttered muffin ring in a quick oven.

Sister Martha Wetherill
Shaker Housekeeper

GRAHAM MUFFINS

One quart of Graham flour, two tablespoonfuls of sugar,
two eggs, half a tablespoonful of butter, one tablespoonful of
baking powder, and a little salt; moisten and mix thoroughly
with a little milk. Bake in a patty pan at once in a quick oven.

The story of the Shakers and some of their
favorite cooking recipes. Calendar 1882—3.

MUFFINS FROM WHEAT MEAL

One quart of wheat meal, one teaspoonful of saleratus, one of salt, half a teacupful of molasses, three teacupfuls milk. Bake in muffin tins.

Sister Mary Whitcher's
Shaker Housekeeper

MUFFINS

One quart milk, two eggs, quarter of a cup of butter, same of lard. Raised with yeast.

The story of the Shakers and some of their
favorite cooking recipes. Calendar 1882—3.

MUFFINS

Two cups flour, two eggs, two heaping teaspoons baking powder, half a cup butter, one tablespoon sugar, salt. Water to make a dough about as stiff as cake dough. Put one spoonful in each buttered ring.

Sister Marian Scott

SALLY LUNN MUFFINS

Sift together four cups flour, one teaspoon salt, two tablespoons sugar, six heaping teaspoons baking powder, four eggs well beaten, two teaspoons melted butter. Add to this two cups milk. Mix all together beat well and bake. (Some kinds of flour require more milk.)

Sister Marian Scott

CHESTER MUFFINS

Four quarts flour, teacup sugar, teacup butter, cup yeast, four eggs, little salt, two quarts sweet milk. Let rise all night.

Manifesto—1880

BUTTERMILK MUFFINS

One quart of sour buttermilk, one teacupful of sour cream, two eggs, one teaspoonful of soda, a little salt, flour enough to make as thick as pound cake. Bake in muffin rings placed upon tins in the oven, from 20 to 30 minutes, according to the temperature of the stove.

Sister Abigail Crossman

CREAM MUFFINS

Mix one pint sour cream (not very sour), one pint of flour, three eggs, one teaspoon salt; half a teaspoonful of soda or saleratus; whites and yolks of eggs beaten seperately. Stir in the whites the last thing. They are much nicer baked in new cups, which can be bought of a cheap kind. Wipe them clean with a dry cloth, never wet or grease them, in a short time the muffins will shine like varnish on the side to the cup.

Sabbathday Lake Shakers

HOMINY MUFFINS

Two cups boiled hominy; beat it smooth, stir in three cups of sour milk; half cup melted butter, two teaspoons salt, two tablespoons of sugar, add three eggs well beaten; one teaspoon of soda, dissolved in hot water, two cups flour. Bake quickly.

The story of the Shakers and some of their favorite cooking recipes. Calendar 1882—3.

MUFFINS

One pint sweet milk, two eggs, three cupsful of flour, and three teaspoonfuls of baking powder.

Sister Mary Whitcher's Shaker Housekeeper

144

APPLE FRITTERS

Make a batter, not very stiff, with one quart of milk, three eggs, and flour to bring to a right consistency. Pare and core a dozen large apples and chop them to about the size of a small pea, and mix them well in the batter. Fry them in lard as you would doughnuts. For trimmings use powdered sugar.

The story of the Shakers and some of their favorite cooking recipes. Calendar 1882—3.

CORN FRITTERS

Take about one pint of sweet corn after it is grated. To this add one egg well beaten, a small teacup of flour, half a cup of butter, salt and pepper. These are well mixed and fried a light brown. A tablespoonful of the batter being the size of an oyster when fried.

Sister Abigail Crossman

GREEN CORN PATTIES

Grate as much corn as will make one pint, add one teacupful of flour and one teacupful of butter, one egg, pepper and salt to taste. If too thick add a little milk. Fry in butter.

The story of the Shakers and some of their favorite cooking recipes. Calendar 1882—3.

CORN OYSTERS

One pint green corn, one cup flour, one spoonful of salt; one teaspoonful of pepper, one egg. Drop by the spoonful in hot lard and fry.

The story of the Shakers and some of their favorite cooking recipes. Calendar 1882—3.

Constantine Kermes

SHAKER WOMAN PEELING APPLES

SHAKER WOMAN
MAKING APPLESAUCE

Constantine Kermes:

WAFFLES

Take one pint of milk lukewarm, add four tablespoonfuls of baker's yeast, one teasponful of brown sugar, one tablespoonful melted butter, a little salt and flour enough to make a batter the consistency of thick cream. Let it rise over night. In the morning just before baking add two well beaten eggs. If any flour is added after the batter is raised the waffles will surely be tough. A little difference in the consistency of the batter will affect them very much. If they seem leathery use less flour next time.

Sister Abigail Crossman

RICE WAFFLES

One cup boiled rice, half a teaspoonful soda, one pint milk, one teaspoonful cream of tartar, two eggs, one teaspoon salt, lard size of a walnut, flour for a thin batter.

The story of the Shakers and some of their favorite cooking recipes. Calendar 1882—3.

RICE WAFFLES FOR TEA

One quart of thin sour milk, poured over one teacupful of cold boiled rice. Do this two or three hours before the waffles are wanted. When ready to bake add a pint and a half of flour, two or three beaten eggs and soda. Oil the waffle-irons each time they are used, with lard that is perfectly sweet. The rice used for rice griddle cakes and waffles should be salted when boiling.

Manifesto—1879

DOUGHNUTS

CRULLERS

These dainties are easily and quickly made. A piece of butter about the size of an egg, a nutmeg, a cupful of sugar and three eggs are to be made stiff with flour, cut in fancy shapes and fried in boiling lard.

Sister Mary Whitcher's
Shaker Housekeeper

DOUGHNUTS

One and a half cupfuls of milk, the same quantity of sugar, two eggs, a scant teaspoonful of soda, a teaspoonful of salt, and half a nutmeg. Very toothsome doughnuts are made by this rule.

Sister Mary Whitcher's
Shaker Houskeeper

DOUGHNUTS

One heaping cup sugar, three eggs, one cup sour cream, one small teaspoonful soda, flour sufficient to roll out. If cream is not attainable sour milk will do, or use sweet milk adding a small piece of butter, and a little less soda.

Manifesto—1883

DOUGHNUTS

Four cups rolled sugar, one cup buttermilk, one teaspoon soda, six eggs, well beaten, one nutmeg, a little salt, two table-spoons butter, flour enough to make a soft dough.

Sister Marian Scott

DOUGHNUTS

One cup sugar, two eggs, one cup milk, one tablespoon butter, three teaspoons baking powder. Flour to roll.

Sister Martha Wetherill

DOUGHNUTS WITHOUT SALERATUS

Use one half pint of ferment, one half pint new milk, large cup of sugar, one teaspoonful of salt, mix at night as for bread. In the morning mould in flour enough to roll and cut them and fry in hot fat.

Sabbathday Lake Shakers

CALLIE'S DOUGHNUTS

One quart of flour, one teacupful of sugar, one teaspoonful of cream of tartar, three-fourths of a teaspoonful of soda dissolved in a teacupful of sour milk, one and one half teaspoonful of salt, two eggs. The above is an old and excellent New England recipe for doughnuts.

*Sister Mary Whitcher's
Shaker Houskeeper*

INDIAN DOUGHNUTS

A correspondent says: I send you a recipe for making Indian meal doughnuts, which are much nicer than those not initiated are aware of. A teaspoonful and a half of boiling milk poured over two teacupfuls Indian meal; when it cools add two cupfuls wheat flour, one of butter, one and a half of sugar, three eggs and a tablespoonful of nutmeg or cinnamon; if not stiff enough, add equal portions of wheat and meal; let it rise till very light; roll it about half an inch thick; cut it into diamond-shaped cakes and boil them in hot suet.

Manifesto—1880

RAISED DOUGHNUTS

To four cups of bread dough add two eggs, one-fourth cup of butter—one cup sugar—one teaspoon of mace or nutmeg— one cup flour. To dough which is ready to shape into loaves, add the above ingredients and work into a smooth dough. Let rise until double in bulk, roll out to one-fourth inch thickness, cut into doughnuts and let stand 5 minutes, fry in deep fat.

Sister Mary Whitcher's
Shaker Housekeeper

RAISED DOUGHNUTS

Two-thirds of a cupful of yeast, one of sugar, one of warm milk, two spoonsful butter. Sponge, and knead over night. In the morning they are ready to fry. Use as little flour as possible after they are raised. They are best twisted.

Sister Mary Whitcher's
Shaker Housekeeper

SOUR MILK DOUGHNUTS

Two eggs, one cup sugar, one tablespoon melted butter, one cup thick sour milk, half a teaspoon nutmeg, half a teaspoon ginger, one teaspoon baking powder, one-third teaspoon salt, four cups flour. Beat eggs thoroughly, add sugar, butter and sour milk, in which soda has been dissolved. Then add two cups flour sifted with baking powder and add two more cups flour.

Sister Martha Wetherill

SISTER BERTHA'S WHITE DOUGHNUTS (with maple syrup)

1½ qts. bread flour	1 yeast cake
1/4 cup shortening	1 pint milk
1/4 cup sugar	Sift flour and add sugar

Mix sponge of ½ cup water and yeast cake. Let to rise in a well in middle of the flour. Let sponge rise for about an hour. Then add melted shortening and cooled milk which has been scalded. Knead well and let rise in a warm place until double in quantity. Punch the dough back and knead again. Let it rise again. Then roll the dough out and shape it into fingers about 3 inches long and an inch wide. It is now ready to fry in deep fat. Serve with maple syrup.

Canterbury Shakers

PIES

Pie Crust

Two cups flour, one half cup of butter and lard mixed; two-thirds cup of water, ice cold, a little salt. Mix with a knife, using the hands as little as possible. Roll one way, from you, brush over the tops of the pies with white of egg, or milk.

Sabbathday Lake Shakers

Flake Pie Crust

Take one half cup of lard to a pint of flour, rub well together, take water sufficient to make a dough (not too stiff); roll out and spread with butter, fold over evenly and make a second fold in the opposite direction, roll out again, being careful not to squeeze the butter out.

Sabbathday Lake Shakers

Apple Custard Pie

The nicest pie ever eaten. This recipe is hardly in season, but our readers can keep it for reference when needed. Peel sour apples and stew until soft and not much water left in them; then rub them through a collender; beat three eggs for each pie to be baked, and put in at the rate of one cup of butter and one of sugar for three pies; season with nutmeg. One egg for each pie will do very well, but the amount of sugar must be governed somewhat by the acidity of the apples. Bake as pumkin pies, which they resemble in appearance. Dried apples are very nice by making them a little more juicy. You can frost them and return them to the oven for a few moments, which will improve their appearance.

Manifesto—1878

GREEN APPLE PIE

Pare, quarter, core nice tart apples, and stew in water enough to prevent burning. When tender, make very sweet with sugar. Fill the pie-plate, which has been lined and edged with paste, grate on a little nutmeg, cover and bake three-fourths of an hour.

Sister Mary Whitcher's
Shaker Housekeeper

A NICE PAN DOWDY

Pare and slice enough tart apples to fill a flat earthen or tin pan to the depth of two inches. To three quarts of apple add one cupful of sugar, a grated nutmeg, one cupful of cold water, and butter the size of a walnut. Cover this with plain pie-crust (have the crust about an inch thick), and bake slowly two hours and a half; then cover and set for an hour where it will keep hot. Serve with sugar and cream. When done the apple will look red.

Sister Mary Whitcher's
Shaker Housekeeper

SLICED APPLE PIES

Line the plates with a bottom crust and full them with quartered apples. For a plate of common size allow two spoonfuls of sugar, a little nutmeg, and two spoonfuls of water. Cut the upper crust a little larger then the plate, and raise the under crust with the blade of the knife and lay it under it. Bake one hour in a moderate oven. When molasses is preferred, use three spoonfuls and a little cinnamon instead of nutmeg.

Sister Mary Whitcher's
Shaker Housekeeper

CUSTARD PIE

Take three eggs, beaten thoroughly, two tablespoonfuls of white sugar, one pint of milk, nutmeg to suit the taste, a little salt, stir all together, adding the eggs last.

Sabbathday Lake Shakers

CUSTARD PIE

Three eggs, one pint milk, three teaspoons of sugar, a little salt; flavor with nutmeg or lemon.

Sabbathday Lake Shakers

GRAHAM CUSTARD PIE

One quart of milk, two eggs, half a cup of sugar, half a cup of graham flour. Beat the eggs and stir all together. The graham flour sinks to the bottom of the pie dish as the custard bakes and forms a good crust. It may appear to be soaked as custard pie crust often is, but it is not in the least "clammy." It dissolves easily in the mouth and is entirely digestible. A pleasant cream pie is made from the same recipe leaving out the eggs and using creamy milk or thin cream.

Manifesto—1881

CLEAR LEMON PIE

Dissolve three tablespoons corn starch in a little cold water. Stir in one and one half pints boiling water until it thickens. Before putting to cool, stir in one dessert-spoon butter. Grate rind and squeeze juice of two lemons. Stir with it one and one half cups sugar. Line two pie tins, prick to prevent being uneven and bake. When done, fill with the mixture, return to the oven till hot.

Meringue: three whites, one and one-fourth cups sugar.

Sister Marian Scott

LEMON PIE

Juice of two lemons, one cup sugar, one cup of water, two eggs, two large spoonfuls of flour, a littlt salt. Bake with one or two crusts.

Sabbathday Lake Shakers

LEMON PIE

One grated lemon, two and one half cups of boiling water, one half cup of cold water, one and one half cups of sugar, three tablespoonfuls of cornstarch, and butter the size of an egg. Put the cornstarch in the cold water and stir in the boiling water. This makes two pies. Bake with under-crust. Beat the whites of three eggs for frosting.

Manifesto—1879

LEMON PIE

Grate one lemon, mixing the juice with the grated rind, and take also one cupful of water, one of sugar, the yolks of two eggs, a piece of butter the size of an egg, one slice of bread, broken fine, without the crust. Bake only with an under crust. When done, beat the whites of the eggs with four tablespoonfuls of sugar and a few drops of lemon and spread over the top; then return to the oven to brown slightly. This makes one pie and is very nice.

Sister Mary Whitcher's
Shaker Housekeeper

LEMON PIE

These three modes of making lemon pies are all good. The first is to take the yolks of three eggs, two teaspoonfuls of corn starch dissolved in a little cold water, a cupful of boiling water, one of sugar, the juice and grated rind of a lemon. When the pie is nearly cold cover with the beaten whites, with a spoonful of powdered sugar added. Brown nicely.

Sister Mary Whitcher's
Shaker Housekeeper

LEMON PIE

A cupful of sugar, the yolks of two eggs, the juice of one lemon, a little extract of lemon, three tablespoonfuls of flour. Just before putting into the oven add a cupful of milk. Use the whites of the eggs for frosting.

Sister Mary Whitcher's
Shaker Housekeeper

LEMON PIE

Rub together two spoonfuls of flour and one of butter, and add one cupful of sugar, one egg, one teaspoonful of water, and the juice and grated rind of one lemon. Bake in a crust of pastry, either barred across the top, or with plain cover.

Sister Mary Whitcher's
Shaker Housekeeper

LEMON PIE

Five eggs, laying aside the whites of three for frosting; a heaping teacupful of sugar, two tablespoonfuls of flour, a little extract of lemon, tartaric acid to suit the taste, two quarts of milk. Two pies can be made with these quantities.

Sister Mary Whitcher's
Shaker Housekeeper

LEMON PIE

Four crackers rolled fine, one cup sugar, two eggs, one and one-third cups boiling water, pour over crackers and sugar and cover. When cold add eggs, juice and rind of lemon.

Sister Martha Wetherill

LEMON PIE FILLING

Four Uneeda biscuit crackers, rolled fine, pour over two cups of hot water, add one cup sugar. When cooled a little, dissolve one tablespoon corn starch and one of flour with same liquid. Yolks of three eggs, reserving whites for frosting, a spoonful of butter, a little salt and rind and juice of large lemon.

Sister Martha Wetherill

LEMON MERINGUE PIE

One lemon grated, one cup sugar, one cup of milk, one tablespoonful of flour, the yolks of three eggs. To make the meringue, take the whites of the three eggs and one-third of a cup of powered sugar. Beat the whites to a froth and stir in the sugar. Bake the pie first then spread on the meringue and bake only 5 minutes.

Sister Abigail Crossman

FAMILY MINCE MEAT

Chop the meat fine and add twice its weight of apple. To ten pounds of this mixture add two pounds of raisins, a cup and a half of brown sugar, the same of molasses, two tablespoonfuls of cinnamon and allspice.

Sabbathday Lake Shakers

Mock Mince Pie

One cup chopped raisins, one cup apple, one cup rolled crackers, two tablespoons butter, one tablespoon vinegar, one tablespoon hot water, two and one half tablespoons sugar, one teaspoon each of cloves, cinnamon, nutmeg and allspice.

Sister Marian Scott

Pumpkin Pie

When making pies of canned pumpkin, use as little milk as possible, then one egg will be enough for a pie; otherwise, the custard must be thickened with several eggs.

Manifesto—1882

Pumpkin Pie

Take one quart of pumpkin stewed and pressed through a sieve, two quarts of milk, two cups of sugar, seven eggs, beaten very light, a teaspoonful of butter, ginger and cinnamon to suit the taste, stir well together and bake with plain crust.

The story of the Shakers and some of their
favorite cooking recipes. Calendar — 1882-3

Rhubarb Pies

Do not cut the rhubarb until the morning it is to be used, or, if you have to buy it, keep it in a cool place. Strip off the skin and cut the stalk into pieces about an inch long, and stew in just enough water to prevent burning. When cold, sweeten to taste. Cover the pie-plates and roll the upper crust about half an inch thick; cut into strips an inch wide, and after filling the plate with the rhubarb put on four cross pieces and the rim. Bake half an hour.

Sister Mary Whitcher's
Shaker Housekeeper

Squash Pie

Run the squash through a sieve, milk to make a thin batter, three eggs to every quart of mixture; sweeten and flavor to suit the taste. A quart will make two pies.

Sabbathday Lake Shakers

Squash Pie

Two teacupfuls of boiled squash, three-fourths of a teacupful of brown sugar, three eggs, two tablespoonfuls of molasses, one tablespoonful of melted butter, one tablespoonful of ginger, one teaspoonful of cinnamon, three teaspoonfuls of milk and a little salt.

The story of the Shakers and some of their favorite cooking recipes. Calendar 1882-3

Tomato Pies

Peel and slice ripe tomatoes and sprinkle over them a little salt. Let them stand a few minutes; then pour off the juice and add sugar, half a cupful of cream, one egg, and nutmeg, and cover with a paste. Bake in a moderate oven over half an hour. This makes an excellent and much-approved pie.

Sister Mary Whitcher's Shaker Housekeeper

PUDDINGS AND OTHER DESSERTS

Apple Pudding

Strain one pint of stewed apples. Beat the yolks of six eggs with two cups sugar, to which add one quart of milk and two teaspoons of vanilla. Stir one-half a cup of butter into the hot apples, mix with the milk and eggs. Pour into a deep pudding dish and bake half an hour. Beat the whites of the eggs and add six tablespoons of sugar. Heap over the top of pudding and set in the stove to brown. Serve with cream and sugar.

Sister Marian Scott

APPLE PUDDING

Peel and quarter enough apples to cover the bottom of a baking dish. Make a batter of sour milk, soda, flour and one spoonful of butter. This should not be thicker than for pancakes. Turn bottom up. Add sugar, cinnamon and nutmeg.

Sister Marian Scott

APPLE PUDDING

Pare and chop fine six large apples. Put in a pudding dish a layer of grated bread crumbs one inch deep, then a layer of apple. On this put bits of butter, sugar and a slight grating of nutmeg. Continue as before, and finally pour on a teacupful of cold water. Bake half an hour. Use in all two tablespoonfuls of butter and a small cupful of sugar.

Sister Mary Whitcher's
Shaker Housekeeper

APPLE BATTER PUDDING

Core and peel eight apples, put in a dish, fill the places from which the cores have been taken, with sugar, cover and bake. Beat the yolks of four eggs light, add two teaspoonfuls of flour, with three even teaspoonfuls baking powder sifted with it, one pint milk with a teaspoonful of salt; then add the whites of the eggs well beaten.

The story of the Shakers and some of their favorite cooking recipes. Calendar 1882-3

BERRY PUDDING

A pint of milk, two eggs, a saltspoonful of salt, a quarter of a teaspoonful of soda (dissolved in a little hot water), half a teaspoonful of cream of tartar, sifted through a cupful of flour. To these ingredients add flour enough to make a thick batter. Finally, stir in a pint of blackberries, or raspberries, well dredged with flour. A sauce should be served with this pudding.

Sister Mary Whitcher's
Shaker Housekeeper

BIRD'S NEST PUDDING

Pare and core apples sufficient to fill a pudding dish. Make a batter of one quart of milk, three eggs, two cups of flour. Pour over the apples, and bake in a quick oven. Eaten with a sauce.

The story of the Shakers and some of their favorite cooking recipes. Calendar 1882-3

BIRD'S NEST PUDDING

One cup sugar, one cup sweet milk, half a cup butter, two cups flour, two eggs, two teaspoons baking powder. Have ready some sour apples, partly cooked. Pour on the batter while boiling hot. May be either baked or steamed.

Sister Martha Wetherill

BLACK PUDDING

One cup blackberry jam, one cup sugar, two and one-half cups flour, half a cup butter, three eggs well beaten, four tablespoons of water, two tablespoons of baking powder. Bake 40 minutes in moderate oven.

SAUCE: One quart boiling water, two heaping teaspoons cornstarch, four tablespoons sugar, half cup butter, juice of half a lemon. Eat all warm.

Sister Marian Scott

QUEEN OF PUDDING

One pint fine bread crumbs, one quart sweet milk, three ounces of loaf sugar, small piece of butter, yolks of four eggs, grated rind of one lemon; bake till done then spread over a layer of preserves or jelly, whip the whites of the eggs stiff, add three ounces of pulverized sugar, in which has been stirred the juice of one lemon. Pour the whites over the pudding and replace in the oven. Let it brown lightly. To be eaten cold

The story of the Shakers and some of their favorite cooking recipes. Calendar 1882-3

BREAD PUDDING

Take one pint of bread crumbs soaked in one quart of sweet milk; half a cup of white sugar, two eggs, beaten thoroughly; one cup raisins, if desired; heaping teaspoonful of butter and salt to suit the taste. Stir well together and bake.

The story of the Shakers and some of their favorite cooking recipes. Calendar 1882-3

BREAD PUDDING

One pint of grated bread crumbs, one quart of milk, yolks of six eggs, well beaten, one grated lemon, and sugar to taste. Bake. When cold spread a layer of jelly over the top then make an icing of the whites of the eggs and white sugar, and spread smoothly over the jelly to be eaten cold with sauce.

Sister Abigail Crossman

BREAD AND BUTTER PUDDING

Cut a small loaf into thin slices, and after buttering these, put a layer of them into a deep pudding dish, already buttered. Sprinkle with raisins, currants, and then slices of citron; then put in another layer of bread and more of the fruit. Continue in this way until the bread is all used. Cover with a custard made with nine eggs, one cupful of sugar, three pints of milk, two teaspoonfuls of salt and one nutmeg. Let this stand three hours, and then bake one and a half hours in a moderate oven. It is desirable that a rich sauce be served with this pudding.

Sister Mary Whitcher's
Shaker Housekeeper

CAPE ANN PUDDING

Pare, boil and mash six good-sized potatoes, and pour over them a quart of boiling milk. Stir and let the mixture get cold; then add the yolks of five eggs and the whites of three, beaten with one large cupful of sugar, the grated rind and juice of two lemons. Bake half an hour, and frost with the whites of two eggs, and one cupful of sugar beaten to a stiff froth. Set back in the oven until it is a delicate brown; then set away to cool. This should be eaten ice cold.

Sister Mary Whitcher's
Shaker Housekeeper

CHOCOLATE PUDDING

One square of Baker's chocolate, one quart of milk, six tablespoonfuls of sugar, four tablespoonfuls of cornstarch, four eggs, one generous teaspoonful of vanilla. Put the milk on to boil reserving one cupful to mix with the cornstarch. Scrape the chocolate and add two tablespoonfuls of sugar and one of hot water to it Place over a low fire and stir until dissolved, which will be about one minute. Put this in the boiling milk. Mix the cornstarch with the cold milk. Beat the yolks of the eggs into this mixture, and when the milk is boiling stir this mixture, the sugar and about one-fourth of a teaspoonful of salt into it. Cook six minutes, stirring all the time; then add the whites of the eggs, which you must beat to a stiff froth, before you add the cornstarch and eggs to the boiling milk. Remove from the fire and add the vanilla. This pudding can be eaten cold or hot, with or without sugar and cream.

Sister Mary Whitcher's
Shaker Housekeeper

Cocoanut Pudding

Beat the whites of two eggs, add one pint of milk, half a cup of sugar and one grated cocoanut. Flavor with what you please, mix, pour in a pudding pan, bake half an hour and eat cold.

Sister Marian Scott

Cocoanut Corn Starch

Three quarts of milk, bring to a boil. Yolks of six eggs, three cups sugar, eight tablespoons cornstarch, dissolved in a very little cold water. Cook five minutes, stirring all the time. Remove from fire, add three small cups cocoanut and a pinch of salt, and one tablespoon of butter. Whip the whites of the eggs stiff, and put on top. (Would be fine served cold).

Sister Martha Wetherill

White Corn Starch Pudding

One quart milk, let come to boiling, add three and a half tablespoons corn starch in a little milk, a pinch of salt, one and a half teacups sugar. Let cook thoroughly. When done add the whites of four eggs beaten and beat all till light. Put into molds to cool.

SAUCE: To one-third quart milk add beaten yolks of four eggs, three-fourths cup sugar, a little nutmeg. Cook till done. When cold, beat it good (sic) with a Dover egg beater.

Sister Marian Scott

CORNSTARCH PUDDING

One quart of milk, three eggs, two tablespoonfuls of corn-starch, twelve of sugar, half a teaspoonful of salt. Mix the cornstarch with a cupful of milk, and let the remainder come to a boil. Beat the sugar, salt, and yolks of the eggs into cornstarch and milk, and stir into the boiling milk. Cook 5 minutes, beating well; then pour into a pudding dish. Beat the whites to a stiff froth, and beat into them a cupful of powdered sugar. Flavor to taste. Spread this over the pudding, and brown in a moderate oven.

Sister Mary Whitcher's
Shaker Housekeeper

COTTAGE PUDDING

A cupful of milk, one of sugar, a spoonful of butter, one of saleratus, two of cream of tartar, two eggs, one pint of flour. Soften the butter, and beat to a froth with the sugar and eggs; then add the milk, and lastly the flour, in which the saleratus and cream of tartar are thoroughly mixed. Flavor with lemon, put in two shallow pudding dishes and bake half an hour in a moderate oven. Serve with lemon sauce. The pudding is improved by sifting sugar over it before baking.

Sister Mary Whitcher's
Shaker Housekeeper

COTTAGE PUDDING

One cupful of sugar, two of flour, one of milk, one egg, butter the size of an egg. One teaspoonful of soda, well beaten, then the milk, and finally the flour, in which the soda and cream of tartar have first been well mixed. Bake in a pudding dish for half an hour in a moderate oven. To be eaten with sauce. The lemon sauce is good.

Sister Mary Whitcher's
Shaker Housekeeper

Milk Cracker Pudding

Twelve milk crackers, three eggs, one quart of milk. Sweeten and flavor to suit the taste. Break the crackers fine, heat the milk to boiling and stir in the eggs, sugar and flavoring. Immediately pour over the broken crackers and let stand a few minutes, then set upon the ice until cold. Eat cold.

P. S. This is a delicious and refreshing dessert for warm weather.

The story of the Shakers and some of their favorite cooking recipes. Calendar 1882-3

Whipped Cream Pudding

Cover half an ounce of gellatin with cold water and let soak one hour. Whip one pint of cream. Put one pint of milk on to boil, to which add the gellatin and strain. Beat the yolks of four eggs and one cup of sugar together and stir in the boiling milk. Take from the fire and flavor and pour in a bowl to cool. Stand on ice and stir until thick, then add the whipped cream, mix and put on ice to harden. Turn out and serve with whipped cream.

Sister Marian Scott

Cream Batter Pudding

Half a pint of sour cream, half a pint of sweet milk, half a pint of flour, three eggs, a little salt, half a teaspoonful of soda. Beat the whites and yolks separately, add the whites last. Bake in a moderately hot oven, this is the Queen of batter puddings.

A very nice sauce is made for it by adding to a coffee cup of boiling milk a tablespoonful of flour, first wet with cold milk. Have ready a teacupful of sugar and half a teacupful of butter thoroughly stirred together; and when the flour and milk have boiled two or three minutes, add the sugar and butter. Stir well but do not boil. Flavor to taste.

Sister Abigail Crossman

LEMON CUSTARD

Two white potatoes grated, the rind and juice of two lemons, two eggs, one cup sugar. Line the pie-plate with good crust, pour in the custard and bake.

Manifesto — 1878

RICE CUSTARD

Boil two ounces of ground rice, a pint and a half of new milk, add four oz. of sugar, four of sweet cream and bake in a slow oven. Rice may be ground in a coffee mill.

Sabbathday Lake Shakers

STARCH CUSTARD

To one quart of new milk, three tablespoons of starch, wet up with cold milk, boil the milk, stir in the starch, flavor it with lemon or vernille, put in custard cups and bake the same as eggs custard.

Sabbathday Lake Shakers

BOILED CUSTARD

To one quart of milk take five eggs, if large four will do. Half a teacup of sugar put it in a pot, cover it close, place it within a pot of boiling water which has a close cover. Stir it occasionally, in a half hour it will be a fine custard.

Sabbathday Lake Shakers

ENGLISH PUDDING

One cup molasses, one cup sweet milk, one cup chopped raisins, half a cup butter, one teaspoonful soda, three and a half cups flour, all kinds spices, steam 3 hours.

Sabbathday Lake Shakers

DELIGHTFUL PUDDING

Butter a dish, sprinkle the bottom with finely minced candied peel, and a very little shred suet; then a thin layer of light bread, and so on until the dish is full. For a pint dish make a liquid custard of one egg and half a pint of milk, sweeten, pour over the pudding and bake as slowly as possible for two hours.

The story of the Shakers and some of their favorite cooking recipes. Calendar 1882-3.

DELMONICO PUDDING

From E. W. — Aunt Addie

One quart milk, four eggs, five spoonsful (sic) sugar, two heaping tablespoons corn starch, lemon flavoring. Heat milk in double boiler. Separate eggs, beat yolks with sugar. Add starch wet with a little cold milk, one-fourth teaspoon salt, stir into hot milk. Cook 3 minutes and pour into pudding dish. Beat whites stiff and two spoons sugar and the lemon flavoring. Spread on pudding, bake till a light brown.

Sister Marian Scott

ENGLISH PLUM PUDDING

Nine cups flour, three cups suet, two-thirds cup butter, three eggs, one pint molasses, two cups sugar, three cups each of raisins and currants. Spice to taste. Mix with sweet milk, adding one teaspoon of soda. Steam three hours.

Sister Martha Wetherill

FARINA PUDDING

Boil one quart of milk, thicken with Farina, add a teacup of sugar. Take from fire and stir in the beaten whites of four eggs, flavor with nutmeg. Bake. Sift sugar over the top and set back in the stove to brown. Serve cold.

Sister Marian Scott

FARMER'S PUDDING

Take one pint of bread crumbs and a quart of milk, half a cup of sugar, four eggs, taking only the yolks, butter the size of a walnut, one lemon grated, bake until done, but not watery; then spread a layer of currant jelly or any preserved fruit over it. Take the whites of the eggs and sugar in which has been stirred the juice of the lemon, beat to a stiff froth, pour it over the pudding and brown it. Serve cold with cream. It can be made without a lemon. Flavor with nutmeg.

Sister Abigail Crossman

FLOATING ISLAND

Heat quart of milk to the boiling point; stir in the yolks of five eggs, well beaten, and let them cook, while you stir them often, three minutes. Cool and add a little lemon or vanilla. Beat the whites to a stiff froth, and dip by the spoonful into a kettle of boiling water; and when stiffened lay them over your custard.

Manifesto — 1879

FLOUR PUDDING

Four spoonsful of flour, six eggs, two pints of milk. Line a basin with buttered paper, boil an hour.

Sister Abigail Crossman

FRUIT PUDDING (VERY GOOD)

Three eggs, one cup milk, one cup sugar, half a cup molasses, half a cup suet chopped fine, one teaspoon salt, two and a half cups flour, two and a half teaspoons baking powder, half a teaspoon each of cinnamon, (or one teaspoon cinnamon), nutmeg, allspice and mace, two cups chopped raisins, one and a half cups currants, two-thirds cup citron. Pour all on floured cloth and steam 5 hours.

Sister Marian Scott

BOILED INDIAN PUDDING

A cupful of molasses, one of beef suet, chopped fine, four of Indian meal, a little salt, and enough boiling water to make a thick batter. Tie loosely in a cloth, and boil two hours or more. Put in the pot before the water quite boils. Serve with butter and syrup.

Sister Mary Whitcher's
Shaker Housekeeper

LEMON PUDDING

Six eggs, butter the size of an egg, the rind and juice of two lemons, a teaspoonful of salt, a cupful of ground rice, a heaping cupful of sugar, a quart of milk. After putting aside one cupful of the milk, put the remainder in a tin pail, which set into a basin of boiling water. Wet the rice with the cupful of cold milk, and when the milk begins to boil, stir the rice into it, together with the salt; let this boil 10 minutes, then take off and let it get blood warm. Beat the eggs, sugar, and lemon together, and stir into the mixture. Bake in a buttered dish half an hour. This pudding should be eaten cold.

Sister Mary Whitcher's
Shaker Housekeeper

COWELL PUDDING

One coffee cup of milk, one cup raisins, half cup molasses, half teacup of brown sugar, one teacup suet, one teaspoonful of saleratus, half teaspoonful salt; flour to make stiff batter. Boil 3 hours. Serve with sauce.

Sabbathday Lake Shakers

MT. BLANC

Sweeten one quart of cream, flavor with lemon extract. Dissolve one tablespoon of moss Farina in cold milk and stir in the sweetened cream. Set on the stove and heat and put in a cool place.

Sister Marian Scott

QUAKING PUDDING

Put a teacup of grated bread crumbs in a bowl. Beat four eggs with two tablespoons of sugar, small pinch of salt and two tablespoons of corn starch. Stir into one quart of milk. Pour over the bread crumbs and put in a greased pudding mold and steam one hour. Serve with lemon sauce.

Sister Marian Scott

MOUNTAIN DEW PUDDING

One pint milk, yolks of two eggs, three tablespoons sugar, cocoanut, half a cup rolled-crackers, 1 teaspoon lemon. Mix and bake half an hour. Meringue of the whites of two eggs and one cup sugar.

Sister Marian Scott

ORANGE PUDDING

Take four good-sized oranges, peel seed and cut into small pieces. Add a cup of sugar and let it stand. Into one quart of *nearly* boiling milk, stir two tablespoonfuls of cornstarch, mixed with a little water and the yolks of three eggs. When done let it cool, and then mix with the orange. Make a frosting of the whites of the eggs and half a cup of sugar. Spread it over the top of the pudding and place for a few minutes in the oven to brown.

The story of the Shakers and some of their favorite cooking recipes. Calendar 1882-3

Orange Pudding

Peel three large or four small oranges, cut them in thin slices, removing the seeds. Put them in a pudding dish sprinkle over them a cup of sugar. Beat the yolks of two eggs with one tablespoonful of corn starch and two of sugar. Add a quarter teaspoonful of salt and stir into a pint of boiling milk. As soon as is thickens, remove from the fire, when cool spread it over oranges. Beat the whites of the eggs to a stiff froth with two heaping tablespoonfuls of powered sugar, put it over the pudding, brown it in a hot oven.

Sister Abigail Crossman

Poor Man's Pudding

One cupful of sour milk, half a cupful of molasses, two eggs, a little salt, half a teaspoonful of soda, flour enough to make a thick batter, one cupful of seeded raisins. Boil in a mould for two or three hours.

Sister Mary Whitcher's
Shaker Housekeeper

Potato Pudding

Boil three large mealy potatoes. Mash them very smoothly, with one ounce of butter, and two or three tablespoonfuls of thick cream. Add three well beaten eggs, a little salt, grated nutmeg, and tablespoonful of brown sugar. Beat all together, bake in a buttered dish for half to three-quarters of an hour, in a Dutch oven. A few currants may be added to the pudding.

Sabbathday Lake Shakers

Sweet Potato Pudding

Boil the potatoes and mash them very smooth. Two cups full of potatoes, add one cup sugar, one of butter, and glass of wine, five eggs, one nutmeg and the grated rind of one lemon. Bake with an under crust.

Sabbathday Lake Shakers

YANKEE PLUM PUDDING

Take a tin pudding boiler that shuts all over tight with a cover. Butter it well. Put at the bottom some stoned-raisins, and then a layer of baker's bread cut in slices, with a little butter or suet, alternately, until you nearly fill the tin. Take milk enough to fill your boiler (as they vary in size) and to every quart add three or four eggs, some nutmeg and salt, and sweeten with half sugar and half molasses. Drop it into boiling water and let it boil three or four hours, and it can be eaten with a comparatively clear conscience.

The story of the Shakers and some of their favorite cooking recipes. Calendar 1882-3

STEAMED PUDDING

One cupful of molasses, one of sweet milk, one of raisins, half a cupful of butter or two-thirds of a cupful of chopped suet, one teaspoonful of mixed spice, one of soda, half a teaspoonful of salt, four cupsful of flour. Dissolve the soda in the milk. Mix all the ingredients thoroughly and steam 3 hours in a buttered mould. To be eaten with lemon sauce.

Sister Mary Whitcher's Shaker Housekeeper

ROCK CREAM

Boil one cup of rice in milk until tender. Pour in a dish and ornament with currant jelly. Beat the whites of four eggs with half a cup of sugar and three tablespoons of cream. Flavor and pour over rice.

Sister Marian Scott

Velvet Cream

Take two tablespoonfuls each of currant and strawberry jelly, two tablespoons sugar, beaten whites of two eggs. Mix with a pint of whipped cream.

Sister Marian Scott

A Nice Pudding

Boil one teacup of rice in a pint and a half of water. Pour over one quart of milk, beat the yolks of five eggs and add five tablespoonfuls of sugar; let it come to a simmer, then pour into a pudding dish and flavor, beat the whites of five eggs with five tablespoonfuls of sugar to an icing, spread over the top of the pudding and brown it.

Sabbathday Lake Shakers

Rice Pudding

Put half a cup of rice in one and a half cups of cold water, let it swell on the stove, then put in one pint of milk and let it come to a jelly, but not cook down too much. Beat the yolks of three eggs with five spoonfuls of sugar, stir it while boiling. Put in a pudding dish and bake, then beat the whites of three eggs to a froth with five spoonfuls of sugar, spread it on the top, and set it in the oven to brown lightly. Put in raisins if desired.

The story of the Shakers and some of their favorite cooking recipes. Calendar 1882-3

Boiled Rice Pudding

Pick and wash one cupful of rice, and boil in one quart of boiling water for 15 minutes; then drain dry. Wring a pudding-cloth out of boiling water, and spread in a deep dish, and turn the rice into it. Sprinkle in one cupful of raisins, and table-spoonful of salt; tie the cloth loosely, that the rice may have room to swell, and boil two hours. Serve with lemon sauce, or sugar and cream. Or, apples may be used in place of the raisins.

Sister Mary Whitcher's
Shaker Housekeeper

SNOW PUDDING

Soak half a box of gelatin for one hour in half a pint of cold water; then add two cupfuls of sugar, the juice of two lemons, and half a pint of boiling water. When cool, but not thick, add the whites of three eggs, beaten to a stiff froth. Set the dish in another of ice water and beat thick and white. Turn into a mould and set away to harden.

Sister Mary Whitcher's
Shaker Housekeeper

SNOW PUDDING

Soak half a box of gelatin for ten minutes in a coffee cupful of cold water; then pour on a pint of boiling water, and add two cupfuls of sugar and the juice of a lemon. Let stand until cool. Beat the whites of four eggs to a stiff froth, and, putting them with the other things, beat the whole one hour. This makes the snow. Make a soft custard of the yolks of the eggs and a quart of milk, and pour it into the dish. It may appear as if considerable time and patience is required for making this pudding, but the result ought to satisfy one.

Sister Mary Whitcher's
Shaker Housekeeper

SNOW PUDDING

Soak half a box of gelatin in half a pint of cold water half an hour. Then add half a pint of boiling water, juice of one lemon, two cups of sugar. Strain and let cool. When nearly cold, add whites of three eggs, beaten to a stiff froth, then beat all well again and set on ice.

SAUCE: Make a thin boiled custard of the yolks and pour around pudding when served.

Sister Marian Scott

SNOW CREAM

Add to one quart of cream the whites of three eggs well beaten, four spoonfuls (sic!) of sweet wine, sugar to taste, and bit of lemon peel. Whip to a froth, remove the peel, and serve.

Sister Marian Scott

SUET PUDDING

One pint of milk, one pint of syrup, half a pound of raisins, half a pound of currants, half a pound of suet, add prepared flour as stiff as pound cake. Spice to taste.

The story of the Shakers and some of their favorite cooking recipes. Calendar 1882-3.

APPLE TAPIOCA PUDDING

One large cupful of tapioca, three pints of cold water, one cupful of sugar, one teaspoonful of salt, one teaspoonful of essence of lemon, three pints of pared and quartered apples. Wash the tapioca and put it to soak in the cold water. Three hours will do, but it is better to soak it over night. Cook for 20 to 30 minutes; then add the seasoning and apples. Turn into a buttered dish and bake one and a quarter hours. Let the pudding stand in a cool room half an hour before serving. Serve with sugar and cream.

Sister Mary Whitcher's
Shaker Housekeeper

APPLE TAPIOCA

Put a teacupful of tapioca and a teaspoonful of salt into a

pint and half of water. Let stand two hours in a warm place. Pare and core six tart apples. Fill with sugar in which is grated a little nutmeg and lemon peel. Put them in a pudding dish. Over them pour the tapioca, first mixing with a tablespoonful of melted butter and little cold milk. Bake one hour.

Sister Marian Scott

Tapioca Cream

Four tablespoons of pearl tapioca soaked over night in water enough to cover. In the morning put a quart of milk in a double boiler, and when hot add the tapioca, letting it cook until the tapioca is clear; then carefully the beaten yolks of four eggs with a cup of sugar, and a dash of salt. Let cook a few minutes and turn it out into a bowl or pan and carefully fold in the whites of the eggs beaten to a stiff froth. Flavor the tapioca with lemon before putting in the whites in which is a little vanilla. Set aside to cool. Three quarts of milk is enough for our family at present. 27.

Sister Amelia J. Calver

Tapioca Cream

Cover four large spoonfuls of tapioca with one cupful of cold water, and soak over night. Set one quart of milk on the fire to boil. Beat together the yolks of four eggs, and one cupful of sugar. Stir into the boiling milk, with a pinch of salt, and then stir in the tapioca. Beat the whites to a stiff froth and stir into the custard; then turn into a dish. Flavor with lemon or vanilla.

Sister Mary Whitcher's
Shaker Housekeeper

Boiled Tapioca Pudding

Wash one cupful of tapioca, and soak it an hour in a pint

of cold water; then stir in one quart of milk and one teaspoonful of salt. Put the basin in another of hot water, and set on the fire; cook one hour and a half. Serve with sugar and cream.

Sister Mary Whitcher's
Shaker Housekeeper

TAPIOCA PUDDING #2

Put three tablespoonfuls of tapioca to soak over night in lukewarm water. In the morning, pour onto this one quart of milk. Set on the stove till it comes to a boil, add a pinch of salt, four or five tablespoons of sugar and yolks of nine eggs which when you pour it cook it let it thicken (sic!) stirring all the time. Pour in your pudding dish, beat the whites of the eggs, add four tablespoons powdered sugar, spread over the top, put in the oven and bake a light brown.

Sister Marian Scott

TAPIOCA PUDDING

Take one and a half cups of tapioca and soak over night, three eggs beaten thoroughly, and reserving the white of one for frosting, one cup of white sugar, one teaspoonful of butter, one and one-half pints of milk, a little salt and nutmeg. Bake until well done. Frost same as directed for lemon pie and return to oven until brown.

The story of the Shakers and some of their
favorite cooking recipes. Calendar 1882-3.

VELVET CREAM

One teacup cream, two tablespoons strawberry jelly, two tablespoons currant jelly, two tablespoons powered sugar. Whites of two eggs beaten stiff. Beat all to a cream. Fill a wineglass half full of the whipped cream, then the jelly.

Sister Marian Scott

Virginia Pudding

Put on a quart of milk, and when it is scalding hot, add a little salt and four tablespoonfuls of flour wet in a little cold milk; then add the yolks of three well beaten eggs, with a little sugar. Bake the pudding slowly. When done, pour on the top the whites of the eggs used beaten stiff with half a cupful of sugar, and flavored with vanilla.

Sister Mary Whitcher's
Shaker Housekeeper

Charlotte Russe

Cover the bottom and sides of a mold with slices of stale cake. Put half a box of gelatine in a pint of milk and let it dissolve. Whip one quart of cream. Beat the yolks of three eggs and mix in half a pound of sugar. Then beat the whites of the eggs and add. Strain the gelatine on these and stir quickly, add the cream, flavor with vanilla. Pour in a mold and set on ice. Pour over whipped cream when ready to serve.

Sister Marian Scott

Charlotte Russe #2

One pint cream, half a box gelatine. Whip the whites of three eggs with eight teaspoonfuls of sugar. Put two teaspoonfuls of vanilla in the gelatine.

Sister Marian Scott

Shaker Boiled Apples

About the nicest morsel that ever tickled the palate is a boiled apple; not boiled like a potato nor steamed like a pudding, but as follows: Place a layer of fair-skinned Baldwins, or any nice varieties, in the stew-pan, with about one-fourth of an inch of water. Throw on about half a cup of sugar to six good-sized apples, and boil until the apples are thoroughly cooked and the syrup nearly thick enough for jelly. After one trial no one would, for any consideration, have fair-skinned apples peeled. The skins contain a very large share of the jelly-making substance, and impart a flavor impossible to obtain otherwise. It is also said that "a wise housekeeper, instead of throwing away the skins and cores of sound pie-apples, would use them for jelly." A tumblerful of the richest sort can thus be obtained from the dozen apples. Boil the skins, etc., a few minutes and strain. Add a little sugar to the liquid and boil until right to turn into the tumbler.

Sister Mary Whitcher's
Shaker Housekeeper

Shaker, or Boiled Cider Apple Sauce

For one bushel of sweet apples use one gallon of boiled cider. Put the cider into a brass or tin boiler. Wash and drain the apples, put them into the boiler, and cover tight. If the boiler will hold one bushel of apples, two hours should be given for cooking. Care should be taken that they do not cling to the boiler or scorch. Cook very slowly over a moderate but steady heat. Do not stir the apples while cooking.

Sister Mary Whitcher's
Shaker Housekeeper

Baked Apples

Wash one dozen medium-sized sour apples. Put them in a deep baking tin, stems up, and pour over them one cupful of sugar (if very sour add more) and two cupfuls of water. Bake quickly.

Sister Mary Whitcher's
Shaker Housekeeper

Rice Souffle

Wash half a cupful of rice and put it on to boil with one cupful of cold water. As soon as the water is all absorbed, add a quart of milk, and cook one hour in the double boiler; then add four tablespoonfuls of sugar, one teaspoonful of salt, and the yolks of six eggs. Let the mixture cool; then add one teaspoonful of flavor, and the whites of six eggs beaten to a stiff froth. Turn into a buttered pudding dish, and bake in a moderate oven 25 minutes.

Sister Mary Whitcher's
Shaker Housekeeper

Orange Souffle

Five oranges, five eggs, three tablespoonful of powdered sugar, one-fourth of a cupful of granulated sugar, a pint of milk, a speck of salt. After putting the milk on to boil, beat the yolks of five eggs, and the whites of two eggs, with the granulated sugar. Stir into the boiling milk, and stir until it begins to thicken. It will be about two minutes. Add the salt, and set away to cool. Pare the oranges, remove the seeds, cut up the pulp fine, and put in a glass dish. Pour on the cold custard. Just before serving, beat the three remaining whites with the powdered sugar, and heap this upon the custard.

Sister Mary Whitcher's
Shaker Housekeeper

Swiss Cream

Half a box of gelatin, one quart of cream, one cupful of boiling water. Soak the gelatin one hour in half a cupful of cold water. Whip the cream; then put half a cupful of boiling water into the gelatin and strain into the whipped cream. Add the sugar and vanilla; stir until it begins to thicken and put into moulds and keep cold four hours before serving. Use a whip churn.

Sister Mary Whitcher's
Shaker Housekeeper

SPANISH CREAM

One quart of milk, three eggs, one cupful of sugar, one-third of a box of gelatin, one generous teaspoonful of vanilla flavor. Put the gelatin in a bowl with half a cupful of cold water, and when it has stood an hour add it to a pint and a half of the milk, and then place the sauce pan in which it is to be cooked (it should hold two quarts), into another of boiling water. Beat the yolks of the eggs with the sugar and one-fourth of a teaspoonful of salt. Beat the whites to a stiff froth. Add the half pint of cold milk reserved from the quart to the yolks and sugar, and stir all into the boiling milk. Cook 5 minutes, stirring all the time; then add the whites and remove from the five. Add the vanilla and pour into moulds. Place on ice to harden.

Sister Mary Whitcher's
Shaker Housekeeper

FLOATING ISLAND

One quart of milk and five eggs. Boil the milk and sweeten and flavor to taste. Beat the whites to a froth and add three tablespoonfuls of sugar. Flavor, and pour on the milk while boiling. Let it remain a minute or two. Beat the yolks of the eggs. Stir in one tablespoonful of cornstarch mixed with a little cold milk, and stir this mixture into the boiling milk, letting it cook a short time.

Sister Mary Whitcher's
Shaker Housekeeper

APPLE DUMPLING

First procure good, sour, juicy apples, pare and core, leaving them in halves. Get all your ingredients ready before beginning to mix your dough, sugar, soda, milk, lard, salt, flour and apples.

Now make a dough as for soda biscuits, only adding a little more lard to make it shorter. Take a bit of dough out on the kneading board, and after kneading, roll this as for pie crust. Put in two of your apple halves, sweeten according to taste, and cover the apple and sugar with dough. Lay your dumplings in your bread-pan, the smooth side up, first having your pan well buttered. Proceed in this manner until you get your pan well filled (be sure it is a large-sized pan, for they will go off like hot cakes) then place a small bit of butter on the top of each dumpling, sprinkle a handful of sugar over all; then place in a moderate oven and allow them to bake one hour. Serve (not too hot) with pudding sauce or with cream and sugar. Dumplings made in this way are really delicious.

Manifesto — 1879

WINE JELLY

Soak one box of gelatin in half a pint of cold water two hours; then pour on a pint and a half of boiling water, and stir until the gelatin is all dissolved, but do not set near the fire; now add the juice of two lemons, one pint of sugar, and one pint of wine. Wring a napkin out of hot water, and lay in a fine strainer; strain the jelly through this. Make the day before using.

Lemon jelly can be made by using juice of eight lemons and one pint more water instead of the wine.

Sister Mary Whitcher's
Shaker Housekeeper

FROZEN DESSERTS

TO MAKE ICES

If you have not a freezer the process may be very easily accomplished by putting the cream into a tin pail, and setting it into a pail or small tub filled with coarse salt or lumps of ice. When the cream begins to freese around the edge stir it thoroughly and then shake the pail about until it is well frozen.

Sabbathday Lake Shakers

Boston Ice Cream

Squeeze one dozen lemons and strain the juice upon as much cruhed sugar as it will absorb; pour three quarts of cream into it very slowly, stirring very hard all the time.

Sabbathday Lake Shakers

CANDIES, SUGARED NUTS, and ROOTS

Candy

Boil in a granite sauce-pan slowly without stirring three cups granulated sugar and half of cold water, test the syrup by dropping a little in cold water. If it becomes waxy, it has boiled long enough. When partly cool, stir with a large bright spoon, till it begins to roll, then add a tablespoon of thick sweet cream. Knead with the hands till soft and pliable. This is *fondant*. To color brown, add a tablespoonful of melted Baker's chocolate to the fondant. Form the fondant into little balls and roll in red sugar.

Sister Marian Scott

After Dinner Mints

Two cups granulated sugar, sufficient hot water to dissolve, cream of tartar size of a bean. Boil until it hairs, without stirring; then add one half teaspoon peppermint. Set in a cool place until nearly cold, then stir rapidly until fine and white. Form into little balls or cakes. May also be colored pink and flavored with wintergreen or vanillia; also used for stuffing dates.

Amelia Calver,
Lebanon Valley Cookery—1926

COFFEE CARAMEL

Three cups sugar, one half cup milk, one half cup strong coffee, one tablespoon butter.

Sister Marian Scott

CREAM CANDY

Two cups sugar, one half cup of water, one-fourth teaspoonful cream of tartar, butter size of a walnut, flavor with vanilla. Boil until it hardens in water, and pull while quite soft.

Sabbathday Lake Shakers

COCOANUT CARAMELS

Two cups of dissiccated cocoanut, two tablespoons of flour, the whites of three eggs beaten stiff, cup of sugar; bake on buttered paper in a quick oven.

Sabbathday Lake Shakers

GINGER DROPS

One cup butter, one cup molasses, one cup sugar, three eggs, one tablespoon ginger, one tablespoon soda dissolved in two-thirds cup of boiling water. Five cups of flour. Drop in tablespoons on buttered paper in tin.

Sister Marian Scott

MOLASSES CANDY

Two cups of molasses, one of white sugar, one tablespoonful of vinegar, a small piece of butter. Boil from 20 minutes to half an hour, or until it hardens in cold water. Pour into buttered dishes and when cold work with the hands.

Sabbathday Lake Shakers

SNOWBALLS

Mix together one cup flour, one half cup cornstarch, one cup sugar, one-third teaspoon salt, three level tablespoons baking powder. Stir in gradually two-thirds cup milk, three tablespoons melted butter, stiffened whites of four eggs. Divide at once into six buttered cups and steam a half hour. Turn out gently and roll in powered sugar.

West Pittsfield Shakers,
Lebanon Valley Cookery—1926

SPONGE DROPS

Beat to a froth three eggs, add one teacup sugar, beat 5 minutes. Stir into this one and one half cups flour in which one teaspoon cream of tartar and one half teaspoon soda have been thoroughly mixed. Butter cookie sheets and drop in spoonfuls three inches apart.

Sister Marian Scott

SUGAR KISSES

Whites of two eggs, beaten as for frosting, one cup of sugar added to them. Mix well and drop in small cakes on a buttered tin. Bake in a moderate oven until lightly touched with brown.

The story of the Shakers and some of their
favorite cooking recipes. Calendar 1882-3.

CHOCOLATE DROPS

Two cups of powdered sugar, nearly a cup of water. Boil about 5 minutes, then beat until it turns to a cream, after which make into drops and dip into melted chocolate. Melt three-fourths of a cake of chocolate, grate into a bowl and place over the teakettle or in a pan of hot water.

Sabbathday Lake Shakers

CHOCOLATE CREAM DROPS

These are simple but delicious. Boil together for four minutes two cupfuls of sugar and one half a cupful of flour and beat to a cream. When nearly cold, flavor to taste. Mould in little balls and roll in chocolate that has been grated and melted.

Sister Mary Whitcher's
Shaker Housekeeper

SUGARED BUTTERNUTS THE SHAKER WAY

Two cups of brown sugar—one half cup water. Boil till it spins a dry thread; care should be taken not to over boil. Let cool a trifle then place in pie tin with enough nuts to cover bottom. Dip syrup on them—enough to coat all sides of nuts. Then empty them into granulated sugar while still wet. Stir till well covered, then drop one or two at a time in a pan of confectioners sugar. Stir well and place on plates to dry. This amount of syrup will coat one lb. of nuts or perhaps more.

Sister Jennie M. Wells—1953

SUGARED SWEET FLAG *(Acorus calamus)*

Scrape or peel sweet flag root and cut in small cross sections. Soak these sections for three days and three nights, changing water three times a day. Cook four or five hours, changing to fresh cold water every hour. After this cooking process they could be tender enough to pierce with broom straw. Drain overnight and then spread on a plate to dry another night. To each cup of flagroot add one half cup of sugar. Cook slowly until all moisture is dried up and then sugar. Pack in glass jars.

Sister Jennie M. Wells—1953

MAKE YOUR OWN SYRUP

To make a gallon of syrup of beautiful whiteness and crystal-like transparency, such as is known in our markets as silver drips, or rock candy drips, there are required eight pounds of refined sugar, such as is known by its various names and grades of A or B or extra C, and costing from ten to twelve and one half cents per lb., according to locality and distance from the sugar refinery. To this quantity should be added three pints of boiling water, and the whole subjected to slow boiling for a period of fifteen to twenty minutes, after which the solution while warm, should be strained through a fabric of moderately close texture. This will produce a gallon of syrup, at much less cost than the price demanded in market for the grades of syrup named. For a light yellow or golden syrup, the same quantity of light brown sugar may be employed, and so on through the lower grades of sugar and syrup; but no grade of sugar can be found which will produce so worthless an article as the Cuba molasses generally offered in our markets.

Manifesto—1879

FRUITS

FRUIT

There is no doubt but that pure fruit acids are excellent for the system. One orange eaten before breakfast occasionally, without sugar, is recommended by the best physicians as an excellent corrective for the system.

Manifesto — 1878

HOW TO EAT A BANANA

The banana yields more food to the acre than any other plant, and yet it disagrees with no end of Northern stomachs. This is because we eat it the wrong way. But the wife of a missionary to the tropics tells the glad tidings from heathen shores of how to eat a banana. When you have stripped off the willing rind, just scrape off the stringy and hairy coat that lies beneath the rind, and you may eat your banana without tasting it all the rest of the day.

Manifesto — 1897

STEWED PRUNES

Wash the prunes in warm water and rub them well between the hands. Put them in a kettle that you can cover tight with two quarts of water to one of punes. Stew them gently two hours. These will not keep more than two days in warm weather. If you like you can add one cupful of sugar to a quart of prunes and they will keep much longer.

Sister Mary Whitcher's
Shaker Housekeeper

DAIRY PRACTICES

BUTTER

Butter may be kept sweet for two years by the following process: Mix one part of sugar, one of saltpetre and two of the best salt, one ounce to a pound of butter. Mix thoroughly and put it in a clean cask. Pack it down well sprinkle with salt, and pour melted butter over. It does not taste well till it has stood for a fortnight; after that it has a rich marrow taste.

A Collection of Useful Hints for Farmers
and Many Valuable Recipes,
by James Holmes

LAYING DOWN BUTTER FOR TABLE USE

For twenty lbs. of butter take twenty ounces of salt down weight, five ounces of sugar weight, two ounces of saltpetre light weight, the saltpetre must be ground fine and sifted through a sieve, before it is put into the butter. The butter must be worked dry or be made as free from buttermilk as possible before this composition is put into it. It must be well mixed in the butter, then covered air tight and set away till the next day, then worked dry with a paddle made for the purpose and packed down into a firkin or cask, made perfectly sweet by cleansing with wheat bran (if it can be procured) scalded, then sprinkle on salt while it is wet to keep the butter from sticking to the cask, it must be thoroughly dried before the butter is put into it. We generally sprinkle a little salt between each laying, or churning of butter, so that we can take it up more easily. After the cask or firkin is filled, or as much in it as you desire, cover it with fine salt and lay on a clean linen cloth, large enough to completely cover the top, then make it air tight and put it in a cool place. It should never be taken from the cask long before it is put on the table if it can be avoided, it should always be kept as free from air as possible, the more it is kept from the air, the sweeter it will be.

Shaker Manuscript,
Fruitlands and Wayside Museum, Harvard, Mass.

To Make Good Butter in the Spring or Winter When the Cows are Feeding on Hay

For a sufficient quantity of cream to make ten or twelve lbs. of butter, take four or five carrots (according to size) make them perfectly clean by washing and scraping, grate them with or on a grater such as you would use for horseradish; then put a quart or three pints of new milk, squeeze out the juice and put it into the churn with the cream. It gives the butter a fine color and a very sweet taste.

Shaker Manuscript,
Fruitlands and Wayside Museum, Harvard, Mass.

To Cure and Preserve Butter

Reduce separately to a fine powder, in a dry morter, two lbs. of the best or whitest common salt, one lb. of saltpetre and one lb. of lump sugar. Sift these ingredients one above another on a sheet of large paper and then mix them well together. Preserve the whole in a covered jar placed in a dry situation. When required to be used one ounce of this composition is to be proportioned to every pound of butter, and well worked into the mass. Butter cured by the above composition, has been kept three years and was as sweet as at the first. It requires to be kept three weeks or a month before it is used, because earlier salts are not sufficiently blended with it. It ought to be packed in wooden vessels, or in jars vitrified throughout which do not require glazing, because during the decomposition of the salts they corrode the glazing and the butter becomes rancid.

Shaker Manuscript,
Fruitlands and Wayside Museum, Harvard, Mass.

Method of Making Cheese

We set our cheese at 5 o'clock in the morning, our milk being about as warm as it comes from the cows, adding about the proportion of about one quart of water to five pails of milk. Now we let it stand one and one half hours, then cut it up and let it stand 21 minutes longer, then dip off the whey and stir it up and let it stand again three-fourths of an hour. Now we whey it down in the tub and put it into the basket, and break and tie it up three or four times according as need requires, leaving it half an hour, space between each breaking up, then tying it up the strainer we press it as clean as we can from the whey without the hoop, then cut it in pieces about half an inch square and put into water a little more than milk warm if common curd, if tender, let the water be warmer, after we take it out of the warm water we pour on cold. We believe it is essential that the milk be sweet to avoid strong cheese, as soon as the curd is out of the tub we wash it. NB. We scald our curd in another tub.

Shaker Manuscript,
Fruitlands and Wayside Museum, Harvard, Mass.

FIRM BUTTER WITHOUT ICE

In families where the dairy is small, a good plan to have butter cool and firm without ice is by the process of evaporation, as practiced in India and other warm countries. A cheap plan is to get a very large-sized, porous, earthen flower-pot with a large saucer. Half fill the saucer with water, set it in a trivet or light stand—such as is used for holding hot irons will do; upon this set your butter; over the whole invert the flower-pot, letting the top rim of it rest in and be covered by the water, then close the hole in the bottom of the flower-pot with a cork, then dash water over the flower-pot, and repeat the process several times a day, or whenever it looks dry. If set in a cool place or where the wind can blow on it, it will readily evaporate the water from the pot, and the butter will be as firm and cool as if from an icehouse.

Manifesto — 1879

A GOOD TEST OF THE PURITY OF MILK

A German paper gives a test for watered milk which is simplicity itself. A well-polished knitting needle is to be dipped into a deep vessel of milk, and immediately withdrawn in an upright position. If the milk is pure, some of the fluid will hang to the needle, but if water has been added to the milk, even in small proportions, the fluid will not adhere to the needle.

Manifesto — 1879

Sour Cream—Sour Milk & Buttermilk

There is no end to the nice articles of food that may be made by using sour cream, sour milk, and buttermilk, in a judicious way. There are several things in their use about which care should be taken:

1st.   Cream that is to be used in cooking should be thoroughly separated from the milk.

2nd. It should be sour.

3rd. If in any recipe milk or buttermilk is to be employed with the cream it should also be entirely sour, as the mixture of sweet and sour milk or cream tends to make the article heavy.

4th. The amount of soda or saleratus should only be just enough to sweeten and lighten the cream, any more than this imparts the green color and soapy flavor which are so disagreeable and unwholesome in articles of food.

Sister Abigail Crossman

PICKLES & PRESERVES

To Keep Cucumbers Fresh

When the cucumbers are in their best they should be cut and laid in a box just to fit them, and bury the box in some dry sand, covering it over to the depth of a foot. There should not be any hay or moss put with them in the box, as it will cause them to turn yellow. If laid in a box without hay or moss, the color and bloom may be preserved for two weeks to look as fresh as the day they were cut. Melons may also be kept in the same way.

Sister Mary Whitcher's
Shaker Housekeeper

To Keep Small Fruits From Rising to the Top of the Jar When Canned

Screw down the cover tightly while the fruit is hot, and keep turning the cans from top to bottom until the fruit is so filled with the juice as to compel it to settle to the bottom.

Sister Mary Whitcher's
Shaker Housekeeper

A Recipe for Making Apple Butter

We will give you a recipe how to make Apple Butter as we first learned of the Pennsylvanian as near as we can recollect. Take sweet cider from the press, boil and skim it, then commence feeding in sweet apples, and continue to do so until it gets to a proper consistency, meanwhile stirring it that it may not adhere to the bottom of the kettle. It requires to be boiled 12 or 14 hours. Some persons boil it to the consistency of jelly. We have practiced making it more the thickness of marmalade. But it should always be boiled enough to prevent the cider and apples from separating. Most persons prefer cassia for seasoning, some few would like cloves. It is better to season it when partly cooled otherwise much of the strength of the spice will evaporate. About one hour before you finish boiling add two gal. molasses to a barrel.

Shaker Manuscript,
Fruitlands and Wayside Museum, Harvard, Mass.

Apple Jelly

To make the finest quality of apple jelly, the apples must be good and fully ripe; the temperature cool, never higher than 60 to 70 degress is preferred, slightest fermentation of the juice spoils the jelly; hence the whole process must be confined to three or four hours, and with the mercury at 60 degrees to one hour. A copper evaporator is used; it must be washed every day thoroughly.

Manifesto — 1880

GRAPE MARMALADE

Put the grapes in a stone pot and put this into a kettle of cold water. Set the kettle on the fire and boil until the fruit can easily be mashed. Stir often, and press with the bowl of the spoon. Strain the grapes through a sieve, and to every quart of pulp, allow a pint of sugar. Boil 40 minutes.

Sister Mary Whitcher's
Shaker Housekeeper

PINE-APPLE JAM

Pare and weigh the pine-apples, and grate them down on a large grater. To one pound of fruit put three-fourths of a pound of powdered sugar. Set over the fire and when it comes to a boil, stir till clear. Put it in jars and cover carefully.

Sister Mary Whitcher's
Shaker Housekeeper

CANNING RHUBARB

To any of the readers of the Manifesto who have never tried it, we will give a very simple method for canning rhubarb. Peel the stalks and cut in pieces one half inch in length, fill the glass sealers as full as it can be pressed in and pour on water until the jar is full so as to exclude the air, and put the cover on tight. It will keep perfect condition.

Manifesto — 1893

RHUBARB

In preparing rhubarb for the table it is much more palatable if baked by itself than if stewed with water. After the stalks are sliced pour boiling water over them and leave for one half hour, then put them in the colonder and drain the water off, after which put a layer of rhubarb in a pudding dish, then some sugar, then some rhubarb until there is sufficient quantity, putting the sugar last. Do not add any water as it is better without. Bake until the rhubarb is tender. If the dish is covered while baking it will be much nicer and it does not require as much sugar as when there is water with it.

Sister Abigail Crossman

FRUIT PRESERVED WITH HONEY

Fruit may be preserved with honey by putting the fruit first in the can, then pouring honey over it, and seal air tight; when the honey is poured from the fruit it will have the flavor and appearance of jelly, making a delicious dessert.

Manifesto — 1882

CHILI SAUCE

48 ripe tomatoes	4 tablespoons salt
10 peppers	2 teaspoons each of cloves, cinnamon,
2 large onions	nutmeg and allspice
2 quarts vinegar	1 cup sugar

Slice the tomatoes, chop the peppers and onions together; add vinegar and spices and boil until thick enough. Mustard and curry powder improves this.

The story of the Shakers and some of their favorite cooking recipes. Calendar 1882-3.

TO MAKE CHILI SAUCE

6 tomatoes	1 tablespoonful sugar
2 onions	1 tablespoonful salt
3 green peppers	1 cup and a half of vinegar

Shaker Manuscript,
Fruitlands and Wayside Museum, Harvard, Mass.

How to Make Chow Chow

Twelve ripe tomatoes, two peppers, two onions, one table-spoonful salt, one of sugar, one teaspoonful cloves, one of cinnamon, one cup of vinegar, one teaspoonful of ginger, one nutmeg. Boil it well a little more than half an hour. Chop the tomatoes, peppers and onions very fine.

Shaker Manuscript,
Fruitlands and Wayside Museum, Harvard, Mass.

Tomato Chow Chow

One bushel of green tomatoes, one dozen green peppers, one dozen onions. Chop fine as desired, add one pint of salt, let it stand over night. In the morning strain out this brine, put it into a copper kettle with just vinegar enough to cover it. Boil till tender. Strain from this vinegar, take new vinegar, add four lbs. of sugar, two spoonfuls of cloves ground, two of white mustard, four spoonfuls of cinnamon ground, boil all together and pour over the mass in stone jar. This is chow chow, leave out the onions and you have sweet pickle.

Sister Abigail Crossman

Piccalili

A peck of tomatoes should be sliced and sprinkled with a handful of salt. They should stand over night, and in the morning all the liquor should be turned off. Then chop them together with a cabbage head, seven onions and four green peppers. Mix with this mass half a pint of whole mustard, half a teacupful fine sugar, half a teacupful of horseradish and vinegar enough to cover the whole. Stew until soft.

Sister Mary Whitcher's
Shaker Housekeeper

Spiced Vinegar for Pickles

Take two ounces of bruised black pepper, one ounce of bruised ginger, half an ounce of bruised allspice, and one ounce salt. If a hotter pickle is desired, add half a drachm of cayenne. Put these in one quart of vinegar and simmer gently in an enameled saucepan until extracted, and pour on the pickles or other vegetables.

Sister Mary Whitcher's
Shaker Housekeeper

Bread and Butter Pickles

Eight thinly sliced green cucumbers, two cups of onions chopped fine, three cups of sugar, two teaspoons of celery seeds, two of tumeric, two of white mustard seed, three green sweet peppers cut fine and seeded. Cover with salt and allow to stand over night. In the morning, drain, put on stove one quart of vinegar, if it is strong, add a little water as these are better not too sour. Add the spice and sugar. When hot put in vegetables, and allow to boil one minute. If they cook too long they will not be crisp.

Sabbathday Lake Shakers

Sweet Pickles

Seven pounds of fruit, two pounds of sugar, one quart of vinegar, two ounces of cassia buds or cloves.

Sister Mary Whitcher's
Shaker Housekeeper

Pickled Beets

Take a peck of young beets, the size of large hickory nuts, or no larger than walnuts. Wash thoroughly, drain. Cook in clear water till tender, not mush. Make a vinegar of two-thirds

196

vinegar and one-third water, add little sugar to taste. Skin beets, drop in cold water then drop one or two at a time in boiling vinegar. Fill jars and seal while hot.

Sister Jennie M. Wells

BEST METHOD FOR PICKLING CUCUMBERS

They are neither affected by age, season nor climate. To each hundred of cucumbers, put in a pint of salt and pour in boiling water sufficient to cover the whole. Cover them tight to prevent the steam from escaping, and in this condition let them stand 24 hours. They are then to be taken out and after being wiped perfectly dry (care to not break the skin), place them in a cask. Boiling vinegar is then to be put to them, and the cask closed tight and in two weeks delicious hard pickles are produced, as green as before pulled from the vines. The best vinegar to be used.

CUCUMBER PICKLES

Take small sized cucumbers and scald them three successive mornings in weak brine. Drain them dry, have ready a brass kettle and some nice strong vinegar, with cloves, allspice and a small piece of alum, which will make green and brittle, a little horseradish root improves them. Pickles made in this way will keep through the year.

Manifesto — 1883

CUCUMBER PICKLES

For one gal. cucumbers, take one qt. salt, with cold water sufficient to cover them. Let them remain in this brine three days, then remove from the brine, and pour over them weak vinegar, scalding hot. After four days, remove this liquor and pour over them a good strong vinegar, heated, adding pepper, spice, mustard, etc., to your taste.

Manifesto — 1883

PICKLED PEARS

Ten lbs. of pears, three lbs. of light brown sugar, one quart of vinegar, one oz. cinnamon, one oz. cloves (ground), one quarter lb. of citron put all together and boil until the pears are tender, skim out and let the syrup boil a half hour longer.

Sister Abigail Crossman

PICKLED SECKEL PEARS

Wash pears, leave whole and boil in clear water till they can be pierced with a broom straw. Drain. Prepare spiced vinegar half vinegar and half water, if pure cider vinegar is used. Half a cup brown sugar to every quart of vinegar and water. Use whole cloves and stick cinnamon, boil, skim, then add pears. Boil a few minutes then fill jars and seal.

Sister Jennie Wells

MUSK MELON PICKLE

Take melon slices that are tasteless, yet ripe and drop them into a spiced vinegar: 1 cup vinegar, two cups water, half a cup sugar, half dozen whole cloves, one stick cinnamon. Boil together 5 minutes. When partly cooled pour over melon slices.

Sister Jennie Wells

PICKLED ONIONS

Peel small silver button onions, and throw them into a stewpan of boiling water; as soon as they look clear, take them out with a strainer ladle, place them on a folded cloth covered with another and when quite dry put them into a jar and cover them with hot, spiced vinegar. When quite cold bring them down, and cover with bladder wetted with the pickle.

Sister Mary Whitcher's
Shaker Housekeeper

Mustard Pickles

One quart of small onions, one quart of cucumbers, one quart of green tomatoes, one large head of cauliflower, one bunch of celery, two green peppers. Cut all of these in pieces that will look nice to serve, allow to stand over night in a brine made of one cup of salt to nine cups of water; in the morning put on stove and let come to a boil in the brine. Do not let boil only come to a boil. Make a paste of one cup of flour, five tablespoons of dry mustard, one tablespoon of tumeric powder, two cups of vinegar. To make a smooth paste, sugar and vinegar enough to make two quarts. Cook until smooth and thick, add the vegetables, and again bring to a boiling point. Put in sterilized jars and seal while hot. Put in enough salt as the seasoning is the making of it.

Sabbathday Lake Shakers

Mustard Pickles

(N.B. What she wrote was "1 cucumber.")
One quart green tomatoes, one quart cucumbers, one head cauliflower, one quart green beans boiled till tender. Slightly boil cauliflower and cucumbers, one root of celery cut into small pieces. Divide cauliflower and scald three minutes. Cover all with a brine four quarts water, one cup salt and stand over night. Mix one cup sifted flour and one cup sugar, six tablespoons mustard, one tablespoon tumeric powder in a little vinegar to make a paste. Add one quart boiling vinegar. Cook until it thickens. Heat through, seal in airtight vessels.

Sister Marian Scott

Pickled Green Peppers

Take large green peppers, cut off top, leaving the stem on. Remove seeds and loose membrane, drop all into boiling water, set aside to let all cool together. Have prepared raw cabbage chopped very fine. Salt to taste. Next day drain the scalded peppers and pack solid with the chopped cabbage. Prepare vinegar scalded and cooled enough to cover peppers which have been stuffed and tops tied on, place in layers in earthen crock and pour the vinegar over, cover with grape leaves that have been washed, set in dark place. Good served with roasts.

Sister Jennie Wells

PICKLED PLUMS

Take seven lbs. of blue plums, three lbs. of brown sugar, one quart of vinegar. Boil the sugar and vinegar together with one ounce of cloves and nearly as much cinnamon, pour it boiling hot over the fruit, cover the jar, let it stand over night. Pour off the juice, boil again and pour it on the fruit boiling hot, repeat the third time seal for winter use.

Sister Abigail Crossman

A RECIPE FOR MAKING TOMATO KETCHUP

To a gallon of juice add eight tablespoonsfuls of salt, two do. black pepper, half a tablespoonful of allspice, four pods red pepper, three do. mustard. Grind these articles fine and simmer them slowly in sharp vinegar in a pewter basin 3 or 4 hours, then strain thro a wine sieve and bottle close. Use vinegar enough to make half a gallon of liquor when the process is over.

Shaker Manuscript,
Fruitlands and Wayside Museum, Harvard, Mass.

TOMATO CATSUP

Wash the tomatoes, press thro a fine sieve to six quarts of juice and pulp; add half the quantity of best vinegar; then set it over the fire to boil. When it begins to thicken add pimento, cloves and pepper each half an ounce, cinnamon a quarter of an ounce and two nutmegs finely grated. Boil to the consistency of thin mush, then add four tablespoonfuls of salt and take it out of the vessel. When cold, bottle and cork tight. Boil it in a tin lined vessel. This can't be beat.

Sister Abigail Crossman

Tomato Catsup

The Journal of Commerce gives the following directions as having been in use in the editor's family for fifty years—which is going back to quite an early period in the general introduction of the tomato for culinary purposes: "Take a bushel of tomatoes, cut them in small pieces; boil until soft; then rub them through a wire sieve; add two quarts of the best cider vinegar, one pint of salt, one-quarter pound of whole cloves, one-quarter pound of allspice, one tablespoonful of black pepper, one good-sized pod of red pepper (whole), and five heads of garlic. Mix together and boil until reduced to one-half the quantity. When cold strain through a colander, and bottle, sealing the corks. It will keep two or three years as fresh as when first made."

Manifesto — 1881

Tomato Catsup

To a peck of tomatoes boiled soft and strained in a sieve that will allow the pulp to run thro add four tablespoonful of salt, four of ground pepper, four of mustard, two of allspice, two of cloves, one of cayenne pepper and one gallon of strong vinegar and boil gently 3 hours. Then cool and bottle.

Shaker Manuscript,
Fruitlands and Wayside Museum, Harvard, Mass.

Tomato Chow Chow

Slice one peck green tomatoes, six green peppers, four onions; stir in a cup of salt and let them remain over night. Then pour off the water, put them in a kettle with vinegar enough to cover them. Add one cup of grated horse-radish, one tablespoonful of cloves, one tablespoonful of cinnamon, one tablespoonful of allspice, one cup of sugar; cook until soft.

Canterbury Shakers

Canning Tomatoes

After scalding and pealing, put them into sieve, and let the water part drain off. Then pack the cans full, leaving but room enough for a large spoonful of syrup. The syrup is made by dissolving two and one half lbs. of salt, 2½ lbs. of sugar in in one gallon of water. Then solder the can's vent and all if leaky make tight before boiling. Then boil 30 minutes for two and one half lb. cans, if larger cans are used boil longer. After taking out, and cooling a little open the vent with soddering iron (to let out the steam excess and close again).

(From the Oneida Circular)
Shaker Manuscript,
Fruitlands and Wayside Museum, Harvard, Mass.

Green Tomato Pickle (good)

One peck green tomatoes sliced, six large onions sliced, a teacup of salt over both, mix thoroughly, let it stand over night. Pour off the brine in the morning and throw it away. Mix two quarts water with one quart vinegar and boil 20 minutes. Drain and throw away juice. Three quarts vinegar, two pounds sugar, two tablespoonfuls each of allspice, cloves, cinnamon, ginger and mustard, twelve large ripe peppers chopped fine. Boil one and one half hours. Put away in stone crock.

Sister Marian Scott

To Pickle Ripe Tomatoes

Take ripe tomatoes, put them down in a vessel, first, a layer of tomatoes, sprinkling salt on each layer, let them remain two days or more. Then take them and wash them, put them in weak vinegar or cider for 24 hours. Take them from this, slice onions, put your tomatoes in a barrel, putting in first a layer of tomatoes, then of onions, some allspice, whole cloves, mustard seed, cinnamon and pepper according to your own judgement. After this is done fiill it up with the best cider vinegar, be sure and have the vinegar cold, if it is hot it will take off the skin.

Sabbathday Lake Shakers

Green Tomato Pickle

Take the seeds out of green tomatoes, cut fine if you choose or let them be just cut in two. Untill you have six lbs. of them add four or five good sized bell peppers green after taking out the seeds and cutting fine. Add also two and one half lbs. of white sugar and one quart of vinegar, one and one half oz. of cloves a little mace. Cook all about 1 hour and you will have something.

Sister Abigail Crossman

Green Tomato Pickle

Take green tomatoes, wash and cut round way. Put in a weak brine over night. Next morning drain through a culender, when drained, boil them in vinegar and water until soft then put them into syrup made of good vinegar and sugar spiced with cloves, cinnamon and allspice, boil all together a short time, until the tomatoes are struck through with the syrup.

Shaker Manuscript,
Fruitlands and Wayside Museum, Harvard, Mass.

How to Pickle Tomatoes

Pick them when they are ripe, put them in layers in a jar, with garlicks, mustard seed, horseradish, spices, &c. as you like, filling up the jar; occasionally putting a little fine salt proportionally to the quantity laid down, and which is intended to preserve the tomato. When the jar is full, pour on the tomato cider vinegar (it must be pure) till all is covered and then cork up tight and set away for winter.

A Collection of Useful Hints for
Farmers and Many Valuable Recipes
by James Holmes

Pickling Tomatoes

J. H. S. would like to know how to put up green tomatoes in brine. The way I do is to put them down with my cucumbers; every time that I lay down a picking of cucumbers I throw in a lot of tomatoes ,every size. When I want to use them, I take them out of the brine, cut them in two and let them soak a day or two; than I put them in more fresh water and boil until tender; then drain them and put in good vinegar same as cucumbers, with a few spices. I also put ripe tomatoes down in vinegar. I put small red ones in a glass can, all that will go in and not break the skin, with a little brown sugar, a few cloves and cinnamon. I use the best cider vinegar, as it eats the fruit and makes it soft.

Manifesto — 1881

Tomato Pickle

Slice one peck of green tomatoes, four onions, six green peppers, one teacupful of salt, let them remain over night. Add a teacupful of sugar, one tablespoonful of cloves, one of allspice and one of horseradish root grated.

Sabbathday Lake Shakers,
M. B. G.,   E. M. H.
Nov. 27, 1859

TOMATO PICKLES

As you take them from the vines put them into cold vinegar, after a few hours remove them. Tie some spices in a bag and scald them thoroughly in the vinegar, pour this over the tomatoes while boiling hot.

Sister Abigail Crossman

TOMATO PICKLES

To one gallon of chopped tomatoes put one teacup of salt, let them stand 24 hours, then let them drain very dry, then add to them the following: To one gallon of the tomatoes, three tablespoons of ground pepper, three of mustard, three of cinnamon, two of allspice, two of cloves, all ground, three of green peppers and three small onions, one gill of white mustard seed not ground, put in layers and cover with cold vinegar.

Shaker Manuscript,
Fruitlands and Wayside Museum, Harvard, Mass.

TOMATO FIGS

Take six pounds of sugar to one peck (or 16 lbs.) of the fruit. Scald and remove the skin of the fruit in the usual way. Cook them over a fire, their own juice being sufficient without the addition of water, until the sugar penetrates and they are clarified. They are then taken out, spread on dishes, flattened and dried in the sun. A small quantity of the syrup should be occasionally sprinkled over them whilst drying; after which, pack them down in boxes treating each layer with powdered sugar. The syrup is afterwards concentrated and bottled for use. They keep well from year to year and retain surprisingly their flavour, which is nearly that of the best quality of fresh figs. The pear shaped or single tomatoes answer the purpose best. Ordinary brown sugar may be used, a large portion of which is retained in the syrup.

A Collection of Useful Hints for
Farmers and Many Valuable Recipes,
by James Holmes

Tomato Figs

Pour boiling water over the tomatoes in order to remove the skins; then weigh them, place them in a stone jar, with as much sugar as you have tomatoes, and let them stand two days; then pour off the syrup and boil and skim it until no skum arises. Then pour it over the tomatoes and let them stand two days as before and then boil and skim again. After the third time they are fit to dry, if the weather is good, if not let them stand in the syrup until drying weather. Then place on dishes or plates, and put them in the sun to dry, which will take about a week, after which pack them down in small wooden boxes with fine white sugar between each layer. Tomatoes prepared in this way will keep for a year.

Sister Abigail Crossman

Tomatoes Preserved in Brine

Dissolve salt in spring water until it is strong enough to bear an egg, select perfectly ripe tomatoes and place them well without pressing them in a stone jar with a deep plate in such a manner that it presses upon the fruit, and by this simple method tomatoes may be preserved more than a year.

Sister Abigail Crossman

Tomato Preserve

Take the round yellow variety as soon as ripe, scald and peel; then to seven pounds of tomatoes add seven pounds of white sugar and let them stand over night. Take the tomatoes out of the sugar and boil the syrup removing the scum. Put the tomatoes in and boil gently 15 or 20 minutes; remove the fruit again and boil the syrup until it thickens. On cooling put the fruit into jars and pour the syrup over it and add a few slices of lemon to each jar, and you will have something to please the most fastidious.

Sister Abigail Crossman

To Make Tomato Preserves

Take them while quite small and green, put them in cold clarified syrup with an orange cut in slices to every two pounds of tomatoes. Simmer them over a slow fire for 2 or 3 hours. There should be equal weights of sugar and tomatoes. If very superior preserves are wanted, allow two fresh lemons to three pounds of tomatoes, pare thin the rind of the lemons juice and cold water sufficient to cover the tomatoes, and put in a few peach leaves and powdered ginger tied up, boil the whole gently for three-fourths of an hour, take up the tomatoes, strain the liquor and put with it one pound and a half of white sugar for each pound of tomatoes, put in the tomatoes and boil them gently till the syrup appears to have entered them. In the course of a week turn the syrup from them, heat it scalding hot and turn it on the tomatoes, prepared in this way they resemble West India sweet meats.

A Collection of Useful Hints for
Farmers and Many Valuable Recipes,
by James Holmes

Dried Tomatoes

Take ripe tomatoes, scald them in the usual way and strip off the skins, or mash and squeeze through a sieve; then stew the pulp slowly so as to evaporate as much juice as possible without burning; spread it on a platter and dry it in a slow oven or hot sun. When wanted for use you have only to soak it soft, cook a few minutes and serve it up as you would tomatoes stewed fresh from the garden.

A Collection of Useful Hints for
Farmers and Many Valuable Recipes,
by James Holmes

To Keep Tomatoes the Year Around

Take them full ripe, and scald in hot water to facilitate the operation of taking off the skin; when skinned, boil well in a little sugar and salt, but not water and then spread in cakes about an eight of an inch thick in the sun. They will dry enough in three or four days to pack away in bags, which should hang in a dry room.

A Collection of Useful Hints for
Farmers and Many Valuable Recipes,
by James Holmes

General Directions for Making Sweetmeats and Jellies

In preparing sugar for sweetmeats, let it be entirely dissolved before you put it on the fire. If you dissolve it in water, allow half a pint of water to a pound of sugar. If you boil the sugar before you add the fruit to it, it will be improved in clearness by passing it through a flannel bag. Skin off the brown scum, all the time it is boiling. If sweetmeats are boiled too long they will lose their flavor and become a dark color. If boiled too short a time, they will not keep well. You may ascertain when jelly is done by dropping a small spoonful in a glass of water. If it spreads and mixes with the water it requires more boiling. If it sinks in a lump to the bottom it is sufficiently done. This trial must be made after the jelly is cold. Raspberry jelly requires more boiling than any other sort—black currant jelly less.—Keep

208

your jellies, &c in glass jars or in those of white queensware.

A Collection of Useful Hints for
Farmers and Many Valuable Recipes,
by James Holmes

PEACH JELLY

Wipe the wool well off your peaches, which should be free of stones and not too ripe, and cut them in quarters. Crack the stones and break the kernels small. Put the peaches and kernels into a covered jar, set them in boiling water and let them boil till they are soft. Strain them through jelly bag until all the juice is squeezed out. Allow a pint of loaf sugar to a pint of juice. Put the sugar and juice into a preserving kettle and boil them 20 minutes, skimming them carefully. Put the jelly warm into glasses and when cold tie them up with brandied papers. (Plum and greengage jelly may be made in the same manner with the kernels, which greatly improve the flavor.)

A Collection of Useful Hints for
Farmers and Many Valuable Recipes,
by James Holmes

GRAPE JELLY

Pick the grapes from the stems, wash and drain them. Mash them with a spoon. Put them in the preserving kettle and cover them with a large plate; boil them 10 minutes; then pour them into your jelly bag and squeeze out the juice. Allow a pint of juice to a pound of sugar, put the sugar and juice into a kettle and boil 20 minutes, skimming them well. Fill your glasses while the jelly is warm, and tie them up with papers dipped in brandy.

A Collection of Useful Hints for
Farmers and Many Valuable Recipes,
by James Holmes

Gooseberry Jelly

Cut the gooseberries in half, they must be green and put them into a jar closely covered. Set the jar in oven or pot filled with boiling water. Keep the water boiling round the jar, till the gooseberries are soft, take them out, mash them with a spoon and put them into a jelly bag to drain. When all the juice is squeezed out, measure it and to a pint of juice allow a pint of loaf sugar. Put the juice and sugar into the preserving kettle and boil them 20 minutes, skimming them well. Then put the jelly warm into glasses, closely covered with brandied peppers. (Cranberry jelly is made in the same manner.)

A Collection of Useful Hints for Farmers and Many Valuable Recipes, by James Holmes

To Make Currant Jelly

Pick your currants very carefully and if it be necessary to wash them, be sure they are thoroughly drained. Place them in a stone jar, well covered, set in a pot of boiling water. When cooked soft strain them through a coarse cloth, add one pound of fine Havana sugar to each pound of jelly, put into a jar and cover as above. Or you may break your currants with a pestle and squeeze them through a cloth, put a pint of clean sugar to a pint of juice and boil it very slowly till it becomes ropy. This is an excellent article, especially in sickness and no family need or ought to be without a supply.

A Collection of Useful Hints for Farmers and Many Valuable Recipes, by James Holmes

Cherry Jam

To twelve pounds of Kentish or duke cherries, when ripe, weigh one pound of sugar; break the stones of part and blanch them; then put them to the fruit and sugar and boil all gently till the jam comes clear from the pan. Pour it into China plates to come up dry to table. Keep in boxes with white paper between.

Currant jam, black, red or white. Let the fruit be very ripe, pick it clean from the stalk, crush it and to every pound put three-fourths of a pound of loaf sugar; stir it well and boil half an hour.

A Collection of Useful Hints for
Farmers and Many Valuable Recipes,
by James Holmes

Preserving Cucumbers

Cucumbers for pickles may be preserved as follows: When fresh gathered, wash them in cold water, then put them in a pail with salt and let them stay 12 hours; then put them into a tub or barrel of brine as strong as it can be made and some salt left at the bottom. After a time more salt should be added so that some is always left undissolved at the bottom. To pickle them, take them out of the brine, soak them over night in fresh cold water; then drain them, put them in a jar or bottle, with spice and red peppers, and pour hot vinegar over them and seal them up at once. They will keep for years thus preserved.

Manifesto-1881

Preserving Grapes

Travellers say that the Chinese have a method of preserving grapes so as to have them at hand during the entire year, by cutting a circular piece out of a ripe pumpkin, or gourd, making an aperture large enough to admit the hand. The interior is then completely cleaned out, the ripe grapes are then placed inside, and the cover replaced and pressed in firmly. The pumpkins are then kept in a cool place, and the grapes will be found to retain their freshness for a very long time.

Manifesto-1880

To Preserve Raspberries

Pick your raspberries in a dish, beat and sift their weight
of fine sugar and strew them over them. To every quart of
raspberries, take a quart of red currant jelly, and put to its
weight of fine sugar; boil and skim it well, then put in your
raspberries and give them a scald. Take them off and let them
stand over two hours; then set them on again and scald until
they look clear.

A Collection of Useful Hints for
Farmers and Many Valuable Recipes,
by James Holmes

Watermelon Preserve

To thirty lbs. of melon add thirty-four lbs. of sugar. Cut
the melon in pieces an inch thick, or larger if preferred, and
boil in nine quarts of cider, or acid water, until it is soft, then
skim out into a collender to drain. Pour out the cider and put
in the sugar with water enough to dissolve it readily and skim
it well. Then put in the melon, and let it boil until it looks
clear.

Manifesto-1883

Spanish Pickled Onions

Cut onions into slices; put a layer of them in a jar; sprinkle
with salt and cayenne pepper; then add a layer of onions and
season as before; proceed in this way until the jar is full and
pour cold vinegar over all till covered. Will be fit to use in a
month.

Manifesto-1880

Vinegar from Beets

It is said that good vinegar can be made from beets. The
juice of one bushel sugar beets, worth twenty-five cents, and

which farmers can raise without cost, will make them five or six gallons of vinegar, equal to the best made of cider or wine. Grate the beets, having first washed them, and express the juice in a cheese-press or in any way which a little ingenuity can suggest, and put the liquor into an empty barrel, cover the bung hole with gauze and set it in the sun, and in twelve or sixteen days it will be ready for use.

A Collection of Useful Hints for
Farmers and Many Valuable Recipes,
by James Holmes

RASPBERRY VINEGAR

To two quarts of raspberries put one pint of cider vinegar. After two or three days mash the fruit and strain through a bag. To every pint allow a pound of sugar. Boil 20 minutes and skim. Bottle when cold.

Sister Mary Whitcher's
Shaker Housekeeper

SAUCES, DRESSINGS, FROSTINGS, ICINGS

ACCOMPANIMENTS FOR FISH, MEAT & DESSERT

TO BROWN BUTTER

A simple recipe but a useful one. Put a lump of butter, as large as the gravy demands, into a frying pan. When it is melted, dredge it with browned flour, and stir to a smooth batter until it boils. Use this to color and flavor gravies. It makes a nice sauce of itself.

Manifesto-1878

LEMON OR ORANGE BUTTER

Take one lemon, grate the rind, add the entire juice; add two well beaten eggs, and one cup of sugar; mix thoroughly, and use as an accompaniment to bread and butter, or separately as a preserve. For Orange butter, use an orange instead of a lemon.

Manifesto-1878

TOMATO BUTTER

To seven pounds of very ripe tomatoes, take three pounds light brown sugar, half a pint of vinegar and half an ounce of cinnamon; boil slowly for five or six hours. It may then be put into jars. A spoonful of this added to almost any soup or sauce gives it a most delicious flavor.

Manifesto-1878

CRANBERRY SAUCE

Discard the poor fruit, and wash the rest. Put in the preserving kettle, with half a pint of water to one quart of berries. Now put the sugar on top of the berries, allowing a pint of sugar to a quart of berries. Set on the fire, and stew 20 minutes. Stir often to prevent burning. They will not need straining, and will preserve their rich color, cooked in this way. Never cook cranberries before putting in the sugar. Less sugar may be used, if you choose.

Sister Mary Whitcher's
Shaker Housekeeper

FROSTING WITHOUT EGGS

Four tablespoons milk, one cup sugar. Boil 5 minutes then stir constantly until cooked enough to spread on cake. If chocolate is desired, one teaspoon chocolate after taking from fire.

Sister Martha Wetherill

COOKED ICING

Nine heaping tablespoons sugar, three tablespoons hot water, one heaping teaspoon cornstarch. Boil two minutes, then pour it on one egg beaten to a stiff froth, beat until smooth and white, flavor to taste.

Sister Marian Scott

FROSTING CAKE

Allow for the white of one egg, nine heaping teaspoonfuls of double refined sugar, and one of nice Poland starch. The sugar and starch should be pounded, and sifted through a very fine sieve. Beat the whites of eggs to a stiff froth, so that you can turn the plate upside down, without the eggs falling off—then stir in the sugar gradually with a wooden spoon—stir it ten or fifteen minutes without cessation—then add teaspoonful of lemon juice (vinegar will answer, it is not so nice). Lay the frosting on the cake with a knife soon after it is taken from the oven—smooth it over, and let it remain in a cool place till hard. To frost a common sized loaf cake, allow the white of one egg and half of another.

Sister Abigail Crossman

CREAM SALAD DRESSING

Two even tablespoons dry mustard, one teaspoon each sugar and salt, mix with a little hot water and two tablespoons butter, beat well. Three unbeaten eggs, one at a time, beating well in between. Half a cup vinegar, two-thirds cup sweet cream. Cook in double boiler. Slice potatoes thin. Chop three onions very fine, sprinkle with parsley, and garnish with pickled beets and parsley, with three hard-boiled eggs, sliced over the top.

Sister Martha Wetherill

ANTI-FOWL POTPIE

Prepare the dough as you would for bread, either Graham or white; when it is light cut it off in small pieces and put it on a steamer in a tightly covered cooker; it takes an hour and a half to steam; have ready a gravy made of hot water thickened with drawn butter, or cream and flour paste to season to the taste, and add a little fresh parsley, put the dumplings in a large dish and pour the gravy over them.

Sister Martha Anderson
Manifesto-1892

DUMPLINGS

One pint of unsifted flour, one teaspoonful of cream of tartar, half of soda, one of sugar, one of salt, a small teacupful of milk. Run the dry ingredients through a sieve and with the milk cut into small cakes and cook just 10 minutes in the soup or stew, which must boil rapidly all the while.

Sister Mary Whitcher's
Shaker Housekeeper

FISH SAUCE

Yolks of two raw eggs. Add salad oil, drop by drop, until it is of the consistency of thick cream; add the juice of half a lemon.

The story of the Shakers and some of their favorite cooking recipes. Calendar 1882-3.

HARD SAUCE

Beat to a cream a quarter pound of butter, add gradually a quarter pound of sugar; beat it until very white, add a little lemon juice, or grate nutmeg on top.

Sabbathday Lake Shakers

LEMON SAUCE

One large cupful of sugar, nearly half a cupful of butter, one egg, the juice and a little of the grated rind of one lemon, one teaspoonful of nutmeg, half a cupful of boiling water. Beat the butter to a cream. Add the beaten egg, and also the sugar gradually, and then beat in the lemon and nutmeg. Set the dish in another of boiling water. Add the half cupful of boiling water and stir for 5 minutes.

Sister Mary Whitcher's
Shaker Housekeeper

LEMON PUDDING SAUCE

One large cup of sugar, nearly half a cup of butter, one egg, one lemon—all the juice and half the grated peel—1 teaspoonful nutmeg, three tablespoonfuls boiling water. Serve with lemon sauce.

The story of the Shakers and some of their
favorite cooking recipes. Calendar 1882-3.

SAUCE FOR SNOW PUDDING

The yolks of three eggs, one pint of milk, two tablespoonfuls of sugar, half a teaspoonful of vanilla. Beat the eggs and sugar together, and when the milk is warm pour it on the mixture.

Put the basin into another of boiling water and stir until it begins to thicken. When cool, add the vanilla flavor.

Sister Mary Whitcher's
Shaker Housekeeper

WHITE SAUCE FOR GAME

Boil an onion in a pint of milk till it is like jelly; then strain, and stir into the boiling milk sifted bread crumbs enough to make it like thick cream when well-beaten. Beat while boiling and season with salt, black and cayenne pepper and a little nutmeg.

The story of the Shakers and some of their favorite cooking recipes. Calendar 1882-3.

STRAWBERRY SAUCE

Take one pint of butter, two cups of sugar and one pint of fresh strawberries. Beat the butter and the sugar to a cream, stir in the beaten whites of two eggs and the berries.

Sister Marian Scott

SYRUP SAUCE

Boil two cups of sugar with three tablespoonfuls of water. When thick, take from the fire, put in a lump of butter with a wine-glass of fruit juice.

Sister Marian Scott

EGG SAUCE

Melt one tablespoonful of butter. Thicken with flour. Pour half a pint of milk and stir until it boils. Chop the whites of two hard-boiled eggs fine, press yolks through a sieve and mix in. Season with salt and pepper.

Sister Marian Scott

CREAM SAUCE

Take one pint of thick sweet cream. Add half a teacup of sugar, one teaspoon of vanilla extract. One grated nutmeg and the juice of one lemon. Stir until the sugar is dissolved and set in a cold place.

Sister Marian Scott

EGG SAUCE #2

Scald half a pint of milk. Stir in one teacup of sugar, the beaten yolks of two eggs, and one teaspoon of cornstarch. Flavor with vanilla.

Sister Marian Scott

BOILED PUDDING SAUCE

Take one pint of boiling water, half a pound of sugar and one ounce of butter. Beat the yolks of three eggs. Let come to a boil, take from the fire and flavor.

Sister Marian Scott

CHURNEY SAUCE

Six large green tomatoes, twelve large apples chopped not too fine, one onion, four green peppers, two cups brown sugar, one cup raisins, one tablespoon cinnamon, one tablespoon salt, one tablespoon cloves, one quart vinegar. Cook slowly 2 hours (N.B. Not quite so much spice).

Sister Martha Wetherill

PART II

DYES

MAY 30, 1843—A NEW DYE COMMENCED AT THE SECOND FAMILY AND REFUSED TO WORK

Not having experience to direct, I began to experiment. First made a tea of wheat bran and madder which in a few hours produced favorable symptoms. This at once revealed the fault, which was undoubtedly too strong of Potash. I dipped five pails of the dye out and replaced them with a lively beer made of hops, woad, and wheat bran, I stirred it well and in two hours fermentation begun to appear. Soon a beautiful dye was ready for action.

Sister Abigail Crossman

FROM HAVING POOR POTASH APRIL 1845

Not having had sufficient experience to know the quality of potash, I chanced to get some that appeared black and soft. Not knowing the difference I commenced using it in the dye as usual. However the fermentation soon ceased. I began to try stimulants and fermenting medicines, but all to no purpose, life was extinct. The Indigo was as inactive as if placed in muddy water. I then commenced scalding and skimming, which process gave the surface a dirty appearance. This was the cause of its sickness. When sufficiently cleaned, I let cool as before and set it up as usual. It was soon ready for use. Poor Indigo will also sicken a dye and the only remedy is the above cleansing. The filth in Indigo may be detected by burning a lump and examining the cinders.

Sister Abigail Crossman

Trouble from Coloring Dirty Wool

June 1845, having nearly finished coloring, and being attended with usual prosperity, I was not a little surprised on opening the kettle to find the dye utterly refusing to work. What must be done. A trial never met with before, but from appearance, we judged the offence was taken from dirty wool. Consequently, a cleansing was the only remedy; this I performed and set up the dye, thinking or hoping the trouble was over. But not so, there was yet filth in the dye to prevent fermentation. Again, repeated scalding and skimming until the surface wore a thin blue skim; then let it cool to about bloodheat and made a lively beer of bran and hops, which, together with some new maddeer tea and a little saleratus well stirred together, the dye we soon began to discover life. Continued thro' the day feeding it with madder tea, bran water and a little potash at evening. It smiled upon us with increasing brightness much to the satisfaction of all concerned.

Sister Abigail Crossman

June 23, 1848—Bad State of the Dye at the East Family

A request from the East Family opened another field of experience. Thro' inexperience and change of dyers, the strength of the dye was exhausted, especially the potash which is an essential preservitive to endure the heat of the summer. Without falling into a state of decomposition which terminated in a proper taint insomuch that it became an attraction for flies and a deposit for maggots. The state was greatly increased through neglect of often stirring the dye well together as well as by its being too weak. When fermentation ceases, to separate, and in warm weather should be thoroughly stirred. Here again was a new case accompanied with gloomy prospects. The scent was almost insupportable, but not being willing to loose so good a subject for experience we commenced cleaning it by scalding and adding small quantities of saleratus as long as it would throw upon offensive skum. When all clarified let it cool down and set it up as usual feeding it at intervals with stimulants lime water and the next day, to our surprise, it began to work and ended its day in perfect subjection.

Sister Abigail Crossman

APRIL 25,1853—A DYE NOT PROPERLY PROPORTIONED

The Church at Hancock has set up a new dye, but it utterly refused to work. Firstly made a beer of bran water and hops also steep some madder in a portion of Indigo about one lb. of potash. Add these to the dye stirring them well. Also, in small quantities more potash with a little lime water, as this appeared to be the greatest cause of the difficulty. Should a dye in this state be strengthened too fast it would prevent fermentation and consequently produce as great an error as when too weak. In twenty-four hours the dye commenced working but appeared to lack matter, steeped half a lb. in wheat bran water and added it at intervals of two hours, stirring it powerfully. This is a great assist to the fermentation, I continued this for twenty-four hours more, and it was ready for use. When I close the dye for the season I put in a little potash lye, but no other ingredient.

Sister Abigail Crossman

STATE OF A DYE WHEN CLOGGED WITH INDIGO

October 1, 1850 having been called upon to prepare a dye at the second Family for coloring worsted yarn, there appeared unfavorable symptoms with which I was unacquainted. I concluded, however to cleanse it, and raise a higher state of fermentation. This being done and coloring commenced, the goods were not only dull but spotted. Again repeated the scalding, which somewhat improved the hue, but not all together; continued coloring by feeding the dye with all the ingredients necessary for dyeing except Indigo. The color improved and on the sixth day coloring without Indigo the hue was brighter than on the first day; thus proving that the difficulty was in over charging the dye with indigo. Therefore it appeared necessary to observe strictly the state of the dye from day to day that each ingredient was proportioned to operate with another. There is some danger of over taxing a dye with potash. Should this be discovered it will show itself by causing the dye to work slow and leave a whitish appearance upon the goods, dip a quantity white yarn which will extract the potash faster than the Indigo and soon bring it to an equilibrium.

Sister Abigail Crossman

PROBLEMS

Dyes sometimes will appear to gender disease entirely unaccounted for and baffle all medical skill. Such was the case at Hancock West Family, July, 1851. The dyer was one of long experience and eminent faculties not withstanding, the dye remained obstanant and all treatment to no effect. Being invited to assist, we dipped as clear from the dregs as possible and commenced boiling and cleansing with saleratus this again was different for no vestage of blue skum could be raised and the liquor appeared thick and of a clayish hue. I had carried with me some dregs from our Dye which, when cool enough, I put into this liquor, together with madder beer hoping to start fermentation, but to no effect. What could be the cause was the question no one could answer, unless an enemy had secretly put in grease or vitriol soap or something of the kind extremely offensive; of this there was no proof. Again we made another beer, steeped therein some more madder, procured more dregs from another dye and once more tried to arouse the dead to life. This was accomplished in twenty-four hours; it revived and worked well until the Indigo was entirely extracted.

Sister Abigail Crossman

Iron Black

For ten pounds of woollen goods, boil them for one hour in thirty ozs. of copperas and ten of Blue vitriol with three of fustic liquor. They are then taken out aired and dripped. The kettle is then cleared out, and the liquor of five lbs. of good logwood introduced into it, the goods entered when boiling. They are kept boiling in this for one hour and a half, when they should be a full black color. If they have a slatey appearance they require more logwood. If they have a full brown rusty appearance it is a sign they have received too much logwood. By running them through a sour of very dilute sulphuric acid some of the logwood will be stripped off and the color will assume a clear good shade. Goods intended to be fulled with soap are dyed with a very full color as the fulling strips off some of the logwood. The old fashioned way of dyeing black was to boil the goods in a very strong liquor of logwood first and in the copperas liquor last. By giving two or more dips the color is rendered more durable. The fustic is employed to throw the color on the jet shade. If this be left out of the bath, the color will be a blue black.

Sister Abigail Crossman

For Colouring Black

To one run of double and twisted thread, take one oz. of blue vitrol, desolve it in cold water, then put the thread into this, and boil it half an hour. Take it out and rinse it in cold water. Then put it into a strong logwood dye, boil it a short time in that, take it out and air it, continue so doing; if it is not black enough, strengthen the dye with logwood, too much vitrol will rot it. Dry it before you rinse it the last time. To make a blueish black, put the vitrol into the logwood dye, but this more apt to crock than the other.

Shaker Manuscript,
Fruitlands & Wayside Museum, Harvard, Mass.

BLACK ON COTTON

Two pounds of logwood, four ounces of copperas, four ounces of allum for eight pounds of black after collourd pail blue.

Manuscript Tyringham Shakers

DEEP BLUE ON COTTON

Four ounces of Indigo, four ounces of madder, one ounce of allum, eight ounces of lime or pearlash, eight gallons of water for eight pounds of deep blue.

Manuscript Tyringham Shakers

FURTHER REMARKS FROM EXPERIENCE

A dye calculated for colouring wool, cotton, silk, linnen is not a little difficult to manage judiciously by the most experienced. It being necessary that every ingredient used in forming the dye should be of good quality, rightly proportioned. This, as has been observed, must be directed more from judgement than rule after the first setting up of the dye. Sometimes our dyes become troublesome in consequence of having poor materials, especially Potash which when new is very strong, and if added too freely will stop fermentation; colouring *blue* is at an end, the blue will be a dirty drab; should such or similar symptoms appear make wheat bran water and steep therein madder, woad and hops; Madder should be steeped by itself as it never should be allowed to boil; Woad and hops may be boiled together or seperate as you choose. I practice steeping the ingredients in bran water to prevent filling or weakening the dye. Add a portion of the above liquor to the dye once in two hours, stirring it well. Keep the heat gradual, and if the dye is not injured by any other means, it will soon commence fermentation. In 24 hours will be ready for use. Grease and soap are both extremely offensive to a dye and the filth naturally existing in wool not thoroughly cleansed out will not only prevent the dye from colouring but cause what you may attain to wash out. The head in this case will not evaporate, and no permanent colour can be procured with the following treatment. Heat the dye gradually to a boiling point in which time the grease or whatever is offensive will rise to the surface and should be taken off; continue this process until a clear blue colour then let the dye cool to a lukewarm state, and add the usual setting up of the dye as practiced daily in colouring. The only criterion to judge the state of a dye is the fermentation. Consequently, if this is not carefully attended to the colour will not only be dull, but not permanent the heating or scalding entirely kills fermentation it must have time to commence anew and work itself into the state discribed in the Receipt before ready for use. I practice scalding the dye after colouring wool, unless I have a quantity of yarn either cotton or wool to continue soon after which will have a tendancy to cleanse from it all impurity.

Sister Abigail Crossman

ARTICLES BEST CALCULATED FOR DYEING BLUE

Indigo Bengal, madder French grape potash which on breaking looks red: lime hard and well burnt. Those who are experienced can ascertain by the looks or taste by touching a drop upon the tongue otherwise a measuring glass called a Hydrometer will test the strength of all alcolies. For a general rule for working, the glass in the dye would stand at No. 6. Great care should be taken when colouring, not to overtax the dye, by colouring too large quantities at once, nothing is gained by this, for instance, if you tire it too much through the morning dip, it will be stuped and lazy throughout the day. It quits colouring when it begins to show white bubbles. Whether the period be one hour or two let it rest, thus continue throughout the day and you will find a good days work accomplished, and the dye in first rate order for the next day. If by any means the fermentation be much below the proper medium the speed not only immediately lessens, but the dye altogether refuses to bring the goods to the desired point and cause it to appear incapable. In reality nothing is the matter but over taxation. If you wish to perform a long journey in a day drive slow in the morning.

Sister Abigail Crossman

DIRECTIONS FOR CLEANSING THE BLUE YARN FROM THE BLUE DYE

After the yarn be well dried from the dye it should be packed closely from the air and remain two or three months. Then, in a loose manner be placed in water nearly boiling hot and remain about half an hour then drain the water carefully off and repeat the same letting it stand until you can wring it from this water dry it in the shade.

NOTE: For deep blue make a weak brine of the first scalding water, then proceed as above.

Sister Abigail Crossman

RECEIPT FOR DYEING BLUE ON WOOL COTTON SIZE OF VAT CONTAINING 8 BARRELS

Fill the kettle or vat about two-thirds full leaving room to add according to necessity of clean soft water. Heat it a little above blood heat. Then add four lbs. good potash (that which is red inside is preferable) dissolve in boiling water and well settle from the sediment; a small piece of quicklime added to the potash when dissolved is a fine thing in cleansing it. Reset all of four lbs. of madder well steeped but not boiled and carefully strained from the dregs. The full strength of the madder may be extracted by repeating the steeping. Also four lbs. of ground Indigo Bengal is best adapted to coloring, six quarts of wheat bran soaked in warm water strained and well settled from the starch, should now be put in and all stirred together; covered as tight as possible and left to commence fermentation. Should you wish to hurry the work, make a lively beer of hops and wheat bran before setting up the dye and put it in with the other ingredients, thus dispensing with the wheat bran tea. Keep the heat gradual but do not bring it to a scald unless the dye becomes injured by dirt or grease which if this be the case, fermentation will cease and the only remedy is to cleanse it by scalding, skimming, etc. and let it cool to a lukewarm state before setting it up. When all the ingredients are put in the dye should be stirred once in two hours. When fermentation begins to appear add a little lime water made perfectly clear by pouring boiling water upon quick lime and let it settle. Should it not ferment as fast as desirable procure some dregs from another Dye and stir them in together with a little warm Madder tea made of wheat bran water. I have learned from experience that lime water too is a good thing to put in between dippings, as it has a setting quality and acts against the natural consequences of Hot Dyes in collecting nitres which will prevent the colour from being permanent. Woad tea is used as a stimulant and is considered an assistant to Indigo. Also hops steeped in bran water is a good medicine when the dye appears inactive. To know when the dye is fit for use, there will appear upon the surface a purple froth and the liquor be upon a yellowish green. When in this state plunge it well from the bottom which will produce a heavy foam or head, let it stand two hours, and it is fit for use. When colouring yarn a good dye will bear working six hours or more in a day by working two hours and resting two. Wool extracts the strength of the dye much faster, consequently the time must be limited according to the judgment of the colourer. Also the dye should be made weaker of potash when dyeing worsted yarn or wool then for cotton goods. A large dye will perform more business if well managed in a week to recruit every night in small quantities than to colour two or more days between settings. The quantity coloured and the adding of ingredients must be regulated altogether from judgment as some kinds of goods extract more of one material than another. For instance, wool re-quires larger portion of Madder than cotton, and less of lime and potash than when dyeing cotton or silk. Also, coarse cotton fabrics weaken the dye much faster on the first days colouring than the 2nd. Consequently, great care is necessary that the strength of the dye be not too much exhausted as this will cause the colour to wash out, if too strong, stop fermentation, and injure the strength of the goods, especially Worsted yarn.

Sister Abigail Crossman

LONDON BROWN

To twenty yards of cloth, take two pounds of fustick and seven pounds of red wood chips, boil moderately one hour and add half a pound of allumn, run your cloth three-fourths of an hour, then slacken your dye and add three pounds of madder. Let it stand and simmer with often stirring every half an hour, run your cloth one hour and if the strength is not out of the dye, run again. The cloth must be a good red before you sadden, then add copperas to sadden with by little and little till your colour suits.

Shaker Manuscript, E. Benniss,
Fruitlands and Wayside Museum, Harvard, Mass.

A SHORT AND GOOD WAY TO COLOUR BUTTERNUT ONE-FOURTH QUICKER

Boil the bark in four different waters and get out all the strength, then throw the bark away and store the liquor away, and colour with it anytime when most convenient. Keep the heat of the dye when colouring about 130 degrees. It will colour faster to take it out and air it once a day.

Calvin Goodell — Canterbury,
Fruitlands and Wayside Museum, Harvard, Mass.

To Color a Drab

One hundred lbs. of clean wool, take four lbs. fustic, three lbs. camwood, one half lb. nutgalls. Put all these into a bag. Boil them well, then add eight lbs. madder, steep 20 minutes, enter your wool or cloth and boil two hours and then sprinke in two lbs. of copperas. Drain off the liquor and let it stand over night.

Shaker Manuscript,
Fruitlands and Wayside Museum, Harvard, Mass.

To Dye with Hemlock Bark

1st dip the thread or silk into the dye and then into some weak lye next into some copperas water rinse the thread or cloth in warm water. If too dark dip it into some weak lye again.

Sister Abigail Crossman

Directions for Colouring Green on Cotton or Tow Yarn

Take one pound of logwood, two lbs. of fustic boil them seperately until the strength is out of the chips then put the clear liquor together and add one oz. of blue vitriol for each pound of yarn, this will colour nine lbs. of yarn.

Sister Abigail Crossman

Green on Cotton

Take cherry tree bark, four oz. of allum for eight lbs. of deep green after coloured pail blue.

Tyringham Shakers

For Green on Wooling

To twenty yds. of cloth, take six lbs. of fustick chip and boil them well, then add one-fourth lb. of alum, run your cloth with a hot fire 15 or 20 minutes, then air and add a little of your blueing and run again the same manner as before, add your blueing, little by little till your colour suits. If you have a considerable cloth to colour, it will be necessary to boil your fustick till your colour is strong, then put it into a tub for the convenience of dipping it off as it is wanted to mix with the blueing. The quantity of yellow dye to be dipped off, must be left to the discretion of the dyer; according to the quantity of cloth in colouring; let the chips remain in the kettle and fill your copper with water. Boil again and yellow your cloth till a good colour yellow, by adding alum every dipping, then take the chips out of the dye and add your blueing and yellow dye, having your dye hot and well mixed together, run your cloth and add your compound and yellow dye little by little, mix well and stir together; and if the colour does not appear bright enough, add a little alum, keep it in much longer, and this will add lustre to your colour. This is the best method of dyeing a bright green.

Tyringham Shakers

Logwood Dye

To three lbs. of cotton yarn take one lb. of Logwood and three oz. of blue vitriol. Dip the yarn in the vitriol before putting it in the dye.

Sister Abigail Crossman

True Purple

Dye madder red then dip the goods in the working blue vat this will not fade.

Sister Abigail Crossman

To Dye Cotton Madder Red

For every lb. of yarn, scald with boiling water, two oz. of Sicily sumach. Strain this through a hair sieve and put in your yarn and wash it well in cold water, and then dry it thoroughly. Then take a gallon of clear liquor from the red standard and twelve oz. of flour and make a paste by boiling it 30 minutes. When this is nearly cold, size your yarn and let it dry perfectly. Now it is ready for dyeing.

Take for every lb. of yarn half an oz. of sal soda and dissolve it in gallon of cold water and rinse your yarn well in this, afterwards, wash it well in cold water. Then dye as follows: for a lb. of yarn, half a lb. of french madder to six quarts of hot water put in your yarn when at 160 degrees of heat and bring it to a boil in an hour moving your yarn once in ten minutes. Boil 30 minutes. After it is dyed wash thoroughly in cold water and dry it in a cool place. Should you think it not deep enough take a pint of murite of tin and one gallon of cold water. Mix it well and keep your yarn in this far an hour, and wash it in cold water and then steep it in a good red wood liquor 15 or 20 minutes. Have your red wood dye as hot as you can bear your hands in. Afterwards wash in cold water.

Tyringham Shakers

Recipe to Dye a Fine Permanent Red on Cotton in Which There are 5 Processes

1st Process. After the cotton has been well boiled and washed, dry and divide it into handsful of half a lb. each; tie a string around each parcel loosely, so as to have room for the dye to penetrate under the strings; for each pound of cotton take four ounces of well pounded nutgalls, boil them half an hour, or, until all the galls are soft and for every pound of cotton, add five quarts of water; take five quarts of this liquor into which dip one lb. of cotton until thoroughly soaked, repeat the operation three times, then put the cotton into another tub and pour the gall liquor on it; proceed in the same way with every pound of cotton, until all is done, let the whole lie till the next morning, then wring it out evenly so that the hanks may be evenly pressed in all parts, then dry it, warm the gall liquor proceed as before and let the cotton lie in another night wring as directed after the first galling and dry.

Sister Abigail Crossman

2nd Process. To every lb. of Cotton dissolve half a lb. of fine pounded alum in five quarts of water in a copper pan, when the alum is dissolved add to every lb. of it two oz. of pearlash, proceed in soaking and drying the cotton twice as directed for galling; with this difference that it lie on the alum four or five days. Before maddering put one lb. and a half on stick, wash it quite clean in running water and wring it well.

Sister Abigail Crossman

3rd Process. Take a tub large enough to wash the Cotton in, fill it with water and dissolve in it one oz. of pearlash for every pound of cotton, turn the Cotton as you would the yarn in the blue dye work it in liquor for 15 minutes, wring out evenly and it will be ready for the following.

Sister Abigail Crossman

4th Process. Take a large copper pan large enough to hold for every lb. of Cotton twelve quarts of water, put into this liquor one lb. of the best Madder for every lb. of Cotton, fill the pan within seven or eight inches of the top when the Madder is in, break the scum on the top place the Cotton on sticks as before directed, and when the liquor is milk warm turn the Cotton as in the blue dye, bring the liquor to a boiling heat in one and one half hours but not to boil out. Let it lie at that heat for 15 minutes then draw the fire place the Cotton on hollow and strait and let it lie so for one hour or more then rinse it out of the liquor and wring gently shaking the Madder well out of it one string at a time from the Madder and wring the Cotton evenly and dry in the summer in the shade, in the winter by a stove.

Sister Abigail Crossman

5th Process. If the Cotton be not dark enough take to every pound of cotton four oz. of Brazilette chips boil them one hour and strain off the liquor into a tub, add to it urine or lime until the liquor has a pink cast, when the liquor becomes warm enough to bear the hand put in the Cotton and turn it over eight or ten times, then heave it out of the liquor and add for every pound of Cotton half an oz. of alum dissolved in hot water, turn in eight or ten times, wring out and dry.

Sister Abigail Crossman

A Preparation for Madder Red

Take five quarts of boiling water and dissolve one pound and a half of sugar lead and three lbs. of alum. Stir it well and when it is scalding hot add two oz. of sal soda. Stir this well together and let it stand a week before using.

Tyringham Shakers

For Coloring Madder Red on Wool

To one lb. of yarn flannel three oz. of alum, one oz. of cream of tartar, eight oz. of Madder. Use the same proportions to dye any number of pounds. DIRECTIONS for preparing the dye. First take a brass or copper kettle with about three gallons of rain water, bring the liquor to scalding heat then add three oz. of alum that is pounded and one once of cream of tartar, then bring the liquor to boil and put in the woolen and boil it two hours. It is then to be taken out and aired and rinsed and the liquor thrown away. Now prepare the kettle with as much water as before then add to it eight oz. of good Madder which should be broken fine and well mixed in water before you put in the woolen. When you have warmed the dye as hot as you can bear your hand in it then enter the woolen and let it remain one hour during which time the dye must not boil but only remain at scalding heat observing to stir about woolen, constantly while in the dye. When the woolen has been in one hour it should be taken out aired and rinsed well and then dried.

Sister Abigail Crossman

CRIMSON RED

To twenty yards of cloth take three-fourths of a pound of alum, three-fourths of a pound of cream tartar and three-fourths of a pound of argal, pulverize and mix them together, fill your copper with fair water heat boiling hot and add this compound; stir and mix it well with boiling water then run your cloths one hour boiling then air rinse and shift your liquor, fill with fair water heat boiling hot then take half a pound of cochineal and half a pound of cream tartar mixed and pulverized. Together then add one half of the chochineal and tartar and run your cloth three-fourths of an hour with dye boiling, then air and add of this compound by little and little with your dye boiling till the colour is well raised on the red then take half a pound of spirits of salarmoniac and run your cloth three-fourths of an hour. This will give it a crimson hue, this is true crimson permanent.

Shaker Manuscript,
Fruitlands and Wayside Museum, Harvard, Mass.

SCARLET RED ON COTTON

Two oz. cochineal, one lb. madder, four oz. alum, one lb. red wool, this is for eight lbs. of scarlet red.

Tyringham Shakers

For Wool

When dark enough, air it a few moments then place it in hot water, let it stand a few minutes then turn it from the wool and pour cool water upon it and rinse it, dry in the sun. The hot water that is turned from the wool is placed in a pail and set in hot water ready for the next parcel of wool and thus proceed thro' the day which liquor I add to the dye at evening.

Sister Abigail Crossman

For Worsted Yarn

Air the yarn well from the dye but not dry it. Then place it loosely in scalding water or nearly so, let it stand a few minutes then rinse clean into warm waters. If you wish it very free from crocking run it thro' a weak suds rinse and dry in the sun.

Sister Abigail Crossman

Receipt for Cleaning Wool

To ten pails of water add six qts. of salt. Heat up to 135 deg. before you put in your wool, which is six lbs. And as you add water to the liquor, add salt also, to keep the same strength as when you begun, keep the wool in the liquor 20 minutes then rinse thouroughly in cold running water. You can vary from this rule, according to your judgements, in point of heat or strength of the liquor, if it does not thouroughly cleanse the wool.

Canterbury Shakers

How to Test the Strength of Lime

Slack one lb. of lime in six quarts of water, it good the hydrometer will stand at No. 1.

Sister Abigail Crossman

HOME TOPICS

How to Kill Insects

A Michigan lady writes, that to kill insects she used one teaspoonful of kerosene to a gallon water, and sprinkles it on the plants with a handbroom. It destroys green flies, currant worms and other pests, and was used without injury to Fuchsias, Geraniums, Callas and other plants. But it must be used with care.

Manifesto — 1879

Red Ants

Shaker Sisters say that there is not a better remedy for dispelling *red ants* than the chalk mark. It is camphor. Saturate a piece of sponge or cloth with spirits of camphor, or wrap a few small lumps of the gum in paper, and place where they inhabit. The disagreeable pests are thus entirtly banished.

Manifesto — 1879

Red Ants

Red Ants may be banished from the pantry or store room by strewing the shelves with a small quantity of cloves, either whole or ground. We use the former as not so likely to get into the food placed upon the shelves. The cloves should be renewed occasionally, as after a time they lose their strength and efficiency.

Manifesto — 1882

Bed Bugs

Alum dissolved in water will kill bed bugs if applied where it is most needed.

Manifesto — 1882

Bed Bugs

A lady found the following remedy for the prevention of bed bugs: After cleaning the bedstead thoroughly, rub it over with hog's lard. The lard should be rubbed on with a woolen cloth. Bugs will not infest such a bedstead for a whole season. The reason for this is the antipathy of insects for grease of any kind.

Manifesto — 1879

Bed Bugs

I see frequently inquiry as to the readiest manner of getting quit of the presence of this pest. A safe, sure and proved way in our family is to get a cup full of fine table salt and fill every joint, opening, crack or crevice very profusely, and keep it so, and your tormentors will very soon be finished without the use of any violent poison.

Manifesto — 1879

To Get Rid of Cockroaches

A correspondent writes as follows: "I beg to forward an easy, clean and certain method of eradicating these loathsome insects from dwelling house. A few years ago my house was infested with cockroaches, or 'clocks' as they are called here, and I was recommended to try cucumber peeling as a remedy. I accordingly, immediately before bed time, strewed the floor of those parts of the house most infested with the vermin with the green peel, cut not very thin, from the cucumber, and sat up half an hour later than usual to watch the effect. Before the expiration of that time the floor where the peel lay was completely covered with cockroaches, so much so that the vegetable could not be seen, so voraciously were they engaged in sucking the poisonous moisture from it. I adopted the same plan the following night, but my visitors were not near as numerous, I should think not more than a fourth of the previous night. On the third night I did not discover one; but, anxious to ascertain whether the house was quite clear of them, I examined the peel after I had laid it down half an hour, and perceived that it was covered with myriads of minute cockroaches, about the size of a flea. I therefore allowed the peel to remain till morning and from that moment I have not seen a cockroach in the house. It is a very old building and I can assure you that the above remedy only requires to be persevered in for three or four nights to completely eradicate the pest. Of course, it should be fresh cucumber peel every night."

People and Patriot, Concord, N. H.

(Perhaps Croton bugs had better be fed on cucumber rinds?- Ed.)

COCKROACHES, CROTON BUGS, ETC.

The Scientific American says: "A mixture, composed of one part of powdered borax and two parts of powdered sugar, sprinkled upon the floor where they frequent, will soon eradicate them."

Manifesto — 1879

CRICKETS

Scotch snuff put on the holes where crickets come out, will destroy them.

Manifesto — 1878

FLY BANISHMENT

It is again freely circulated, that the combined odors of a *geranium* and *calceolaria* in any room, will effectually banish flies. We hope, if any of our trustworthy friends find this a fact, they will report.

Manifesto — 1879

Keep Mice out of Seeds

To keep mice out of seeds, the Druggists' Circular recommends mixing a few lumps of gum camphor with the seeds, in the boxes where they are stored.

Manifesto — 1881

Moths

Red-cedar chips will drive away moths.

Manifesto — 1882

Rats

If rats are about, scatter powdered glass about their holes, or powdered copperas, or fill up the crevices with hard soap, or smear their holes with soft tar, or dip a rat in a cup of tar and let it go and it will tar-plaster every hole in the house.

Manifesto — 1882

The Care of Clothing

A clothes brush, a wisp broom, a bottle of ammonia, a sponge, a hand brush, a cake of erasive soap, a vial of alcohol, should form a part of every toilet. After all dust has been removed from clothing, spots may be taken out of black cloth with the hand brush dipped in a mixture of equal parts of ammonia, alcohol and water. This will brighten as well as cleanse. Benzine is useful in removing grease spots. Spots of grease may be removed from colored silks by putting on them raw starch made into a paste with water. Dust is best removed from silk by a soft flannel, from velvet with a brush made specially for the purpose. If hats and bonnets when taken from the head are brushed and put away in boxes and covered up instead of being laid down anywhere, they will last a long time.

SHAKER WOMAN COOKING

Constantine Kermes

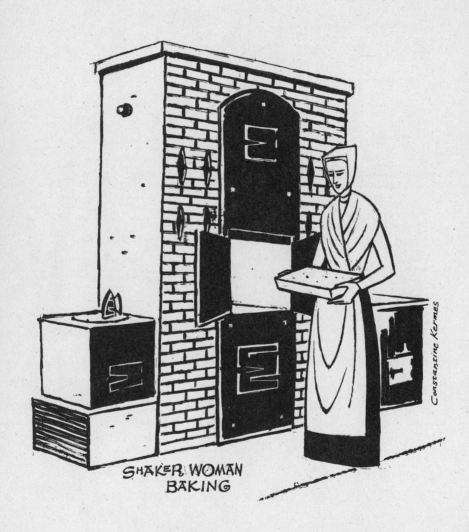

SHAKER WOMAN
BAKING

Constantine Kermes

Shawls and all articles that may be folded should be folded when taken from the person in their original creases and laid away. Cloaks should be hung in place, gloves pulled out length-wise, wrapped in tissue paper and laid away, laces smoothed out nicely and folded, if requisite, so that they will come out of the box new and fresh when needed again. A strip of old black broadcloth, four or five inches wide, rolled up tightly and sewed to keep the roll in place, is better than a sponge or cloth for cleansing black or dark-clothes. Whatever lint comes from it in rubbing is black and does not show. When black clothes are washed, as they may often be previous to making over, fresh clean water should be used, and they should be pressed on the wrong side before being quite dry. If washed in water previously used for white clothing they will be covered with lint.

Manifesto — 1880

PROTECTING FURS

The secret of protecting furs and woolen garments from the depredations of the moth is very simple. In the first place, see that the article you are putting away is thoroughly clean. Re-move all spots of grease and dirt, and brush all dust from the gathers and folds. Take your furs out-doors and beat them thoroughly with a small rod, going over a small part of the surface at a time, till the whole have been beaten. Then seal each article up in double folds of newspaper, pasting so closely that neither air nor insect can get it. This is a better way than any we know of, not excepting camphor, tobacco, pepper, and other pungent preventitives which are commonly used.

Manifesto — 1880

TO MAKE CLOTH WATERPROOF

In a bucket of soft water, put one half pound sugar of lead, one half pound powdered alum—stir at intervals until clean.

Pour off into another bucket put in the garments and let it remain twenty-four hours, then hang up to dry without wringing.

Manifesto — 1878

RIBBONS AND SILKS

Ribbons and other silks should be put away for preservation in brown paper; the chloride of lime used in manufacturing white paper frequently produces discoloration. A white satin dress should be pinned in blue paper, with brown paper outside, sewn together at the edges.

Manifesto — 1879

LEGHORN HATS

Leghorn hats are whitened (otherwise than with the fumes of sulphur) as follows: Immerse in a strong aqueous solution of sulphite of soda or bleaching powder (chloride of lime), and then in diluted sulphuric acid (acid 1, water 5). The bleaching powder treatment requires much subsequent washing, or the use of an antichlore dip, hyposulphite of soda dissolved in twenty parts of water.

Manifesto — 1881

VARNISH FOR SHOES

A coat of gum copal varnish applied to the soles of boots and shoes, and repeated as it dries until the pores are filled and the surface shines like polished mahogany, will make the sole water-proof and it lasts three times longer.

Manifesto — 1882

Varnish for Shoes Impervious to Water

Take one pint linseed oil, six oz. beeswax, two oz. of rosin, half an oz. mutton tallow, melt well together, stirring them well. When milk warm apply it. The leather should be dry. Repeat it a few times; warming it in, and no water can pass thro, it greatly increases the durability of boots and shoes.

Sister Abigail Crossman

To Remove Marks from Tables

Hot dishes sometimes leave whitish marks on varnished tables, when set as they should not be, carelessly upon them. For removing them, pour some lamp oil on the spot, and rub it hard with a soft cloth. Pour on a little spirits, and rub it dry with another cloth, and the whole mark will disappear, leaving the table as bright as before.

Manifesto — 1878

Receipt for Varnish to Loom Harness

Take eight oz. gold leatherage, twelve oz. red lead, twelve oz. gum shelack, four oz. umber, two quarts raw oil linseed, two quarts spirits turpentine. N.B. The shelack, umber and lead must be well pulverized, after which put all the articles (except the spirits) into a kettle capable of six or eight quarts, let them boil very gently for the space of one hour or until such time as the articles are all incorporated then let it cool to blood heat after which add the spirits. Great care should be taken in boiling otherwise it may rise and run over; the fire must be gentle as possible although the gums may adhere to the stick by which it is stir, yet after a little perservance they will mix. After the harness is placed in the frame before varnishing we generally sise it with sising made of fine rye flour as soon as dry, it is ready for varnishing most commonly we put on the varnish at three different times letting it well dry after each varnishing.

Shaker Manuscript,
Fruitlands and Wayside Museum, Harvard, Mass.

Receipt for Boiling Paint Oil

To one gallon of oil; add six oz. of red lead, or three oz. leatherage and half an oz. pulveris umber, gradually while heating, let it heat quite slow till it will snap by spitting in it— it should be frequently stirred while boiling. It should be from one hour to one and one half in going through the process of boiling.

Shaker Manuscript,
Fruitlands and Wayside Museum, Harvard, Mass.

To Make Copal Varnish

One lb. gum when melted add one pint of boiled linseed oil. Mix them hot copal and oil let it stand till it is as cool as boiling water then add one quart of spirits of turpentine and then strain it.

Shaker Manuscript,
Fruitlands and Wayside Museum, Harvard, Mass.

To Remove Old Paint

Wet the place with naphtha, repeating as often as is required; but frequently one application will dissolve the paint, As soon as it is softened, rub the surface clean. Chloroform, mixed with a small quantity of spirit ammonia, composed of strong ammoniac, has been employed very successfully to remove the stains of dry paint from wood, silk and other substances.

Sabbathday Lake Shakers

To Remove Old Paint

Slack three pounds of stone quicklime in water, and add one pound American pearl-ash, making the whole into the consistency of paint. Lay over the old work a brush, and let it remain from twelve to fourteen hours, when the paint is easily scraped off.

Manifesto — 1881

To Bleach Varnish

Take new tin pans and put in the varnish and cover it with glass, set it in the sun till it is white.
One oz. of gum elastic, one pint of spirits turpentine, add half pint linseed oil, boil.

Shaker Manuscript,
Fruitlands and Wayside Museum, Harvard, Mass.

White Spots on Furniture

A bit of butter rubbed on a white spot of varnished furniture, will restore the color.

Manifesto — 1883

Wood Stain

A Carpenter—I want to stain some wood work in imitation of walnut and cherry, please give me directions?
ANS:—Dissolve asphalt in spirits of turpentine and thin it down until when tried on a sample it gives the right walnut shade. If a reddish tinge is desired add a little dragon's blood by de-

grees until the color suits. One coat is enough. For cherry, make
a saturated solution of bi-chromate of potash in hot water, and
when cold, brush this over the work, which should be of clear
pine. Set the work in the light until the shade darkens sufficiently, when it should be covered. The watery solution will
raise the grain of the wood. This should be sandpapered down
and a coat of oil be given.

Manifesto — 1880

MIXTURE FOR CLEANING PAINT

Dissolve two ounces of soda in a quart of hot water, which
will make a ready and useful solution for cleaning old painted
work preparatory to repainting. The mixture, in the above
proportions, should be used when warm, and the woodwork
afterward washed with water to remove the remains of the soda.

Manifesto — 1879

A COMPOSITION FOR PAINTING WOOD

One quart of salt dissolved in a gallon of hot water, one lb.
of coarse brown sugar in a quart of hot water, five lbs. spruce
yellow, two lb. lime.

A Collection of Useful Hints for
Farmers and Many Valuable Recipes,
by James Holmes

CLEANING WOODWORK

An exchange, speaking of the necessity of cleaning wood-
work, comments as follows: it often happens that the woodwork
on doors, particularly near the handles, will become quite dirty
and badly stained by the frequent running back and forth of

careless children. In these cases it is sometimes found impossible to remove the marks with cold water, or without the use of soap, however, undesirable. If this occurs, throw two tablespoonfuls of powdered borax into a pail of hot water, and wash the paint with it. Do not use a brush; but if found impossible to remove the marks in this way, the soap must be resorted to. Rub the soap on the cloth and then sprinkle on the soap dry borax, and rub the spots faithfully, rinsing with plenty of water. By washing woodwork in this way the paint will not be injured, and the borax will keep the hands soft and white. Borax is not half as freely used in domestic labor as it would be if all its usefulness were better known. Its help in increasing the cleansing properties of soap, and at the same time correcting its corrosive tendency, is one of its most valuable properties.

Manifesto — 1883

WASH FOR WOODWORK

As it is now about the time for the cleanly sisterhood to begin their annual "scrubbing" and putting on better appearances, I thought to send for publication a recipe for making a solution to wash wood-work. We have used it and find it a good and "helpful friend" in times of need: To one pint of soft soap add two tablespoonfuls of spirits of turpentine; stir these together thoroughly and put sufficient of it into two quarts of warm water and one pint of skimmed milk to make a weak suds; wash the wood-work with it without any rinsing.

Manifesto — 1881

CLEANING HOUSE PAINT

Old paint work should first be well dusted, then cleaned by washing with lye or pearlash and water; it is sometimes necessary, after the washing to give a coat of weak size, and as soon as it is dry apply varnish, using copal for light work and carriage for dark. Some handrails, doors and so on, are so saturated with grease that no washing will remove it. When this is the case, brush the foul parts over with strong fresh-made lime wash, let that dry, then rub it off; if the grease is not removed repeat the lime washing until the grease is thoroughly drawn out; wash the lime clean off, and afterwards apply the sizing, and lastly the varnish.

Sabbathday Lake Shakers

Washing Floors

Floors should never be flooded with water, as is the too common practice. Use as little water as practicable. Avoid hot soap-suds—it softens the boards and renders them rough; disintegrates the grain of the wood, causing splinters. Oil (or if desirable on old floors, paint) and wipe them with a wrung-out mop in warm water, and your floor will be smooth and hard, and last longer than if drenched with water, or the frequent use of soap. Save your floors, your soap, your muscles and your feelings.

Manifesto — 1880

To Clean Painted Woodwork

To one pint of soap add two tablespoonfuls of spirits of turpentine; then take two quarts of warm water and one pint of skimmed milk; putting enough of the soap in to make a weak suds; with this wash the woodwork. It will cleanse and leave a gloss wherever it is used.

Manifesto — 1882

Whitewash or Cheap Paint

4 oz. lime; 10 lbs. whiting; 4 qts. skim-milk; 1 pt. soap suds. Color to suit. Put the lime in a stone jar; pour on hot water to

slack the lime, and then add milk enough to make it look like cream. Add the whiting and the remainder of the milk. Then stir in the soapsuds and the coloring matter. If to be used without coloring, a small teaspoonful of blueing will make it whiter.

Manifesto — 1882

WATERPROOF WHITEWASH

A waterproof whitewash may be made as follows: "Take half a bushel of lime, slack it with boiling water, and cover to keep in the steam; strain and add seven pounds of salt dissolved in hot water, three pounds of ground rice, boiled to a paste, and added hot, half pound Spanish whiting, and one pound clean glue, previously dissolved to a thin paste; add five gallons hot water, and stir the whole, cover it, and keep it a few days. It must be used hot. One pint covers a square yard.

Manifesto — 1881

LIME FOR WHITEWASH

Lime slacked with a solution of salt in water, and thinned with skimmed milk, from which all the cream has been taken, makes a permanent whitewash for out-door work and it is said, renders the wood incombustible. It is an excellent wash for preserving shingles and for all farm-buildings.

Manifesto — 1881

TO CLEAN BRASS KETTLES

To clean brass kettles, after washing clean, take a teacup of vinegar and a tablespoonful of fine salt; wash every spot on the inside of the kettle with it, then rinse off in pure water.

Manifesto — 1881

Care of Irons

When irons become rough or smoky, lay a little fine salt on a flat surface and rub them well; it will prevent them from sticking to anything starched and make them smooth; or scour with bathbrick before heating, and when hot rub well with salt, and then with a small piece of bees-wax tied up in a rag, after which wipe clean on a dry cloth. A piece of fine sandpaper is also a good thing to have near the stove, or a hard, smooth board covered with brick dust, to rub each iron on when it is put back on the stove so that no starch may remain to be burnt on. Put bees-wax between pieces of paper or cloth and keep on the table close by the flatiron stand. If the irons get coated with scorched starch, rub them over the paper that holds the starch and it will come off. Rubbing the iron over the waxed paper, even if no starch adheres, adds to the glossiness of the linen that is ironed.

Manifesto — 1883

Whitewashing

Good whitewash, well applied to fences, rough siding, and the walls and ceilings of buildings, has a highly sanitary influence, as well as being in the highest degree preservative in its effects. To be durable, whitewash should be prepared in the following manner: Take the very best stonelime and slack it in a tub, covered with a cloth to preserve the steam. Salt—as much as can be dissolved in water used for slacking and reducing the lime—should be applied, and the whole mass carefully strained and thickened with a small quantity of sand, the purer and finer the better. A few pounds of wheat flour mixed as paste may be added, and will give greater durability to the mass, especially when applied to the exterior surface of buildings. With pure lime, properly slacked and mixed with twice its weight of fine sand and sifted wood-ashes, in equal proportions almost any color may be made by the addition of pigments. Granite, slate, freestone and other shades may be imitated, and without any detriment to the durability of the wash. The covering is very often applied and with good effect, underpinning, stone fences, roof and the walls of barns and other out-buildings.

Manifesto — 1879

To Clean Mirrors

Take a newspaper or part of one, according to the size of the glass. Fold it small and dip it into a basin of clean cold water; when thoroughly wet squeeze it out in your hand as you would a sponge, then rub it hard all over the face of the glass, taking care that it is not so wet as to run down in streams. In fact, the paper must only be completely moistened or dampened all through. After the glass has been well rubbed with wet paper let it rest for a few minutes, and then go over it with a fresh dry newspaper, folded small in your hand, till it looks bright and clear, which it will almost immediately and with no further trouble. This method, simple as it is, is the best and most expeditious for cleaning mirrors and it will be found so on trial—giving a cleanness and polish that can be produced in no other process.

Manifesto — 1883

Cement for Joining Metals

To obtain a cement suitable for joining metals and non-metallic substances mix liquid glue with a sufficient quantity of wood-ashes to form a thick mass. The ashes should be added in small quantities to the glue while boiling, and constantly stirred. A sort of mastic is thus obtained, which, applied hot to the two surfaces that are to be joined, makes them adhere firmly together. A similar substance may be prepared by dissolving in boiling water two and one-fourth lbs. of glue and two ozs.of gum ammoniac, adding in small quantities about two ozs. of sulphuric acid.

Manifesto — 1879

CEMENT FOR JOINING GLASS

Dissolve finely powdered Gum Copal in three times its weight of Sulphuric Ether; apply to the edges of the broken glass with a camel-hair pencil, put the pieces together immediately, and press closely till they adhere.

Manifesto — 1878

MUCILAGE

A very clear and transparent mucilage of great tenacity may be made by mixing rice flour with cold water and letting it gently simmer over the fire.

Manifesto — 1879

PASTE FOR PAPER

To ten parts by weight of gum arabic add three parts of sugar in order to prevent the gum from cracking, then add water until the desired consistency is obtained. If a very strong paste is required add a quantity of flour equal in weight to the gum, without boiling the mixture. The paste improves in strength when it begins to ferment.

Manifesto — 1881

TO FASTEN LABELS TO TIN

Put a teaspoonful of brown sugar into a quart of paste, and it will fasten labels as securely to tin cans as to wood. Housekeepers may save themselves much annoyance in the loss of

labels from their fruit cans when putting up their own fruit
by remembering this

Manifesto — 1878

To Remove Oils from Carpets

The following mixture is recommended for taking grease
out of carpets: Aqua ammonia two ounces; soft water one quart;
saltpetre one teaspoonful; shaving soap one ounce; fine scraped.
Mix well, before using to dissolve the soap. When used pour
on enough to cover any grease or oil that has been spilled,
sponging, and rubbing well and applying again if necessary;
then wash off with clear cold water. It is a good mixture to
have in the house for many things; is sure death to bedbugs,
if put in the crevices which they inhabit; will remove paint
where oil was used in mixing it, and will not injure the finest
fabric.

Manifesto — 1882

How to Remove Putty

To remove putty from glass, dip a small brush in nitric or
muriatic acid, and with it paint over dry putty that adheres to
the broken glasses and frames of windows. After an hour's
interval the putty will have become so soft as to be easily
removable.

Manifesto — 1879

Simple Method of Leveling

An exceedingly simple method of obtaining levels is described in *The Manufacturer and Builder*. At each of two
stations, perhaps a hundred feet apart, a pole is driven into the
ground. To each pole, near the top, a glass tube is tied. The
lower ends of the glass tubes are then connected with each other

by means of a sufficiently long piece of india-rubber tubing. Water is to be poured into one of the glass tubes till it fills the tubing and part of the tubes; it will rise to the same level, of course, in both tubes, and the record of this height can be marked on the poles alongside. The method is capable of surprising accuracy, and will serve where obstacles to vision intervene between the stations.

Manifesto — 1879

TOUGHENED LAMP CHIMNEYS

The following recipe is from a Leipsig Journal to the glass interest: Place your tumblers, chimneys, or vessels which you wish to keep from cracking in a pot filled with cold water, add a little cooking salt, allow the mixture to boil over a fire, and then cool slowly. Glass treated in this way is said not to crack even if exposed to very sudden changes of temperature. Chimneys are said to become very durable by this process, which may also be extended to crockery, stoneware, porcelain, etc. The process is simply one of annealing, and the slower the process especially the cooling portion of it, the more effective will be the work.

Manifesto — 1881

LAUNDRY HINT

A hint for the laundry: Linen may be glazed by adding a teaspoonful of salt and one of finely-scraped soap to a pint of starch.

Manifesto — 1879

BITS OF SOAP

Instead of throwing away the pieces of soap which become too small for convenient handling, make a square flannel bag

of suitable size; leave one end partly open, and put in the pieces
as they collect; when it is full, baste.

Manifesto — 1879

OIL-CLOTH

Oil-cloth is ruined by the application of lye soap, as the lye
eats the cloth.

Manifesto — 1881

TO PURIFY THE HOUSE

A house which has been unoccupied for even a week should
never be moved into without kindling fires to burn day and
night for several days, with doors and windows opened so as to
allow all odors and gases to escape, and to dry all the walls and
wood-work most thoroughly; especially ought this to be done
if beads of water noticed on the plastering anywhere; the
least observant know that the rooms of a house have a damp,
musty heavy, dead atmosphere, even if shut up for a very few
days in the finest weather.

Manifesto — 1882

MILDEW

In damp closets, strong rooms, safes and other places where
mildew is dreaded, a trayful of quick lime placed there will
prevent it.

Manifesto — 1879

FRESH AIR

Some, by nailing down their windows to keep out burglars,
shut out their very best friend—pure atmospheric air. By so
fixing the windows that the upper sash can be dropped a few
inches only, the air can be admitted, while the burglars cannot

enter, but by violent means. It would be better to risk danger from burglars than to procure sure death by shutting out the air.

Manifesto — 1880

To Make Otto of Roses

Take a large jar or a clean wooden sask, fill it with rose leaves *very clean*. On these pour pure spring water until they are covered. Set the vessel in the sun; continue this for seven days in succession. In a few days a scum will gradually form on the surface of an oily matter. This is the otto of roses. Take it off with a little cotton on the end of a stick, squeeze this into a vial and cork tight, repeat this till all the oil is removed.

Sister Abigail Crossman

Petroleum

Petroleum has a strong preservative power, converting soft, perishable woods to the durability of red cedar. It improves all farm implements, baskets, all wooden tools, as rakes, hoe handles, common waterpails or any wooden tool which is exposed to the weather. It may be found valuable, also, for rustic work, rustic furniture or chairs left upon a piazza. Give them a good coat of this oil occasionally. It will harden the wood, give them a dark color and make them last longer.

Manifesto — 1879

Household Notes

Plaster of paris mixed with gum arabic water is used as a china cement.

When in a hurry to boil some preparation for dessert in a double boiler, if the outside portion of the boiler be filled with brine, the inside will boil immediately, owing to the much higher temperature of boiling brine than of boiling water.

A teaspoonful of glycerine to a gill of glue makes a cement for fastening leather, paper or wood to metal, which is said to be excellent.

It is claimed that silverware furnishes one of the most reliable means of detecting defective drainage. If it is covered with a black coating or tarnishes soon after being cleaned, and after a second or third cleaning again becomes quickly darkened one should investigate the drainage system of the house.

Sabbathday Lake Shakers

To file glass—Keep the file wet with spirits of turpentine or benzine.

Manifesto — 1882

That a teaspoonful of turpentine boiled with your white clothes will aid the whitening process.

Manifesto — 1879

To bore a hole easily through a hemlock knot, wet the auger in spirits of turpentine.

Manifesto — 1878

A hot shovel held over varnished furniture will take out white spots.

Manifesto — 1878

A bit of soap rubbed on the hinges of doors will prevent their creaking.

Manifesto — 1878

Oat straw is the best for filling beds. It should be changed once a year.

Manifesto — 1878

If your flat-irons are rough. rub them well with fine salt, and it will make them smooth.

Manifesto — 1878

Keep polished steel tools, enwrapped in wool in a closed box. Razors, etc. should be so kept.

Manifesto — 1878

A gallon of strong lye put in a barrel of water, will make it as soft as rain water.

Manifesto — 1878

Ceilings that have been smoked by a kerosene lamp should be washed off with soda water.

Manifesto — 1882

If you are buying a carpet for durability, choose small figures.

Manifesto — 1878

Old boot-tops lined make excellent ironholders.

Manifesto — 1882

Ribbons of any kind should be washed in cold soap suds, and not rinsed.

Manifesto — 1878

A bit of glue dissolved in skim milk and water, will restore old crape.

Manifesto — 1878

To extract stains from silk: Essence of lemon, one part; spirits of turpentine, five parts. Mix, and apply to the spot by means of a linen rag.

Manifesto — 1882

Never iron a calico-dress on the right side; if ironed smoothly on the wrong side there will be no danger of white spots and gloss, which gives a new dress "done up" for the first time the appearance of a time-worn garment.

Manifesto — 1882

Tar may be instantaneously removed from the hand and fingers by rubbing with the outside of fresh lemon or orange peel, and wiping dry immediately after.

Manifesto — 1882

A teaspoonful of good cider vinegar added to one gill of pure raw linseed oil is said to make an excellent furniture polish.

Sabbathday Lake Shakers

Rub white spots on furniture with essence of spirits of camphor, or hold a hot plate from the stove over them.

Sabbathday Lake Shakers

To Clean out a Stovepipe

An exchange says, to clean out a stovepipe, place a piece of zinc on the live coals in the stove. The vapor produced by the zinc will carry off the soot by chemical decomposition. Persons who have tried the process claim that it will work every time.

Manifesto — 1882

Ashes

Do not allow ashes of any kind to be wasted. It will pay to haul leached ashes several miles, when one has his own team and a laborer at fair wages. Coal ashes when spread around berry bushes of any sort, or around grape vines will add materially in producing large and fair fruit.

Manifesto — 1882

To Purify Oil

To make the oil pure, take a good sized bullet or other piece of lead which has a thick coating of lead rust, cut it up fine, put into the oil, and let it stand for two weeks. This causes the acid to settle, and it then resembles milk at the bottom. Now pour off the top, and your oil is pure. Common clock oil can be treated in this manner and made better than some watch oil.

Manifesto — 1879

To Loosen Glass Stopper

Put one or two drops of sweet oil round the stopper, close to the mouth of the bottle; then put it a little distance from the fire. When the decanter gets warm, have a wooden instrument with a cloth wrapped tightly round it; then strike the stopper, first on one side, then on the other; by persevering a little while you will most likely get it out. Or you may lay the bottle in warm water, so that the neck of the bottle may be under water. Let it soak for a time, then knock it with a wooden instrument as before.

Manifesto — 1880

To Loosen Glass Stopper

If a glass stopper won't move, hold the neck of the bottle to a flame, or warm it by taking two turns of a string and see-sawing it. The heat engendered expands the neck of the bottle before a corresponding expansion reaches the stopper.

Manifesto — 1882

Elderberry Ink

To twelve pints of juice, half an oz. of sulphate of iron. This will make good ink.

Sister Abigail Crossman

Elderberry Ink

One half gallon of the juice of elderberries, one oz. of copperas, two drams of alum, twenty drops of creosote dissolved in a small quantity of alcohol.

Sister Abigail Crossman

Indelible Ink

Three oz. of caustic dissolved in two tablespoonfuls of water, one teaspoonful of brandy, one half teaspoonful brown sugar, wet the cloth with strong potash water, large enough for writing; dry with a hot flat, after writing dry with the same.

Sister Abigail Crossman

To Make Black Ink

Half a pound of nutgals crude, six oz. of gum arabic, one and one half oz. of copperas, one and one half oz. of fine salt.

Tyringham,
Sister Abigail Crossman

To Remove Ink from Carpets

Ink spilled on carpets may be entirely removed by rubbing
while wet with blotting-paper, using fresh as it soils.

Manifesto — 1882

Oil: or Waterproof Cloth

Take equal parts of yellow ochre and lamp black, mix with
it an equal quantity in *bulk* of very strong soap suds, boiling
hot. Lay on as thick as a stiff brush will spread; after three
days finish with any color paint you choose.

Another

Mix yellow ochre with oil and thin soft soap, a little Japan
in for dryer. Put on as much as paste. When dry paint with good
oil paint.

Sister Abigail Crossman

To Try Out Beeswax

Put the comb into a colander, or a tin pan with the bottom
punched full of small holes, and place it in a warm oven another
pan partly filled with water. The wax will melt and drop into
the water below, perfectly clear.

*A Collection of Useful Hints for Farmers
and Many Valuable Recipes,
by James Holmes*

Nails for Clothes Press

When you drive a nail into a wall, clothes-press or closet
to hang things on, drive it through a spool up to the head.

Manifesto — 1881

FENCE POSTS

Char the ends of your posts before putting them into the holes. They will last much longer. They may be charred a little higher than the ground, although that is likely to make them a little unsightly. There are farmers who even after charring make an application of thin tar.

Manifesto — 1882

BONES

Have these carefully saved. Keep an old barrel beside your ash house, and whenever you find a bone, throw it in. It is wonderful how they accumulate. If you want to dissolve them, make a pile of bones and fresh ashes; wet moderately and leave for a month or so. In every 200 lbs. of bones there is enough animal matter, phosphate of lime and salts to grow an acre of wheat; and we know not how many barrels of apples when you plant a fruit tree, give it bones at the root.

A Collection of Useful Hints for Farmers
and Many Valuable Recipes,
by James Holmes

TO REMOVE MILDEW

Take an ounce of chloride of lime and dissolve it in a stone vessel. Turn off the clear water, but none of the sediment. Rinse the article mildewed in clear water, and lay into this solution; stir often until the spots disappear; then rinse thoroughly to remove every trace of the lime, which will rot the goods. Or take an ounce of oxalic acid; dissolve, and lay the article into the solution for three minutes; then wring out and lay in the sunshine. If the spots do not readily disappear, repeat the process, and afterward rinse very thoroughly.

Manifesto — 1881

To Remove Ink

The ripe tomato will remove ink and other stains from white cloth, also from the hands.

Manifesto — 1879

To Take Ink out of Linen

To take ink out of linen take a piece of tallow, melt it, and dip the spotted part of the linen into the melted tallow, the linen may be washed and the spot will disappear without injuring the linen.

*A Collection of Useful Hints for
Farmers and Many Valuable Recipes,
by James Holmes*

To Remove Grease

The collars of coats become soiled very quickly from contact with hair, but chloroform will clean them very well without any bad odor. Potato starch water, made by grating potatoes in a little water and letting it settle, then pouring it off and rubbing it with a sponge, will also take off the grease and spots. Ammonia in water rubbed on with a flannel or sponge will answer the purpose. In all cases brush thoroughly in the first place. To remove grease from carpets and restore colors, take a handful of crushed soap bark (quillaqa) to a pail of water. Scrub the spots and sponge the carpets all over.

Manifesto — 1879

Yellow Oil Stain

The yellow stain made by the oil used on sewing machines can be removed if, before washing in soapsuds, the spots be rubbed carefully with a bit of cloth wet with ammonia.

Manifesto — 1883

REMOVAL OF STAINS AND SPOTS

Gum, Sugar, Jelly, etc.—Simple washing with water at a hand heat.

Grease—White good, wash with soap or alkaline lyes. Colored cottons, wash with lukewarm soap lyes. Colored woolens the same, or ammonia. Silks, absorb with French chalk or fuller's earth.

Manifesto — 1881

Stearine—In all cases, strong, pure alcohol.

Manifesto — 1881

Oil Colors, Varnish & Resins — On white or colored linens, cottons or wollens use rectified oil of turpentine, alcohol lye and their soap. On silks, use benzine, ether and mild soap very cautiously.

Manifesto — 1881

Lime & Alkalies — White goods, simple washing. Colored cottons, woolens, and silks are moistened, and very dilute citric acid is applied with the finger end.

Manifesto — 1881

Alkaline Inks — White goods, tartaric acid, the more concentrated the older are the spots. On colored cottons and woolens, and on silks, dilute tartaric acid is applied cautiously.

Manifesto — 1881

Tanning from Chestnuts, Green Walnuts, etc. or *Leather* — White goods, hot chlorine water and concentrated tartaric acid. Colored cottons, woolens and silks, apply diluted chlorine water cautiously to the spot, washing it away and reapplying it several times.

Manifesto — 1881

Tar, Cart Wheel Grease, Mixtures of Fat, Resin & Acetic Acid — On white goods, soap and oil of turpentine, alternating with streams of water. Colored cottons and woolens, rub in with lard, let lie, soap, let lie again, and treat alternately with oil of turpentine and water. Silks the same, more carefully, using benzine instead of oil of turpentine.

Manifesto — 1881

Colored Ink for Stamping — The following are commended for the colors most frequently wanted for stamping purposes: *Red.* Dissolve one-fourth oz. of carmine in two oz. of strong water of ammonia, and add one drachm of glycerine and three-fourths of an oz. of dextrine. *Blue.* Rub one oz of Prussian blue with enough water to make a perfectly smooth paste, then add one oz. of dextrine, incorporate it well and finally add sufficient water to bring it to the proper consistence.

Manifesto — 1881

Blood & Albuminoid Matters — Steeping in lukewarm water. If pepsine, or the juice of *Carica papaya* can be procured, the spots are first softened with lukewarm water, and then either of these substances is applied.

Manifesto — 1881

Iron Spots & Black Ink — White goods, not oxalic acid, dilute muriatic acid, with little fragments of tin. On fast dyed cottons and woolens, citric acid is cautiously and repeatedly applied. Silks impossible.

Manifesto — 1881

Scorching — White goods, rub well with linen rags dipped in chloric water. Colored cottons redye is possible, or in woolens raise a fresh surface. Silks, no remedy.

Manifesto — 1881

Acids, Vinegar, Sour Wine, Rust, Sour Fruits — White goods, simple washing, followed up by chlorine water if a fruit color accompanies the acid. Colored cottons, woolens and silks are very carefully moistened with diluted ammonia, with the finger end. (In case of delicate colors, it will be found preferable to make some prepared chalk into a thin paste, with water, and apply it to the spots.)

Manifesto — 1881

To remove *Ink Spots* from any white fabric throw salt and pepper over it in abundance, and all traces of ink will disappear. Soak the stained parts in milk, and the stains will be removed. Either way will work like magic.

Manifesto — 1881

FRUIT STAINS

In the season of fruit, the napkins used at the table and often the handkerchiefs and other articles, will become stained. Those who have access to a good drug store can procure a bottle of Javelle water. If the stains are wet with this before the articles are put into the wash, they will be completely removed. Those who cannot get Javelle water can make a solution of chloride of lime. Four ounces of the chloride of lime is to be put into a quart of water, in a bottle, and after thoroughly shaking allow the dregs to settle. The clear liquid will remove the stains as readily as Javelle water, but, in using this one precaution must be observed. Be careful to thoroughly rinse the article to which this solution has been applied, in clear water, before bringing it in contact with soap. When Javelle water is used, this precaution is not necessary; but with the chloride of lime liquid it is, or the articles will be harsh and stiff.

Manifesto — 1883

To Clean Silk Dresses

Scrape several large potatoes and put a pint of cold water over them. When it has settled, pour it off, spread your silk upon the table, and wet with a sponge a small part of the silk and iron with a flat-iron just a little warmer than you can handle with your hands bare. If it is too hot it will injure the silk. A correspondent says: "I have just done over an old dress that I have had four years, and it looks almost as well as new."

Manifesto — 1880

To Remove Rust

If wire fence, or any rusty wire or iron, is rubbed with boiled oil in which some red lead has been mixed, on a warm day, the rusting process will be arrested.

A Collection of Useful Hints for
Farmers and Many Valuable Recipes
by James Holmes

Soft Soap

3 lbs. potash)
4 lbs. grease) Bring to a boil, after desolving potash, then add
10 gall. water)

Shaker Manuscript,
Fruitlands and Wayside Museum, Harvard, Mass.

Hard Soap

Take three lbs. of unslacked lime, six lbs. of washing soda, four pailsful of water, boiling hot turned over the soda and lime, let it stand over night. In the morning pour it off; then put in one pailful of cold water, boil half an hour; then put in two handsful of salt, let it stand until cold. Cut into bars and dry. If wanted to be striped and scented, melt and stir in anything you desire. For soft soap leave out the salt.

Sister Abigail Crossman

To Make Best Soap

Take twenty lbs. of grease, two lbs. rosin, eighteen lbs. best potash (or more if it is not strong) & thirty gallons of water; melt the grease & rosin together, and strain into a barrel; dissolve the potash in a few gallons of water, pour it off on the grease and stir it well and the remainder of water gradually and keep stirring until it is thoroughly incorporated.

Sister Abigail Crossman

Soap Formula from Canterbury

Take one gallon of water from which take a sufficient quantity to dissolve the following ingredients, four oz. sal soda, four oz. tartuar (Pure granulated Carbonate of Potash, two drachms of Commercial Cyanide potassium.) Heat the remaining portion of the water to nearly a boil, and dissolve one pound of fine soap shavings. (Be particular not to let the water boil.) Then add the chemical solution, and stir thoroughly until well mixed, then remove from the kettle into vessels to cool. I think you cannot have trouble, if you abide by this recipe.

Sister Lucy A. Shepherd,
Sister Elmira H. Hillsgrow

Soap Formula from Canterbury
Another Process

First measure into an iron or copper kettle, the quantity of water desired, as per recipe; when warm, dissolve the chemicals in a separate vessel, put the soap shavings into the kettle of water, stir occasionally till they are thoroughly dissolved, then stir in the chemicals carefully straining them through a coarse linen cloth. Simmer or boil very slowly two hours or until the ingredients are perfectly assimulated so that on cooling, it will have nothing of a porous and spongy appearance. (We find it necessary to cool and examine many times before it is well mixed.)

Sister Lucy A. Shepherd,
Sister Elmira M. Hillsgrow

RECIPE FOR MAKING SHAVING SOAP

Take four pounds of the best white dry bar soap and cut fine; one quart of rain water, half a pint of beef's gall, half a gill of the spirits of terpentine; put them all into a clean iron kettle and boil them 15 minutes after the soap is perfectly dissolved and mixed. Stir it while over the fire.

To color it, take a half a paper of vermilion and put it in when done boiling and stir it in hard while cooking 5 minutes. Scent it with what you please, but use the oil and not the essence and put in half an ounce while stirring and cooking. Then pour it into a box prepared for the purpose, and let it cool twelve hours, cut it into bars and let it dry 12 hours.

Shaker Manuscript,
Fruitlands and Wayside Museum, Harvard, Mass.

RECIPE FOR MAKING SODA ASH SOAP

Take fifteen gallons of soft water in a clean kettle. Add twelve pounds of soda ash and four pounds of pure unslacked lime. Boil until the strength is all out or two hours. Then dip it out in a tub, let it settle well. Then dip off the clear liquor and return to the kettle; and add eight pounds of White Rosen and boil till dissolved, then add eighteen pounds of grease (sixteen will answer the purpose well) and boil till it comes together in good shape, or until it cools smooth then it is done. Dip it off by measure and add water to fill 32 gallons; or if wanted to be hard add no water but cool it in pans or cakes, just as you like. When these directions are carried out washing is not a task but a pleasure.

Canterbury, Sister Abigail Crossman

Washing Fluids

Take five pounds of sal-soda, one of Borax, and one of unslacked lime. Dissolve the soda and borax in one gallon of boiling water; then pour them both in eight gallons of cold water; stir it a little and let it stand all night. In the morning pour off the clear fluid for use. For two pails of water use a half pint of the compound; soak your clothes over night, rubbing soap on the soiled parts. Wring them out and put them over to boil in water containing soap and fluid. After boiling 15 minutes, take them out into cold water, and suds and rinse them. Don't be afraid to boil the clothes before they are washed; it will not hurt them.

Manifesto — 1883

Good Starch

If you want *good starch,* mix it with cold water until it thickens, then add a dessert-spoonful of sugar and a small piece of butter. This makes a stiff and glossy finish equal to that of the laundry.

Manifesto — 1882

Washing Flannel

Enclose new flannel in a bag, put it into a boiler with cold water, heat and boil it. It will never shrink any more after this operation.

A Collection of Useful Hints for Farmers
and Many Valuable Recipes,
by James Holmes

Easy Washing

Make suds as usual then add a teaspoonful of Spirits of Turpentine to each bucket of water, stir it up, put in the clothes, and let them soak and hour and a half, and then boil them as usual. Unless very dirty, they will need no rubbing, the turpentine having the effect to loosen the dirt

A Collection of Useful Hints for Farmers
and Many Valuable Recipes,
by James Holmes

Washing Made Easy

Take six pounds of hard soap, finely cut; a quarter of a pound of borax, and half an ounce of potash dissolved in one quart of water. Place the above over a fire until all dissolved; then put it in the vessel in which you design to keep it and add half a pint of spirits of hartshorn, put the clothes into it while dry; let them remain there half an hour, and then rinse them twice in clean water, besides the blue water.

A Collection of Useful Hints for Farmers
and Many Valuable Recipes,
by James Holmes

SHAKER
OVAL BOXES

SHAKER
SALADS

SHAKER PAILS

SHAKER
TINWARE

Starch Collars & Cuffs

To starch collars, cuffs, etc. so that they will be stiff and glossy as those bought at funishing stores, add to one quart of the well boiled (corn) starch three ounces of water gloss, one ounce of gum arabic, and two ounces of loaf sugar. Use polishing iron.

Manifesto — 1883

Boiled Starch

Boiled starch is much improved by the addition of a little sperm, or a little salt, or both, or a little gum arabic dissolved. Beeswax and salt will make your flatirons as clean and smooth as glass. Tie a lump of wax in a rag, and keep for that purpose. When the irons are hot rub them with the wax rag then scour with a paper or cloth sprinkled with salt.

Manifesto — 1879

Scorched Shirt Bosom

If a shirt-bosom or any any other article has been scorched in ironing, lay it where the bright sun will fall directly upon it. It will take it entirely out.

Manifesto — 1883

Doing Up Shirts

A shirt-board for ironing is a necessity in every well-regulated family. This should be covered with at least two thicknesses of blankets, and have the ironing sheet, also double, smoothly pinned over it, so that it cannot slip. Keep wax tied up in a rag to rub the iron. The polish of collars, etc. done up at

large laundries is given by means of a polishing-iron and by
dint of much rubbing. It may be done by any good laundress,
but it takes much time and is fearfully hard on the linen.
Spermacetti added in small quantities to the starch gives a pretty
gloss.

We insert this recipe:—Melt together with a gentle heat,
one ounce white wax and two ounces spermacetti; prepare in
the usual way a sufficient quantity of starch for a dozen bosoms;
put into it a piece of this enamel the size of a hazelnut. This
gives a beautiful polish.

Manifesto — 1880

To Make Calicoes Wash Well

Infuse three gills of salt in four quarts of boiling water; put
the calicoes in while hot and leave them cold; in this way the
colors are rendered permanent, and will not fade by subsequent
washing. So says a lady who has frequently made the experiment
herself. Nothing can be cheaper and more quickly done.

Manifesto — 1880

Household Hints

Mix a little carbonate of soda with the water in which flowers
are immersed, and it will preserve them for a fortnight. Common saltpeter is also a very good preservative.

Manifesto — 1883

If *tablecoths, napkins and handkerchiefs* are folded an inch
or two beyond the middle they will last much longer; it is on

the edges of folds where they first wear, and folding them not on a middle line, each ironing, they get a new crease.

Manifesto — 1882

Lumps in starch or gravy.—How true it is that, if we observe and remember, we can learn something of everyone we meet. A few days ago I learned from the poorest housekeeper I know something new to me—that salt added to the flour before the water on stirring paste for starch or gravy—would prevent starch, but I never observed the good results of adding the salt first.

Manifesto — 1883

Kerosene will soften boots or shoes which have been hardened by water and render them as pliable as new.

Manifesto — 1879

HUMAN REMEDIES

CURE FOR FITS & IDLENESS

For a fit of passion.—Walk out in the open air: you may speak your mind to the winds without hurting anyone, or proclaiming yourself a simpleton.

For a fit of idleness.—Count the ticking of a clock: do this for one hour, and you will be glad to pull off your coat the next and work at anything

Manifesto — 1878

Eating Too Much

The average farmer or farm laborer are chargeable with two failings, which injure health and shorten life, both heir-looms of the highly barbarous feudal ages just referred to. They eat too much and bathe too little. Some of the food is objectionable as to the quality, but the quality is less harmful than the quantity. The farmer's out door life gives him a vigorous appetite, and not enough restraint is exercised against an excess. His table drinks, too (which may be classed as part of his food) are also objectionable, being very generally strong tea and coffee. The drink failure is particularly prevalent in the females. When a person regards strong tea and coffee as an absolute necessity for a meal, it is in itself a bad sign. An appetite for an unhealthy stimulus is fastened on the stomach, and the path to disease is short and easy. Nature's simplicity is gone and in its place are nervousness, changing moods, and a tendency to enjoy other stimulants, such as the most highly seasoned foods, and condiments, and, not infrequently, intoxicating drinks. Children brought up to tea and coffee, and the whole range of condiments, along with pie and cake to any extent, and their tender stomachs are disorganized at an early age. Then when a dangerous disease sets in—dyspepsia, heartburn, frequent colic, flatulency, nausea, etc., the child is "weakly" unable to work and an early death is regarded as "an inscrutable dispensation of an all-wise Providence." There are thousands today half broken-down prematurely old, complaining that "food does them no good," or that it "distresses them," and who are running after the doctor, or swallowing quack medicines, who could yet be cured by a proper system of diet. Some it is true, are too far gone, and yet hardly one in a thousand will listen with patience to a kind remonstrance against his bad habits.

Manifesto — 1879

For Burns

Strong, fresh, clear lime water, mixed with as much linseed oil as it will cut; shake the bottle before applying; wrap the burn in cotton wadding saturated with the lotion; wet as often as it appears dry, without removing cotton from burn for nine days, when new skin will probably have formed.

Manifesto — 1879

For Burns

Wash the parts, if not deeply burned, with salt and vinegar, it will immediately relieve the pain and soreness.

Sister Abigail Crossman

Soda for Burns

All kinds of burns, including scalds and sunburns, almost immediately relieved by the application of a solution of soda to the burnt surface. It must be remembered that dry soda will not do unless it is surrounded with a cloth moist enough to dissolve it. This method of sprinkling it on and covering it with a wet cloth is often the very best. But it is sufficient to wash the wound repeatedly with a strong solution.

Manifesto — 1880

Cure for Erysipelas

A Correspondent of an exchange paper, gives the public a cure for this distressing disorder, from which he had been a great sufferer. He says, "a simple poultice made of cranberries, pounded fine and applied in a raw state has proved in my case and a number also in this vicinity, a certain remedy." In case the poultice was applied on going to bed, and the next morning,

to his surprise, he found the inflammation nearly gone and in
two days he was as well as ever.

A Collection of Useful Hints for Farmers
and Many Valuable Recipes,
by James Holmes

NEURALGIA

For neuralgia in the face or other acute suffering elsewhere,
the following remedy has been tried with good effect: Cut a
thick slice of bread all across the loaf—fresh bread is best; soak
one side for a minute in boiling water, and rapidly sprinkle
cayenne pepper over the hot side apply while still smoking
hot to the painful surface. The bread retains the heat long
enough for the cayenne pepper to begin to act, and cayenne
does not affect the delicate skin as mustard does. It acts as a
rubefacient, but not as a blister.

Manifesto — 1881

NEURALGIA

One of the simplest remedies for neuralgia, is essence of
peppermint. Bathe the part affected keeping the hand over it.
It will burn and draw, but not blister.

Manifesto — 1878

FOR HEADACHE

Put a handful of salt into a quart of water, add one of spirits
of hartshorn, and half an ounce of camphorated spirits of wine.
Put them quickly into a bottle and cork tightly to prevent the
escape of the spirit. Soak a piece of rag with the mixture and
apply to the head; wet the rag afresh as soon as it gets heated.

Manifesto — 1878

A Cure for Sick Headache

This complaint is the result of eating too much and exercising too little. Often the cause is that the stomach is not able to digest the food last introduced into, either from its having been unsuitable or excessive in quantity. It is said a diet of bread and butter, with ripe fruits or berries, with moderate, continuous exercise in the open air sufficient to keep up a gentle perspiration, would cure almost every case in a short time. To drink two teaspoonfuls of powdered charcoal in half a glass of water generally gives instant relief. The above sovereign remedies may do in some, but not in all cases. A sovereign remedy for this ailment is not easily found. Sick headache is periodical, and is the signal of distress, which the stomach raises to inform us that there is an over-alkaline condition of its fluid; that it needs a natural acid to restore the battery to its normal working condition. When the first symptoms of a headache appear, take a teaspoonful of clear lemon juice fifteen minutes before each meal and the same dose at bedtime; follow this up until all symptoms are passed, taking no other remedies, and you will soon be able to go free from your unwelcome nuisance. Many will object to this because the remedy is too simple, but many cures have been effected in this way.

Manifesto — 1881

Headache Remedy

Simple remedies are frequently the best for headache. A cup of sour milk spread upon a thin cloth and applied to the head will many times give relief. Or, a mustard plaster on the back of the neck will often give relief. Or, a mustard plaster on the back of the neck will often ease the pain.

Manifesto — 1879

How to Preserve Teeth

The following directions for the care of the teeth have been issued by the medical committee of the National Dental Hospital, London:

1. The teeth should be cleaned at least once a day, the best time being night, the last thing. For this purpose use a soft brush, on which a little soap, and then some prepared chalk, brushing up and down and across. There is rarely any objection to the friction causing the gum to bleed slightly.

2. Avoid rough usage of the teeth, such as cracking nuts, biting thread, etc., as by so doing even good sound teeth may be injured.

3. When decay is first observed advice should be sought. It is the stopping in a small hole that is of greatest service, though not unfrequently a large filling preserves the teeth for years.

4. It is of the greatest importance that children from four years and upward should have their teeth frequently examined by the dental surgeon, to see that the first set, particularly the back teeth, are not decaying too early, and to have the opportunity of timely treatment for the regulation and preservation of the second set.

5. Children should be taught to rinse the mouth night and morning, and to begin the use of the tooth-brush early (likewise the toothpick).

6. With regard to food, children who are old enough, whole meal, bread, porridge and milk should be given. This is much more wholesome and substantial food than white bread.

7. If the foregoing instructions were carried out comparatively few teeth would have to be extracted.

Manifesto — 1881

Catarrh

Water, made quite salty, is the best known remedy for nasty catarrh. Use as a douche several times a day; it will remove largely the very unpleasant effect in company of one afflicted with it, and has cured in many cases. It is pretty generally believed, that most catarrhal remedies are composed largely of salt water, with other materials thrown in to hide the simple, but effective agency.

Manifesto — 1878

Causes of Indigestion

Eating too fast often causes indigestion. The food should be masticated and insalivated thoroughly.

Salt, pepper, spice, mustard, cloves, etc. all tend to cause indigestion.

Manifesto — 1897

Stop Bleeding at the Nose

To stop bleeding at the nose, says an exchange, exercise the jaws as if in the act of mastication. In the case of a child give it something to chew—a piece of paper—for instance. The motion of the jaw will stop the flow of blood. It is a sure remedy, simple as it seems.

Manifesto — 1878

Cinder in the Eye

Put one or two grains of flaxseed in the eye, and bind a cloth over the organ. In a short time the eye may be washed and the seeds and cinders removed.

Manifesto — 1878

LIME IN THE EYE

The evil effects of lime in the eye are well known, plasterers and whitewashers not unfrequently having their eyes seriously injured, if not destroyed, by the caustic power of the lime. Wells says: "If the patient is seen soon after the accident an effort should be made at once to neutralize and wash out the lime by a weak solution of vinegar, with a free use of the syringe. Afterwards, cooling and anodyne lotions and general antiphlogistic treatment should be adopted."

Manifesto — 1878

WEAK EYES

Bathe in soft water, that is sufficiently impregnated with spirits of camphor to be discernible to the smell—teaspoonful of camphor to tumbler of water. For inflamed eyes use milk and camphor, adding a little more of the camphor than above. Let the baths enter the eyes freely.

Manifesto — 1878

CORNS ON THE FEET

To cure corns, take one measure of coal or gas tar, one of saltpetre, and one of brown sugar; mix well. Take a piece of an old kid glove and spread the plaster on it the size of the corn and apply to the affected part; bind on and leave two or three days and then remove, the corn will come with it.

Manifesto — 1881

CORNS

A remedy for corns, is as follows: Bathe the feet in tepid water, to soften the corns; pare these off very closely with a sharp knife; then rub on well green peach tree leaves, after continuing the rubbing once or twice a day, the corns will disappear.

Manifesto — 1881

FOR CORNS

Tie a bit of black silk cloth around the toe, or fasten it inside the stocking if the corn is on the bottom of the foot. It seems a simple remedy but is very efficient.

Manifesto — 1881

CHILBLAINS

The best remedy for this disagreeable infirmity is fire. Hold the feet as near the fire, and as long as can be borne. Let them cool, and do so again, and yet again. This followed for three or four successive nights, accompanied by dry stocking in the morning will cure the worst case.

Manifesto — 1878

RECIPE FOR CHILBLAINS
ORIGINAL SIMPLE AND SURE

Put on a pair of cotton socks, dip your feet in cold water and draw on your woolen stockings outside, then go about your business as usual. The torment will be assuaged in about two minutes, and a cure for the season effected in a day or two.

*A Collection of Useful Hints for Farmers
and Many Valuable Recipes,
by James Holmes*

CURE FOR DANDRUFF

The Journal of Pharmacy asserts that a preparation of one ounce of sulphur and one quart of water, repeatedly agitated during intervals of a few hours will, in a few weeks, remove every trace of dandruff from the scalp, and the hair will become soft and glossy. The head should be saturated every morning with the clear liquid. He says, "I do not pretend to explain the modus operandi of the treatment, for it is well known that sublimed sulphur is almost or wholly insoluble, and the liquid used was destitute of taste, color or smell. The effect speaks for itself."

Manifesto — 1881

DYSPEPSIA

We get this remedy for the above distressing complaint from one who cured himself, and is now curing doctors of medicine, who have no faith in their own nostrums, yet who are afflicted—and the success has been simply marvelous.

Get two ounce essence wintergreen. Take after each meal, one teaspoonful in a little water or milk. When relieved, stop taking the dose; but pass the recipe to your nearest afflicted neighbor.

Manifesto — 1881

TO STOP THE FLOW OF BLOOD

To stop a flow of blood, take the fine dust of tea or the scrapings of the inside of tanned leather; bind it upon the wound closely and blood will soon cease to flow. After the blood has ceased to flow laudanum may be applied to the wound. Due regard to these instructions will save agitation of mind running for a surgeon, who probably will make no better prescription if present than this.

Manifesto — 1881

Health Hints

Gentian root is said to be a tobacco antidote. Buy two ounces or more of Gentian root, coarsely ground. Take as much of it after each meal, or oftener, as amounts of a common quid of "fine-cut." Chew it slowly and swallow the juice. Continue this a few weeks and you will conquer the appetite for tobacco.

Manifesto — 1881

The Cure for Warts

Warts are caused by an abnormal growth of certain elements or constituents of the skin. They are more apt to appear in childhood and old age, because at these periods of life the nutrition of the skin is as a rule at its lowest ebb, most inefficient, and is therefore liable to abnormal manifestations. Strictly speaking, they are the result of the excessive growth or hypertrophy of a small group of papillae of the skin, accompanied by greatly increased production of the cuticle forming an integumentary prominence. They may be of various kinds, as flat with but slight prominence, and looking more like dirty blotch on the skin than anything else, or they may have a prominence of a quarter of an inch or even more on some portions of the body. Being caused by perverted nutrition and abnormal growth, the best remedies for direct cure include such proper constitutional treatment as shall increase the vigor and healthy development of the whole body through improved nutrition. In addition to this, local treatment can be given to remove or dissolve the abnormal growth and stimulate the sub-adjacent part to a healthy nutritive activity. Application of acetic or nitric acid or a saturated solution of caustic potash carefully made by means of minute pencils or sponges, are among the best methods of treatments.

Manifesto — 1886

Remedy for Warts

Warts are very troublesome and disfiguring. The following is a perfect cure, even of the largest without leaving a scar. It is a Frenchman's prescription, and has been tested by the writer: Take a small piece of raw beef, steep it all night in vinegar, cut as much from it as will cover the wart, and tie on it. If the excrescence is on the forehead, fasten it on with strips of sticking plaster. It may be removed in the day and put on every night in one fortnight the wart will die and peel off. The same prescription will cure corn.

Manifesto — 1879

A Sure Cure for Warts

Take a little Salamoniac dissolve in soft water wet the warts frequently with this solution and they will disapper in a week or two.

Sister Abigail Crossman

Warts

A friend of ours asserted that by rubbing warts with lard two or three times a day, either those on persons or cattle, they will disappear in a short time.

Manifesto — 1879

To Cure a Felon

As soon as the part begins to swell get the tincture of lobelia strong, saturate a cloth therewith and wrap the part afflicted, wet it thoroughly and the felon is dead. An old physician says he has known it too cure in scores of cases, and it never fails if applied in season.

Journal of Medicine,
Sister Abigail Crossman

Antidote for Poison

A standing antidote for poison by dew, poison oak, ivy, etc., is to take a handful of quicklime; dissolve in water; let it stand half an hour, and then paint the poisoned parts with it. Three or four applications will never fail to cure the most aggravated cases.

Manifesto — 1878

Poisons & Antidotes

ACIDS — These cause great heat and sensation of burning pain from the mouth down to the stomach.
Remedies — Magnesia, soda, pearl-ash or soap, dissolved in water; then use stomach pump or emetics.

ALKALIES — Best remedy is vinegar.

AMMONIA — Remedy, lemon juice or vinegar, afterward milk and water or flaxseed tea.

ALCOHOL — First cleanse out the stomach by an emetic, then dash cold water on the head and give ammonia (spirits of hartshorn).

ARSENIC — In the first evacuate the stomach, then give the whites of eggs, lime water or chalk and water, charcoal, and the preparation of iron, particularly hydrate.

LEAD — White lead and sugar of lead.
Remedies — Alum and cathartics, such as castor oil and Epsom salts especially.

CHARCOAL — In poisons by carbonic gas, remove the patient to open air, dash cold water on the head and body and stimulate the nostrills and lungs by hartshorn at the same time rubbing the chest briskly.

CORROSIVE SUBLIMATE. — Give white of eggs freshly mixed with water or give wheat flour and water of soap and water freely.

CREOSOTE. — White of eggs and emetice.

BELLADONNA or HENBANE. — Give emetics and then plenty of vinegar and water with a dose of ether of handy.

NITRATE OF SILVER. — (lunar caustic)—Give a strong solution of common salt and then emetics.

OPIUM. — First give a strong emetic of mustard and water and then strong coffee and acid drinks. Dash cold water on the head.

LAUDANUM. — Same as opium.

NUX VOMICA. — First emetics, then brandy.

OXALIC ACIDS. — Frequently mistaken for Epsom salts. Remedies: Chalk, magnesia, or soap and water freely, then emetics.

NITRATE OF POTASH. — Give emetics and then copious draughts of flaxseed tea, milk and water, and other soothing drinks.

PRUSSIC ACID. — When there is time administer chlorine in the shape of soda or lime. Hot brandy and water, hartshorn and turpentine are also useful.

MILK as a Preventive of WHITE LEAD POISONING. — A singular fact is given in the Journal de Medecine with regard to the effect of the habitual use of milk in white lead works. In some French lead mills it was observed that in a large working population two men who drunk much milk daily were not affected by lead. On the general use of milk throughout the works the colic vanished entirely. Each operative was given enough extra pay to buy a quart of milk a day.

Manifesto — 1878

Cure for Piles

The following simple application will certainly cure this more distressing complaint. It has been tried by many and found entirely successful: Take three ounces of pulverized alum, and place in a belt of cotton drilling, two inches in width, and wear the belt around the body above the loins. It should be worn next to the skin, its operation is slow but certain.

A Collection of Useful Hints for Farmers and Many Valuable Recipes, by James Holmes

A Syrup for the Summer Complaint

Take one quart of the juice of blackberries and a pound of loaf sugar. Boil it until the skum arises. Then add one ounce of pulverized cloves and after it is cold a half pint of french brandy.
DOSE: One tablespoonful, for a child one teaspoonful. In extreme cases of summer complaint desentery the above is an excellent medicine, and has cured many.

Shaker Manuscript, Fruitlands and Wayside Museum, Harvard, Mass.

Home-made Court-Plaster

The following recipe comes to us well recommended. One ounce French isinglass; one pint of warm water; stir till it dis-

solves; add ten cents' worth of pure glycerine and five cents'
worth of tincture of arnica; lay a piece of white or black silk
on a board and paint it over with the mixture.

Manifesto — 1878

Cure for Chapped Hands

A solution of cider vinegar and pure glycerine in equal
parts will cure the most stubborn chapped hands on even the
thinnest skin.

Manifesto — 1878

Simple Cosmetic

It is not generally know that the juice of ripe tomatoes is
the most simple as well effective agent for giving a soft, smooth
feeling to the hands, adding beauty to the skin and renewed
limberness to the joints.

Manifesto — 1879

An Excellent Hair Wash

One oz. borax, one half ounce camphor, dissolve in one
quart of boiling water, use when cold.

Shaker Manuscript,
Fruitlands and Wayside Museum, Harvard, Mass.

Cough Syrup

Take one oz. of flaxseed, liquorice root, slippery elm bark
and thoroughwort. Simmer in a quart of water until all the
strength is extracted. Strain and add one pint best molasses,
one pint of white sugar and boil down to a thick syrup.
DOSE: One tablespoonful three times a day. It is the best
cough mixture that can be desired.

The Working Farmer,
Sister Abigail Crossman

Tea for Lung Ailments

COMPOSITION TEA — This almost universal remedy of the Shakers, and which has been sought for by so many thousands as a panacea for colds, coughs, lung irregularities and inflammations, is now made public:

Take two pounds of bayberry root bark, one pound of the inner bark of hemlock, one pound of ginger, two ounces of cayenne pepper, all reduced to a powder and sifted through a fine sieve. Mix well together.

DOSE: One teaspoonful in half a teacup of hot water. Add milk and sugar to please the taste and drink as warm as consistent.

Manifesto — 1882

Sore Throat

If you have a sore throat, slight or serious, a piece of camphor gum as large as a pea kept in the mouth until dissolved, will give relief and often-times cure. It is said on good authority, if the gum is used in season, you will never have diphtheria—it is a good preventive.

Manifesto — 1882

Celery for Rheumatism

Celery cooked is a very fine dish, both as nutriment and as a purifier of the blood. Rheumatism is impossible on such diet. Cold or damp never produces rheumatism, but simply developes it. The acid blood is the primary cause, and sustaining power of evil. While the blood is alkaline, there can be no rheumatism, and equally no gout. Cut the celery into inch dices, boil in water until soft. No water must be poured away unless drunk by the invalid. Then take new milk, slightly thicken with flour, and flavor with nutmeg; serve up with diamonds of toasted bread round dish, and eat with potatoes.

Manifesto — 1879

St. John's Oil

White and yolk of an egg, oil of turpentine, six ounces; acetic acid, one ounce; water, five ounces. Mix: This is an invaluable liniment for the household and farm, applicable to every external ailment. Shake thoroughly before using.

Sister Mary Whitcher's
Shaker Housekeeper

Basilicon Ointment

Take ten ounces of resin, four ounces yellow wax, and sixteen ounces lard. Melt them together; strain through muslin and stir constantly until cool. This is the best ointment or healing salve in existence.

Sister Mary Whitcher's
Shaker Housekeeper

Good for Weak Stomack

Take blue cohosh, sweet flag and golden seal. Make a tea, sweeten with sugar, take a little half an hour before eating. It will prevent food distressing the stomach. It has been thoroughly tried and found to be very good indeed.

Jennie Finch

Good for Billious Colic

Skunk cabbage seed, masterwort seed and white root, a small portion of each, to be made into a tea sweetened with loaf sugar and drank freely will cure the billious colic *for sure*.

Sister Abigail Crossman

Mustard Plaster

In making a mustard plaster use no water whatever but mix the mustard with the white of an egg and the result will be a plaster that will draw perfectly, but will not provide a blister even upon the skin of an infant, no matter how long it is allowed to remain upon the part.

Sister Abigail Crossman

A GREAT PAIN EXTRACTOR

Spirits of ammonia one oz., laudanum one oz., oil origam one oz., mutton tallow half a pound., combine the articles with the tallow when it is nearly cool.

The Maple Leaves,
Sister Abigail Crossman

CURE FOR DEAFNESS

Some time ago an old lady recommended the use of heated hen's oil dropping it into the ear internally one or more times daily, and above all to *persevere* in its use, and it would certainly help me. This remedy I have faithfully employed, and I now hear as well as I ever did in my life. This oil is very penetrating and in the case mentioned acted remedially by softening the indurated earwax, which is no doubt the cause of deafness in more instances than is generally supposed.

Manifesto — 1879

INGROWING NAILS

Our much valued eldress of So. Family, Mt. Lebanon, has had an experience in dealing with these very sore pests; and says that a notched cut in the end of the nail at the center, and as deeply as possible without pain, will effect the *desideratum*. There are many painful suggestion for relief going the rounds, but here is one, simple painless and effective, and the informer has our thanks.

Manifesto — 1879

RESTORING THE DROWNED

A New York physician says that any person who has not been in the water more than two hours may be restored to life by thoroughly warming him. Wrap the body in a blanket or quilt and pour hot water on it, and continue to do so until the subject revives.

Manifesto — 1879

DELICATE ALKALI

A small piece of calk put into a pitcher of water, without imparting any taste whatever to the same, will yet exercise a corrective effect upon the stomach of any one afflicted with acidity, or heartburn, as it is familiarly called.

Manifesto — 1878

VIRTUES OF THE LEMON

A recent writer of note has the following to say regarding the virtues of the lemon: "Lemon juice is the best anti-scorbutic remedy known. It not only cures the disease but prevents it. Sailors make a daily use of it for the purpose. I advise every one to rub their gums daily with lemon juice to keep them in health. The hands and nails are also kept clean, white, soft and supple by the daily use of lemon instead of soap. It also prevent chilblains. Lemon is used in intermittent fevers, mixed with strong, hot, black coffee, without sugar. Neuralgia may be cured by rubbing the part affected with a cut lemon. It is valuable also to cure warts, and to destroy dandruff on the head by rubbing the roots of the hair with it. In fact, its uses are manifold, and the more we employ it, externally, the better we shall find ourselves. Natural remedies are the best, and Nature is the best doctor, if we would only listen to it. Decidedly rub your hands, head and gums with lemon, and drink lemonade in preference to all other liquids."

Manifesto — 1881

The Use of the Lemon

There are three ways of making lemonade: To squeeze the juice into cold water—this is the shortest way; or to cut it in slices and soak it in cold water, or to cut it in slices and then boil it. Lemonade is one of the best and safest drinks for a person, whether in health or not. It is suitable to all stomach diseases; is excellent in sickness. The pips, crushed, may also be mixed with water, and used as a drink. We advise everyone to rub the gums daily with lemon juice, to keep them in health. The hands and nails are also kept clean, white, soft and supple by the use of lemon instead of soap. It also prevents chilblains. Lemon is used in intermittent fevers, mixed with strong, hot black coffee, without sugar. Neuralgia may be cured by rubbing the part affected with a cut lemon. It is valuable, also to cure warts, and to destroy dandruff on the head by rubbing the roots of the hair with it.

Manifesto — 1881

What the Microscope Says

Insects of various kinds may be seen in the cavities of a grain of sand.

Mould is a forest of beautiful trees, with the branches, leaves and fruit.

Butterflies are fully feathered.

Hairs are hollow tubes.

The surface of our bodies is covered with scales like a fish; a single grain of sand would cover 150 of these scales, and yet a scale covers 500 pores. Through these narrow openings the perspiration forces itself like water through a sieve.

Each drop of stagnant water contains a world of living creatures swimming with as much liberty as whales in the sea.

Each leaf has a colony of insects grazing on it like cows on a meadow.

Yes, even the ugliest plant that grows shows some remarkable property when closely examined.

Manifesto — 1881

Our Flannels

The value of flannel next to the skin cannot be overrated. It is invaluable to persons of both sexes and all ages, in all countries, in all climates, at every season of the year, for the sick and well; in brief, I cannot conceive of any circumstance in which flannel next the skin is not a comfort and a source of health. It should not be changed from thick to thin before the settle hot weather of the summer, which in our Northern States is not much before the middle of June, and often not before the first of July. And the flannels for the summer must not be three-quarters cotton, but they must be all woolen, if you would have the best protection. In the British army and navy, they make the wearing of flannel a point of discipline. During the hot season the ship doctor makes a daily examination of the men at unexpected hours, to make sure they have not left off their flannels.

Manifesto — 1882

Lime Water

A handy thing to have in the house is a jar or bottle of lime-water. Pour water over unslacked lime (the quantity is not important, as only a certain amount will be slacked), and cork up for use. A spoonful of the clear liquid stirred into milk, cream or bread sponge in danger of souring, will prevent that catastrophe. It also cleanses bottles, etc., that have an unpleasant odor. A person who needs milk, but whose digestion is so weak as not to manage it, will find no inconvenience if into a glass of the lacteal fluid is stirred a wine-glass of lime-water. The difference in taste is not perceptible.

Manifesto — 1879

INDEX

Air, fresh, 255-256
Ashes, 260
Attar (Otto) of Roses, recipe for, 256

Babbit, Tabitha, 28
Baking powder, 94
Barlow, Lillian, 27
Bates, Theodore, 28
Bed ticks, filling for, 257
Beeswax, 262

BEVERAGES: 36-40
    beer, 38; chocolate, 39; cider,
    boiled, 39; cocoa bean shells, 36;
    cocoanut drink, 39; coffee, 36; tea,
    36-37; Turkish beverage, 40
Bishop, John, 16
Blinn, Henry, 18
Boiling, to hasten, 256
Bones, 263
Brass, cleaning of, 249
Bread, as an absorbent of gases, 31

BREADS: 94-110
    making of, 97-98; biscuits, cream
    of tartar, 106; soda, 106-107;
    raised, 106; bread. brown, 100;
    Shaker brown, 99; steamed brown,
    99-100; buns, 102-104; hot cross,
    103-104; bread: corn, 99, 107, 108;
    Graham, 101; Indian, 101; Indian,
    steamed, 102; Johnny cake, 110;
    rolls: Pemigewasset, 104-105;
    Parker House, 105; Graham, 105;
    French tea, 106; White Mountain,
    104; bread: Rye, 101; salt rising,
    102; sponge, without yeast, 98; un-
    leavened loaf, 98-99
Brooms, Shaker, 28-29
Butter, 186-189
Buttermilk, 190

CAKES: 110-129
    almond cream, 112; ambrosia,
    112; angel, 112; angel's food, 112-
113; berwick sponge, 127; blue-
berry, 113, 129; Boston cream, 115;
cheap, 113; chocolate, 114; chocolate, half-hour, 113; circle, 114;
cocoanut, 114; coffee, 114-115;
corn, 108; cream, 115; cup, 116;
delicious, 116; election, 116;
feather, 116-117; fruit, 117-118;
ginger pound, 120; gingerbread,
118, 119; Lancaster, 119; molasses,
New York, 119; soft, 119-120;
sugar, 119; gold, 118; honey, 120-
121; Hot Springs sponge, 128; imitation pound, 124; Indian, 121;
jelly and jelly roll, 121-122; La-
conia, 122; layer, 122; lemon, 122-
123; loaf, 122; marble, 123; Marsh-
field, 123; Mrs. Herbert's sponge,
128; nut, 124; poor man's, 124;
pound, 124; puff, 125; Queen's,
125; raised, 125; Sally Lunn, 108;
scripture, 125-126; seed, 126; silver, 126-127; sponge, 127-129; tea,
128; Sister Harriet John's fruit,
129; union, 128-129; velvet, 129

Calico, ironing of, 259; washing of,
274

Camisards, 13

CANDY: 181-184
    after dinner mints, 181-182; choco-
    late cream drops, 184; chocolate
    drops, 183; cocoanut caramel, 182;
    coffee caramel, 182; cream, 182;
    ginger drops, 182; molasses, 182-
    183; snowballs, 183; sponge drops,
    183; sugar kisses, 183

Carpets, choice of, 258; removal of
ink from, 262; removal of oil from,
253

Carr, Mrs. Fred Parker, 24
Case, Anna, 18
Catsup, tomato, 199-200
Ceilings, cleaning of, 258

298

Cement, for china, 256; for general use, 257; for glass, 252; for metals, 251-252
Chairs, Shaker, described, 27
Cheese, making of, 188-189
Chimneys, lamp, 254
Civil War (American), 17-18
Clinton, George (Governor), 15
Clothing, care of, 240-243
Cocoa paste, 40-41
Coffee, syrup of, 41
Colleges, Pittsfield Medical (Mass.), 26
Collins, Sarah, 27

COOKIES: 129-136
Berkshire, 129-130; best out, 130; Bristol, 130; cream puffs, 135; dropped, 130; fig-filled, 131; filled, 131; fruit, 131; ginger, 132; ginger snaps, 132; Graham, 133; Graham puffs, 133; hermits, 136; jumbles, 136-137; Lafayette jumbles, 137; molasses, 132-133; molasses, soft, 133-134; popcorn, 134; soft, 134; sour cream, 135; sour milk, 135; Spanish drop, 135; very nice, 134
Cosmetics, 290
Court plaster, making of, 289-290
Crackers, 109; Graham, 109
Crape, restoring of, 258
Cream, sour, 190

Dairy practices, 186-190
Darrow, David, 16
DESSERTS: 156-180
frozen Boston ice cream, 181; ices, 180-181; apple dumpling, 179-180; apple sauce, boiled cider, 177; apples, baked, 177; apples, Shaker boiled, 177; Charlotte Russe, 176; lemon jelly, 180; souffles: orange, 178; rice, 178; Spanish cream, 179; Swiss cream, 178-179; wine jelly, 180
Doolittle, Antoinette, 18

DOUGHNUTS: 146-149
Callie's, 147; crullers, 146; Indian, 147; raised, 148; Sister Bertha's

white, 148-149; sour milk, 148
Drainage, defective, 257
Dresses, silk, cleaning of, 268
Drowned, restoring of, 294
Dumplings, 215
Dyes, 220-236

Eads, Henry, 18
Eggs, 67-73; brine for, 68; deviled, 68; dropped, 69; omelettes, 69-71; omelettes, Quaker, 70-71; tomato, 70; scrambled, 71; Spanish, 71; stuffed, 72
Evans, Frederick, 18

FISH: 31, 89-93
baked, 89-90; balls, 90; cakes, 91; lobster, stewed, 91; oysters, creamed, 92; oysters, fried, 92; oysters, pickled, 93; oysters, scalloped, 92; oyster fritters, 93; oyster pie, 93; oyster stew, 93; salt mackerel, 91-92; Shaker and egg, 72-73, 89; Turbot a la Creme, 90
Flannel, value of, 296; washing of, 272
Floors, washing of, 248
Flour, patent, 96-97
Flowers, keeping of, 274
Fluids, washing, 271
Foods, comparative value of, 32; storage of, 32; weights of, 33
Fritters, apple, 44; corn, 144; corn oysters, 144; green corn patties, 144
Frosting, cake, 214; without eggs, 213-214
Fruits, 185-186
bananas, how to eat, 185; canned, 191; rhubarb, 192-193; stewed prunes, 186
Furniture, removal of spots from, 259

Game, partridge, broiled, 81
Glass, filling of, 257
"Gleaning from Old Shaker Journals," 28
Gravy, removing lumps from, 275
Grease, removal of, 264

Rusk, 109
Rust, removal of, 268

Salad Dressing, cream, 214-215

SALADS: 48-51
chicken, 50; cabbage, 49; cole slaw, 49; ham, 50; potato, 50-51; salmon, 51; slaw, 49
Salt, 31
Sanitation, rules for, 32
Sarle, Helena, 24
Saw, cirular, invention of, 28
Sears, Clara E., 28, 30
Seeds, selling of, 25-26

SHAKERS: buildings, 20-21; clothing, 19; collections relating to, 30; colonies, remaining, 13, 23, 29; communities, 16, 23, 24, 28; decline of, 17; furniture, 22, 26, 27; government, 17; industries, 21, 25-28; inventions, 28-29; literature, 23; music, 23-25; principles, 16; remedies, composition tea, 37-38; sources of members, 17
Sauces: boiled pudding, 218; brown butter, 218; chutney, 218; cranberry, 213; cream, 218; egg, 217, 218; fish, 215; hard, 216; lemon, 216; lemon butter, 213; lemon pudding, 216; orange butter, 213; snow pudding, 216-217; strawberry, 217; syrup, 217; tomato butter, 213; white, for game, 217
Scorching, removal of, 273
Shirts, ironing of, 274
Shoes, 275
Soap, 254-255; making of, 268-270

SOUPS: 41-48
asparagus, 41-42; beef, 43; beef tea, 42-43; black bean, 42; clam, 43-44; clam chowder, 44; corn, 44; fish chowder, 45; green pea, 45; mock oyster, 47; okra, 45-46; oyster, 46; potato, 47; tomato, 47-48; turkey, 48
Stains, milk, removal of, 259
Stains, removal of, 264-267

Stains, wood, 245-246
Starch, 271, 273
Stephens, Rosetta, 24
Stoppers, glass, loosening of, 260-261
Stove pipes, cleaning of, 259
Syrup, 184-185; cough, 290

Tablecloths, 275
Tar, removal of, 259
Teeth, preservation of, 280
Toast, 63-64; egg, 69; lumberman's, 63; mock cream, 63-64; white monkey on, 64
Tools, steel, care of, 258
Turpentine, 257

Van Rensselaer, Stephen, 14
Varnish, 243, 245; bleach for, 245
Vegetables: 51-62, 201, 206, 207; cleaning of, 51; beets, 52-53; cauliflower, 53; celery, 53; cucumbers, 190; onions, 54; parsnips, 54; potatoes, 54-59; boiled, 56; baked, 56; mashed, 58; Saratoga fried, 58-59; Shaker creamed, 57; sweet, 58; potato cakes, 57; potato croquettes, 58; rice, boiled, 63; squash, 59; string beans, 52; sweet corn, dried, 62; tomatoes, 59-62, 201, 206, 207; as cosmetic, 290; general storage of, 207; baked, 61; broiled, 61; caned, 201; dried, 206-207; scalloped, 61; Shaker, 60; sliced, 61-62; stewed, 61; turnips, mashed, 62
Vinegar, 31; beet, 211-212; raspberry, 212; spiced, 195

Waffles, 145; rice, 145
Wardley, James and Jane, 14
Water, 36; softening of, 258
Weeks, Estella T., 24
Welch rabbit, 64
Whitewash, 248-250
Whitney, Abraham, 23
Wickersham, George, 20
Williams, John S., 30
Wines: dandelion, 39; grape, 39-40